WASHINGTON PUBLIC LIBRARY
3 6910 51467 8406

ENCYCLOPEDIA OF MAMMALS

VOLUME 3
Bea–Cat

MARSHALL CAVENDISH
NEW YORK • LONDON • TORONTO • SYDNEY

SMALL BEARS

RELATIONS

The small bears are members of the bear family, Ursidae. Other members of the family include:

BROWN BEARS

AMERICAN BLACK BEAR

POLAR BEAR

Michael McKavett/Bruce Coleman Ltd.

Included in the carnivore order, small bears are no more flesh-eating in their feeding habits than the brown bear and American black bear. Of all bears, the polar bear is most carnivorous in habit.

ORDER

Carnivora
(carnivores)

FAMILY

Ursidae
(bears)

GENUS

Ursus

SPECIES

thibetanus
(Asian black bear)

ursinus
(sloth bear)

malayanus
sun bear

GENUS

Tremarctos

SPECIES

ornatus
(spectacled bear)

SMALL AND SCATTERED

SMALLER THAN THEIR MORE FAMILIAR RELATIVES, THE FOUR SO-CALLED SMALL BEARS ARE EQUALLY AS INTERESTING, AND MANY OF THEIR HABITS MIRROR THOSE OF THE BIG NORTHERN BEARS

It is dusk in a dense, remote forest in the Peruvian Andes. The crackle of thin branches snapping joins the early evening noises. Wedged in the fork of a tree is an untidy pile of broken branches, upon which a large, furry animal with pale eye patches is balancing unsteadily: The spectacled bear is beginning its evening raid on a fruit tree.

The spectacled bear is South America's second largest land animal, and the only one of the small bears still to be placed in a genus of its own. It is also said to be the rarest of all the bear species. It was not known to science until the beginning of the 19th century, when a specimen was captured in Chile and shipped to England. It was then that it was classified, being given the species name *ornatus*, meaning "decorated," because of the pale rings that either encircle its eyes or top them, like eyebrows. These pale markings extend down the throat and chest, and in no two bears are they identical.

The spectacled bear's eye markings vary greatly from one individual to another (below).

Mark Newman/Frank Lane Picture Agency

The other three bears known as "the small bears" are the sun bear of Southeast Asia, the sloth bear of India and Sri Lanka, and the Asian black bear, found through northern India and Pakistan, China, and as far north as Mongolia as well as in Southeast Asia. Until recently each of these was placed in a separate genus; the latest thinking, however, is to place them all in the genus *Ursus*, which also contains brown bears, the American black bear, and the polar bear.

These four small bears are fairly similar to their larger, better-known relatives. Although classified as carnivores, they actually eat more fruit and vegetable matter than flesh. The exception to this rule is the sloth bear, which is a specialist termite-feeder. All are ponderous, moving around deliberately on all fours—unless roused, in which event they can move with surprising speed. The sun bear, for example, has a reputation for being one of the most dangerous animals a human can encounter in the jungle. Its skin is so loose that, when it is grabbed by a large predator such as a tiger, it can wriggle its body within its skin to turn around and bite its attacker, or lash out with its sharp claws.

Like all carnivores, the bears' earliest ancestors emerged during the Miocene epoch (25–5 million years ago), although it was to be some time before

Also known as the Himalayan black bear, the Asian black bear is a skillful climber.

S. Nagara/Dinodia/Oxford Scientific Films

in SIGHT

TERMITE-EATERS

Many animals classified as carnivores in no way exist on a diet composed entirely, or even mainly, of the flesh of other animals. However, animals have evolved within at least three carnivore families that rely on termites for their principal food. The sloth bear supports its considerable bulk mainly by eating these tiny, antlike insects. The bat-eared fox of east and southern Africa has also adopted this habit. It lacks the typical canine teeth of its more carnivorous relatives, and has small carnassial teeth. Its large ears are also an adaptation, helping it to detect termites on the march in their subterranean homes. Perhaps the strangest termite-feeder of all is the member of the hyena family, the aardwolf, another inhabitant of Africa. Its close relatives, the three remaining species of hyena, are among the most dedicated flesh-eaters in the animal kingdom.

an animal the size and shape of today's bears evolved. The "typical" bear genus *Ursus* appeared only within the last 2 or 3 million years and split into three lineages, one occurring in Europe and two in Asia. One of these led to the brown and black bears, which lived in China and other parts of Asia before appearing in America. Fossils of the sloth bear have been found in the area it inhabits today, leading experts to believe that this is where it also evolved. The spectacled bear is a descendant of the short-faced bears that roamed North and South America during the last Ice Age *(see Ancestors, p. 292)*. Most of our modern bears are believed to have evolved within the last million years.

NAMES AND APPEARANCES

Each of the small bears has a distinctive appearance, which is often reflected in their names, as in the spectacled bear. The sun bear is the smallest member of the bear family and is known also as the honey bear, because of its great liking for this food, and also the Malay bear, because of its location. In Thailand it is known as the dog bear and is, indeed, almost doglike in appearance; it certainly grows no bigger than a large dog. It takes its most usual name, however, from the creamy horseshoe-shaped mark on its chest—a crescent symbolizing the rising sun, rather than the moon, in Asian folklore. This marking varies in shape and size between individuals and is occasionally absent altogether.

The clue in the sloth bear's name points to its unkempt appearance. When it was first described by European explorers at the end of the 18th century, it was given the name bear sloth—*Bradypus ursinus*—because its shaggy coat, large curved claws, and habit of hanging upside down from tree branches led scientists to classify it with the sloths of South America. They soon realized that it was actually a bear, however, and duly reversed its name!

The Asian black bear is often known locally as the moon bear—another clue to its appearance, for it generally has a striking pale crescent on its chest. This varies from animal to animal, sometimes being very narrow, faint, or even absent altogether. Apart from this, it has a vague resemblance to its cousin the American black bear, although it is significantly smaller. Its soft, luxurious coat is most frequently a glossy black but may also be a dark brown. ■

SLOTH BEAR

Ursus ursinus

(UR-sus ur-SEE-nus)

The sloth bear has a long, shaggy coat and a nearly naked muzzle. Unlike other bears, its ears are very hairy. Its unusual feeding preference makes this the most specialized of the bears. It was previously classified in the genus* Melursus *(MEL-ur-sus).

SUN BEAR

Ursus malayanus

(UR-sus ma-lay-AHN-us)

The smallest of all bear species, with the shortest, sleekest coat, this forest-dweller is also extremely arboreal. Its cautious nature has made it hard to study, and it is one of the least known. It was previously placed in the genus* Helarctos *(hel-ARK-tos).

ANCESTORS

RUNNING BEARS

A prehistoric bear subfamily known as the Tremarctinae (trem-ark-TEE-nye) evolved to exploit the plains. They were great running bears with long, slender limbs. This adaptation, coupled with large, conical canine teeth and powerful biting muscles, made them successful predators and probably considerably more carnivorous than the modern bears. Although running bears originated in Asia, they colonized the Americas, where they dispersed widely, eventually dying out some 10,000 years ago. Their sole descendant today is the spectacled bear.

SPECTACLED BEAR

Tremarctos ornatus

(trem-ARK-tos or-NAH-tus)

This is the only small bear still to be placed in a separate genus, because of the construction of its jaw. This is the rarest and most southerly distributed bear, the only survivor from several prehistoric species that lived in South America.

Color illustrations Kim Thompson

THE SMALL BEARS' FAMILY TREE

Until recently, each of the small bears was placed in a separate genus, but today the Asian black bear, sloth bear, and sun bear are placed in the genus Ursus, *alongside the American black bear, brown bear, and polar bear. Among the bears, only two species now have separate genera: the spectacled bear and the giant panda—which has only recently been recognized as a bear.*

BROWN BEAR

POLAR BEAR

ASIAN BLACK BEAR

Ursus thibetanus

(UR-sus ti-bet-AHN-us)

This species is probably most closely related to the American black bear, although differing in appearance, most noticeably through the white crescent marking on its chest and its widely set ears. The Asian black bear has the most northerly distribution of the small bears. It was previously classified in the genus Selenarctos (sel-en-ARK-tos).

AMERICAN BLACK BEAR

GIANT PANDA

BEARS

B/W illustrations Ruth Grewcock

ANATOMY: THE SPECTACLED BEAR

The sun bear (below right) is about the size of a large dog. The spectacled and sloth bears (below center) are a little larger. The Asian black bear (below left) is probably the heaviest, with a top weight of 330 lb (150 kg), but this is still far short of the polar bear, which can tip the scales at more than half a ton (500 kg).

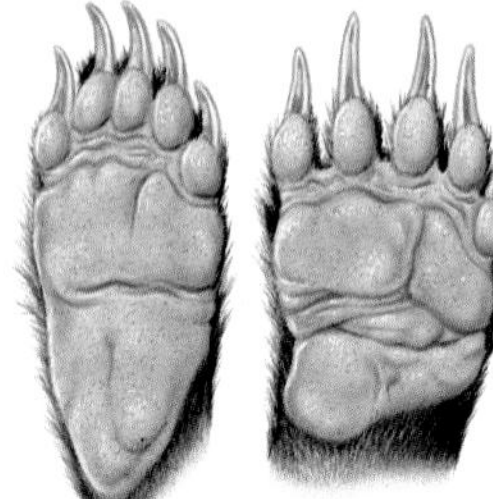

CLAWS

The sun bear and sloth bear both have long, curved claws. These are black and pointed on the sun bear, while those of the sloth bear are ivory in color and quite blunt. The soles of the sun bear's large feet are completely naked, to help it climb trees. The claws on the hind feet of the Asian black bear are much shorter than those on its forefeet.

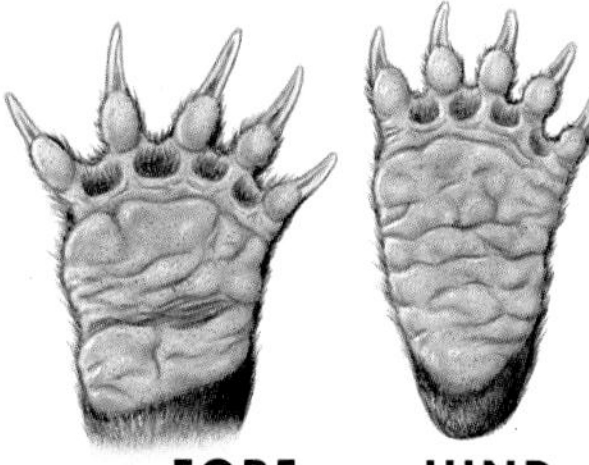

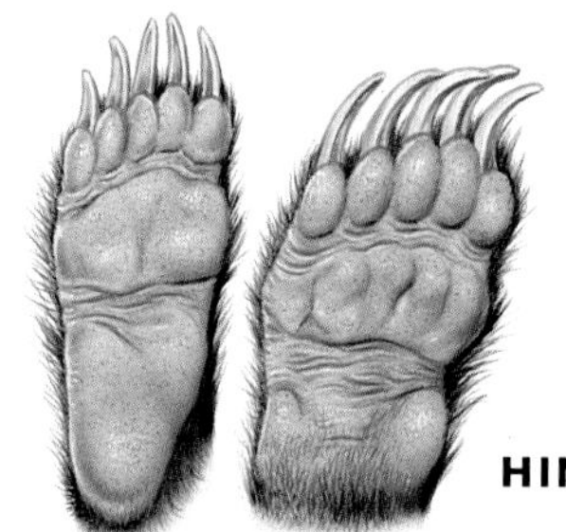

THE FACE

has distinctive pale markings around the eyes; these extend over the chest. The markings around the eyes often form rings that resemble spectacles, but sometimes look more like eyebrows. The markings are never exactly the same in any two bears and occasionally may be lacking altogether.

X-RAY

SPECTACLED BEAR SKELETON

All bears have a heavy bone structure and a short spine which is almost horizontal in profile. The spectacled bear has only 13 pairs of ribs, one less than other bears. The bones of the feet are long and have large heels, reflecting the fact that bears are plantigrade (they walk on the full length of the soles, heels touching down first).

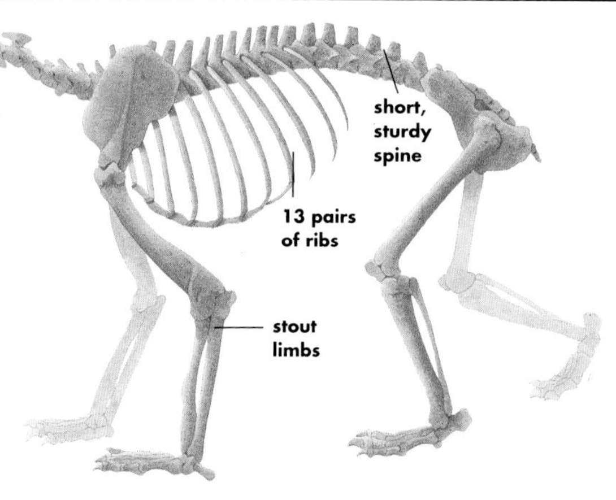

SPECTACLED BEAR FOOT

Bears, like humans, are fairly flat-footed, whereas dogs or antelopes, for example, run on their toes for speed. But bears compensate by having sturdy limbs articulated by powerful muscles: They may not run fast, but they can deal out crushing blows!

long toe bones · tendon · large heel

X-ray illustrations Elisabeth Smith

FACT FILE:

THE SPECTACLED BEAR

CLASSIFICATION

GENUS: *TREMARCTOS*

SPECIES: *ORNATUS*

SIZE

HEAD–BODY LENGTH: 3.9–5.9 FT (1.2–1.8 M)

SHOULDER HEIGHT: 27.5–32 IN (70–81 CM)

TAIL LENGTH: 2.7 IN (70 MM)

WEIGHT/MALE: UP TO 308 LB (140 KG)

WEIGHT/FEMALE: 132–136 LB (60–62 KG)

COLORATION

UNIFORMLY BLACK OR DARK BROWN, EXCEPT FOR WHITE OR YELLOWISH MARKINGS ON FACE AND CHEST

FEATURES

MOST NOTICEABLE FEATURES ARE FACIAL MARKINGS

SIMILAR IN SIZE TO SLOTH AND ASIAN BLACK BEAR

VESTIGIAL TAIL

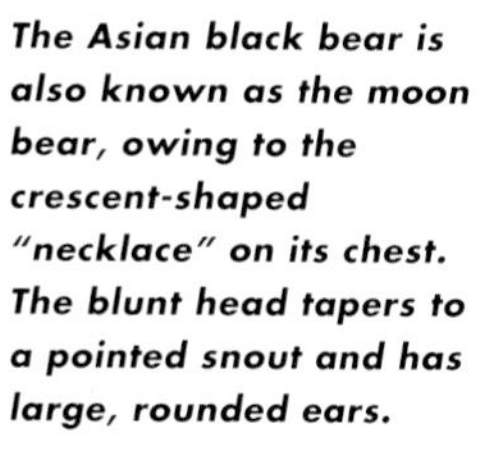

The Asian black bear is also known as the moon bear, owing to the crescent-shaped "necklace" on its chest. The blunt head tapers to a pointed snout and has large, rounded ears.

ASIAN BLACK BEAR

SLOTH BEAR

The sloth bear has a long, almost tubular muzzle with only a sparse covering of pale hair. The lips are extremely mobile and completely naked, and the nostrils can be closed at will.

SUN BEAR

The sun bear has a large, rather flat-crowned head. The pale muzzle is quite short. The ears are small and round, and the tongue is long.

THE LEGS

are longer and more slender than in most other species. Each foot has five long, sharp claws.

THE COAT

is uniformly black or dark brown, apart from the distinctive markings, and the fur is long and dense.

SPECTACLED BEAR SKULL

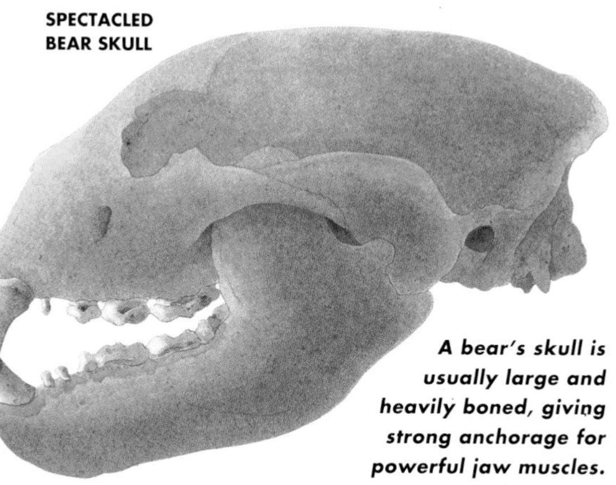

A bear's skull is usually large and heavily boned, giving strong anchorage for powerful jaw muscles.

Although the teeth are strong, they have adapted from the slicing carnassials of a typical carnivore to long canines and grinding molars with broad flat crowns—more suited to a broad diet. The sloth bear lacks the inner pair of upper incisors, giving it a gap in the front teeth, an adaptation to its habit of eating termites.

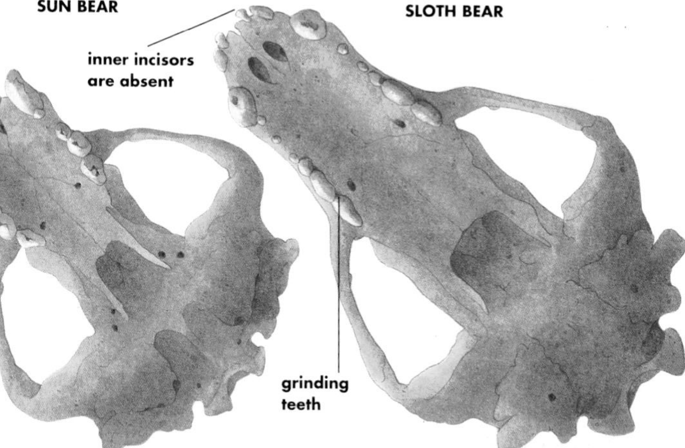

Main illustration Steve Kingston

A POWERFUL PUNCH

THESE BEARS ARE SO SECRETIVE THAT LITTLE IS KNOWN OF THEIR HABITS AND LIFESTYLE IN THE WILD. MOST OF THEM, HOWEVER, HAVE BEEN BRANDED AS BEING PARTICULARLY DANGEROUS

In general, the small bears spend most of their active hours searching for food; they stay as far away from human activity as they can, hiding away in dense woodland or remote pockets of land. While they usually wander over a recognizable area, they tend not to be aggressively defensive or territorial.

Three of the small bears—the sloth bear, spectacled bear, and sun bear—live in the tropics, the latter two actually ranging south of the equator. Although individual food sources are seasonal, overall they are sustained in winter, which means the bears do not need to sleep through the coldest months—unlike their northern cousins, the brown bear, polar bear, and American black bear.

The exception to this is the Asian black bear, which generally "dens" in the northern parts of its range, and often also in the southern areas, although usually for shorter periods, when and if the weather is particularly severe. Pregnant females of this species tend to den whatever their location, giving birth and nursing their young in the safety and warmth of the shelter through their first few critical months. Dens consist either of a burrow excavated by the bear, or a sheltered cave or a hollow in the center of a rotting tree, sometimes as high as 60 ft (18 m) off the ground.

DAILY PATTERNS

The small bears are most active at night, although the Asian black bear keeps more flexible hours. It is active both day and night, although it usually spends the day sleeping in a cave or hollow tree, emerging at dusk to look for food. The shy spectacled bear is active at dawn and dusk in the dense forests of its home, but in the more open country that some frequent, it will venture out to forage only under cover of nighttime darkness. The Asian black bear builds "basking couches"—a heap of twigs and branches, like those of the spectacled bear, located in a secure fork of a tree, sometimes as much as 65 ft (20 m) high. By getting off the ground on cold and wet days, the bear can conserve body heat. Larger adults, particularly males, sometimes appear to lose their climbing ability and stay mainly on the ground.

All these bears are excellent climbers and will frequently choose to spend their time resting and sleeping in roughly assembled nests, similar to that of the Asian black bear, high up in the trees. The sun bear's nest of broken branches, for example, which may be anywhere between 6.5 and 23 ft (2–7 m) above the ground, looks rather like that of the

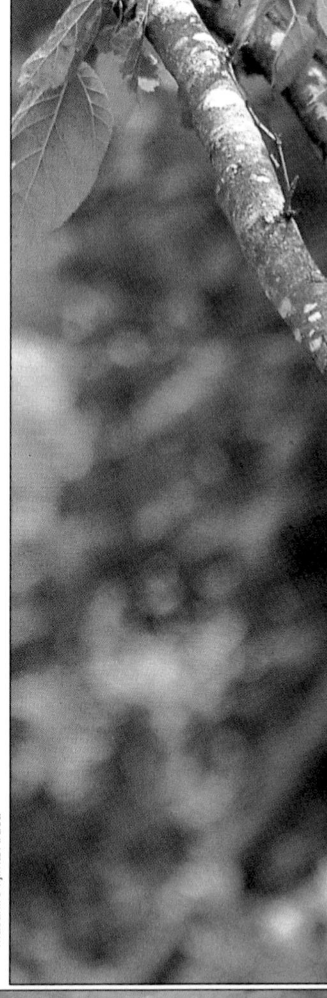

Masahiro Iijima/Ardea

François Gohier/Ardea

Bears are thoroughly at home in water; this spectacled bear is taking a dip to cool off (above).

AGGRESSION

All the small bears have a reputation for being fierce and aggressive. The little sun bear is apparently as dangerous as an enraged elephant and will charge for no apparent reason. It is said that even a tiger treats this animal with respect. The sloth bear also mounts a fearsome attack, rearing up on its hind legs and growling or even roaring. The Asian black bear, too, has a nasty disposition and a short temper. It is feared in Japan, where it is reported to kill two or three people each year.

The truth of the apparently ferocious encounters, however, is proof not so much of these animals' aggressive natures but of the manner of their reactions. The sloth bear, for example, has poor vision and hearing and becomes so engrossed when foraging that an intruder can get very close to it before it is aware of such a presence. Its aggressive response is simply the result of being startled. When an American black bear is disturbed, it usually wakes slowly, but the Asian black bear will awaken with a startled jump—understandably outraged!

orangutan, with which it shares its habitat, although the bear's nest tends to be nearer the trunk of the tree and is more loosely constructed. Heat tolerant, the sun bear often sunbathes in full sun unprotected by any shade. The spectacled bear converts its feeding platform of broken branches into a day bed by adding layers of leaves to make it cozy. It may also choose to sleep in a large tree cavity or in a shallow ground bed which it digs at the base of a cliff or in sheltered vegetation.

As a generalization, bears are solitary, although sun bears may stay together in pairs. Of the small bears, the sloth bear is the most sociable. It communicates with other sloth bears through facial expressions as well as a wide range of vocalizations—roars, squeals, huffs, howls, and gurgles. In spite of its shaggy coat, the sloth bear tolerates extreme heat and often rests during the day in full sunlight. Interestingly, although the sloth bear is an excellent, if cautious, climber, it will not climb a tree as a means of escaping a pursuing predator. This could well be because the leopard is one of its predators—which itself is an agile climber! ■

For the agile Asian black bear, trees are a source of food and resting places.

HABITATS

Bears are generally associated with northern forests, but this is true only of the brown bear and American black bear. The four small bears live mainly in and around tropical woodlands and forests. The Asian black bear has the widest distribution; it is found in Iran, Afghanistan, and northern Pakistan, east through the Himalayas and the Tibetan Plateau extending northward to Manchuria, and other forested areas of China. Bangladesh, Myanmar, and Laos mark its southern borders on mainland Asia. It is found, too, on the Japanese islands of Honshu and Shikoku as well as in Taiwan. Those in the more southerly parts of the range tend to have shorter, thinner coats with less dense undercoats.

Obviously, within this extensive range it occurs in a variety of climatic zones, but it always seeks out forests or moist, brushy areas; wooded hills and mountains are favored spots. In some areas, Asian black bears have an almost migratory pattern to their seasonal lifestyle. In the summer they wander higher up in the mountains, often to an altitude of 11,500 ft (3,500 m) or more. As winter approaches, they descend to the valleys again, although many stop to den at quite high elevations—around 8,850 ft (2,700 m). Others travel down to significantly lower areas, into the warmer valleys, where food may be more plentiful.

ALTHOUGH ITS RANGE IS EXTENSIVE, THE ASIAN BLACK BEAR IS TODAY ALMOST EXTINCT IN BANGLADESH

Although its range is extensive, the Asian black bear exists in scattered, often well-separated populations across it. Although these forests yield a rich diversity of food, a bear may have to travel quite some distance to gather enough. The destruction of forests over much of the Asian black bear's range accounts for the scattered populations, and also the disappearance of this bear from some areas.

In the southern part of its range, the Asian black bear shares its habitat with the sun bear, which then also extends farther south. The sun bear ranges through northeast India—where it was rediscovered in the 1980s—Bangladesh, southern China, Myanmar, Thailand, Cambodia and Vietnam, Malaysia, Java, Sumatra, and Borneo. It is the only bear that truly inhabits the lowland dense tropical rain forests of Southeast Asia, although it is found in forests at all elevations within its range and has

Tom McHugh/Photo Researchers/Oxford Scientific Films

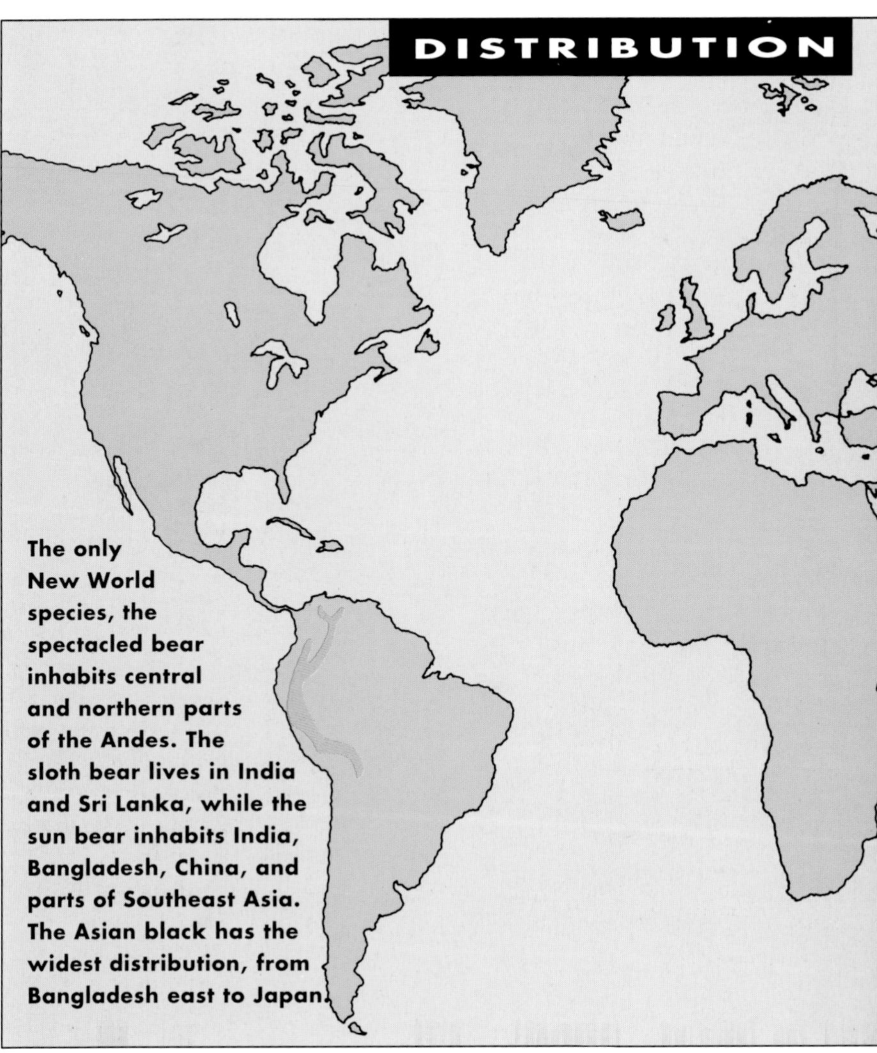

DISTRIBUTION

The only New World species, the spectacled bear inhabits central and northern parts of the Andes. The sloth bear lives in India and Sri Lanka, while the sun bear inhabits India, Bangladesh, China, and parts of Southeast Asia. The Asian black has the widest distribution, from Bangladesh east to Japan.

The sun bear inhabits lush tropical rain forests in India and Southeast Asia (left).

been seen at 4,900 ft (1,500 m) and higher in Borneo. Although the sun bear's distribution may sound extensive, the bear is rare throughout.

The range of the shaggy sloth bear extends to the west of these other two species. It is native to Sri Lanka, India, and Nepal. Although it is found at the base of the Himalayas, it probably does not cover any of the same territory as the Asian black bear—which is sometimes misleadingly known as the Himalayan black bear. In the forests of southern India, the sloth bear has been found up to elevations of 5,500 ft (1,700 m). It likes wooded areas, which suit its tree-climbing habits and skills. It favors both humid and dry conditions, and has been seen in the grasslands and evergreen forests of southern India and the thorn forests of the north, the riverside forests and floodplains in Assam and southern

The Asian black bear manages to keep warmer when huddled up in a tree "nest" (right).

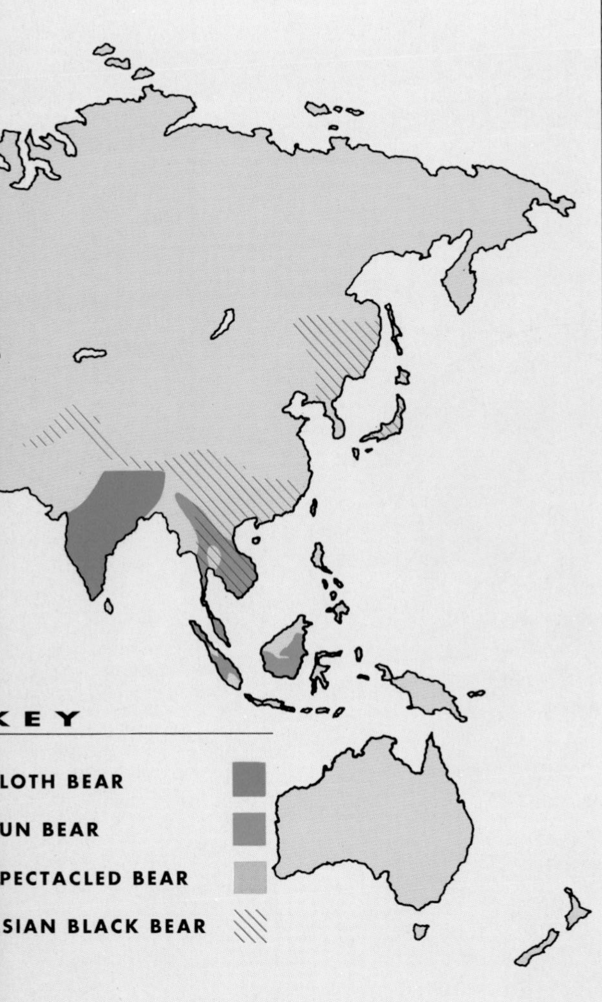

Masahiro Iijima/Ardea

WHY SMALLER?

The fact that all these bears are smaller than the American black bear, brown bear, and polar bear—markedly smaller than the last two—could well be a response to the climate in which they live. Their tropical or semitropical habitats tend not to support such a wide diversity of rich food in one area, such as the salmon rivers frequented by brown bears, for example, where they can gorge themselves. Often the smaller bears have to travel over quite large distances to find food. By and large, when they do find it, it does not have the high fat and protein content of food such as salmon, or the seals which are the staple diet of the polar bear. The sloth bear has a relatively low metabolic rate compared with that of the polar bear, which could well be a reflection on the lower energy—and body-building—content of its diet.

Nepal, as well as the arid-dry lowland national parks of Sri Lanka. It often shows a particular penchant for areas of rocky outcrops within wooded areas.

The spectacled bear straddles the Andes Mountains in South America on either side of the equator. Known also as the Andean bear, it has a range extending north as far as Venezuela, then running south through Colombia, Ecuador, Peru, and Bolivia down into Chile. Some people claim it may also still exist as far north as Panama and as far south as Argentina, but in neither of these areas have sightings been confirmed in recent years.

Within its Andean range the shy spectacled bear has actually adapted to a variety of different habitats, particularly as civilization has driven it away and broken up its populations. It lives, or has at some time lived, in lowland coastal scrubland and savanna at about 600 ft (180 m), the relatively arid alpine prairies flanking the Andes at about 1,640 ft (500 m), and high-altitude grasslands and forested mountains at the 13,800 ft (4,200 m) snow line. Its favorite habitat is the cloud forest at 6,000–8,800 ft (1,800–2,700 m). The bears have to travel in search of food, which is seasonally abundant; they tend to move along the landscape's natural ridge lines to avoid humans.

The small bears are not particularly territorial, and while they wander over a home range, this may well incorporate parts of the home ranges of other bears. Generally, they avoid one another. Some advertise their presence by marking key spots; the sloth bear, for example, has been seen rubbing trees with its stomach and rump, and raking deep claw marks down tree trunks. This could help males to keep clear of one another as well as help them in finding a mate at breeding time. Sun bears also make claw marks on trees, but these could also be associated with feeding or sharpening the claws, which, being nonretractile, become increasingly blunt. ■

FOCUS ON

THE PERUVIAN ANDES

Peru has three main land regions: from west to east, these are the Pacific coast, the Andean highlands—above 6,500 ft (1,980 m), and the *selva*, a region of forests and jungles. The spectacled bear is found in scattered populations throughout these regions.

The Andes form the longest mountain chain in the world, stretching 4,500 mi (7,240 km) along the entire western spine of South America. Several of the highest peaks rise over 20,000 ft (6,100 m) and only some of the Himalayan peaks rise higher. The Andes fall into three regions: northern, central, and southern; the Peruvian Andes occur in the central section. At about 500 mi (800 km) across at the widest point, the central Andes form the broadest part of the mountain chain. Two ranges running northwest and southeast make up this central section and between them lie the wide, high plains or plateaus of Peru and western Bolivia. These extend to some 12,000 ft (3,660 m) above sea level. Their foothills tend to be gentle, and they are crossed with sluggish, meandering rivers. The highest large lake in the world lies in this region, on the border between Peru and Bolivia: Lake Titicaca is 12,506 ft (3,812 m) above sea level and covers an area of 3,261 sq miles (8,446 sq km).

A. Greensmith/Ardea Inset picture Liz Bonford/Ardea

TEMPERATURE AND RAINFALL

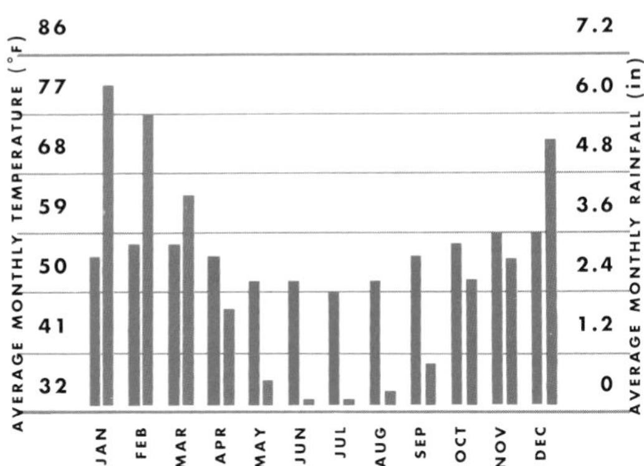

TEMPERATURE

RAINFALL

In Peru a cold ocean current from the Antarctic accounts for the desert conditions that extend down the coast to Chile. Besides bringing little moisture, these tend to produce relatively low temperatures. Eastern slopes tend to be warmer, with higher rainfall.

NEIGHBORS

From the foothills to the peaks, the Andes Mountains are a majestic haven for all kinds of wildlife; Colombia alone contains more bird species than all the rest of South America.

PUMA

The puma has the widest distribution of any cat and is common across North and South America.

ANDEAN CONDOR

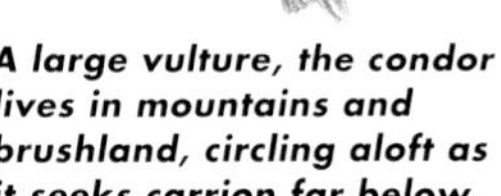

A large vulture, the condor lives in mountains and brushland, circling aloft as it seeks carrion far below.

Neighbor illustrations Louise Boulton and Elisabeth Smith

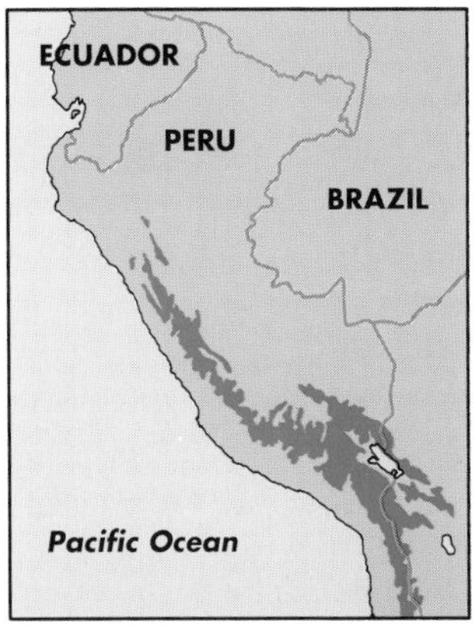

ECUADOR
PERU
BRAZIL
Pacific Ocean

THE ANDES

The mighty Andes Mountains stretch the length of South America, from Panama in the north to Cape Horn in the south. The high Andes, above 13,123 ft (4,000 m), peter out in northern Peru before returning in northern Ecuador.

HIGH ANDES

WHITE-TAILED DEER

When alarmed, this deer raises its tail to flash the white underside and warn others of danger.

EMERALD TOUCANET

This bird ranges from southern Mexico south to Peru, in humid mountain forests and open, tree-studded country.

WILD CAVY

Also known as a guinea pig, the cavy is actually a different species from the familiar domestic pet.

VICUÑA

This member of the camel family lives at very high elevations and is preyed on by the spectacled bear.

COCK-OF-THE-ROCK

Cocks-of-the-rock are startlingly beautiful birds that live near the ground in South American jungles.

FOOD AND FEEDING

Many of the truly flesh-eating carnivores—the big cats, for example—need to hunt for food perhaps only once every few days, gorging themselves to the limit when they make a kill. Not so the bears; they must spend a great percentage of their waking hours foraging for food, for they generally fuel their ample bulk on small, low-protein food items. In consequence, they need to have daily access to high volumes of food.

The Asian black bear's feeding habits tend to vary a little according to its location. In India and Tibet, it is reported to be more carnivorous, killing sheep, goats, and cattle. It can apparently kill a buffalo—an animal considerably larger than itself—by breaking its neck. However, other sources say that most of the Asian black bear's meat-eating habits in these areas involve carrion.

Across most of its range the Asian black bear is omnivorous, with vegetable matter making up a large amount of the diet. In the eastern Himalayas its springtime feasting consists of raspberry canes, cow parsnip, butterbur, and hydrangea, all of which have a high water content. Throughout the summer it searches out the fruits and berries that ripen at different times. It will happily bulldoze through a bramble patch, for example, pulling the branches to its mouth to pick off the berries, then simply plow onward toward the next ripening patch, trampling and flattening the vegetation in the process.

Beechnuts, chestnuts and acorns, hazelnuts, walnuts, and pine nuts are all favorite foods, rich in fat and complex carbohydrates. In autumn the black bear feasts on these wherever able, fattening up in readiness for the semi-dormant months during the winter. During this time the bear leaves its most distinctive feeding "trademark." Climbing high into a tree to gather nuts, the bear stands in a fork of sturdy branches and pulls the thinner limbs toward itself, bending them toward the trunk and cracking them. Picking off the nuts with its lips, it stamps the bent branches underfoot to construct a rough platform. Ragged and untidy, not unlike a crow's nest, these remain high up in the tree, sometimes several in adjacent trees.

In parts of its Chinese range, the Asian black bear and giant panda are found close together. Bamboo is the giant panda's main food, and it removes the fibrous, hairy sheath with the "thumb" on its forepaws before eating. The black bear will also tackle bamboo, but its feeding is less systematic; instead it eats the whole shoots, sheaths and all, chewing them thoroughly. The Asian black bear will also eat termites, beetle larvae, and honey. It enrages farmers in some areas by feeding on the grain of domestically grown crops.

HONEY-LOVERS

One of the sun bear's common names—the honey bear—gives a clue to the fact that it is a consummate honey-feeder. Its forepaws and strong, hooked claws are crucial to its feeding style; it rips open the trunks of trees to feed on

GET TO THE ROOTS

The spectacled bear will eat just about anything; it even digs up juicy roots and tubers from the soil (right).

FOOD FIGHT

Breaking into a bees' nest is no trouble for a sun bear. Ignoring the stings, it thrusts its long tongue into the nest and licks out the sweet honey (left).

Illustration John Morris/Wildlife Art Agency

the honey and larvae, as well as to search for insects and grubs. It has a particularly long tongue, which it pokes into the bees' nest to extract the food.

The sun bear also feeds on termites, using its foreclaws to break through the rock-hard, earthen underground nests. To collect the insects, it dips its forepaws alternately into the hole it has made in the nest, and licks off the termites that crawl onto them. Another food source that yields to the forepaws and claws is the soft growing bud of the coconut palm, known as palmite, which the bear rips open to consume. Since this action often kills the tree, sun bears can cause serious damage to a plantation of coconut palm trees, particularly as one bear is likely to return to the same place night after night until it has worked its way through the trees.

Small rodents, lizards, small birds, earthworms, insects, and fruit all supplement the sun bear's diet. It works over the forest floor with remarkable rapidity

BEARS HAVE AN ACUTE MEMORY OF THE LOCATIONS OF FOOD RESOURCES AND WILL RETURN TO THEM REGULARLY

in its search for food, stopping at the odd log or bush. In contrast to a temperate forest, where the forest floor may yield food in the way of fallen fruit and nuts or even carrion, these treasures quickly rot or decay in a tropical forest. The bear's search, therefore, is far less thorough than the systematic, slow foraging of bears in cooler climes.

The spectacled bear is often said to be more vegetarian than most bears, but in truth it will eat whatever it can find. It even devours a few plant species so tough that few other animals compete for them. Among these are palm leaves and nuts, cacti, orchids, and various bromeliads.

SUCCULENT PLANTS

Bromeliads are a family of plants with straplike and often spiny leaves. Many of them grow high up in trees, rooted to the mossy branches and nourished by organic debris. These plants make up an important part of the bear's diet—possibly as much as a 50 percent annual average; the bear tears away the

Andy Rouse/NHPA

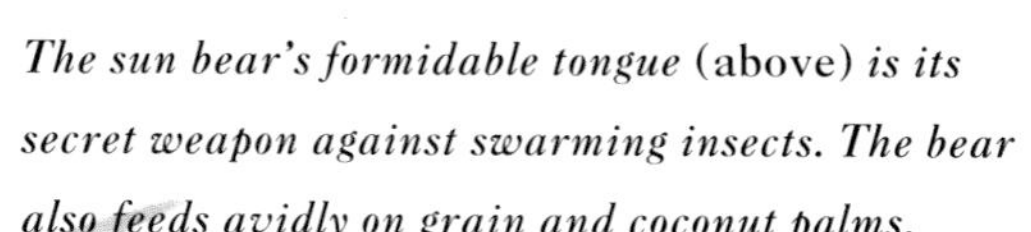

The sun bear's formidable tongue (above) *is its secret weapon against swarming insects. The bear also feeds avidly on grain and coconut palms.*

leaves to feed on the base and get to the edible heart, shredding the entire plant in the process. Bromeliads also provide a source of water as rain collects within the well formed by the rosette of their tightly packed leaves. The bear even climbs up into large cacti to reach the fruits that grow at the top, and it tears away the tough outer stalks of palms to get to the soft inner leaves. It will also strip bark from trees to feed on the cambium layer underneath. It is not averse to raiding sugarcane and corn from cultivated areas.

The spectacled bear reaches fruits by standing in the fork of a tree and pulling the laden branches inward in the way that the Asian black bear does. The spectacled bear, too, piles branches together to make a platform that gives it extra stability in its foraging activities. Small mammals, such as rabbits and mice, and larger prey, such as llamas, vicuñas, and domestic cattle, all make a tasty meal for the spectacled bear, as do birds, ants, and honey.

Sucking termites

The sloth bear will eat berries and the easy pickings of cultivated crops—sugarcane, maize, and yams. Occasionally it picks at the remains on the carcass of some other predator's kill.

Robin Budden/Wildlife Art Agency

J. van Gruisen/Ardea

It is not certain whether the Asian black bear kills large prey, such as deer (above), but it certainly feeds on carrion.

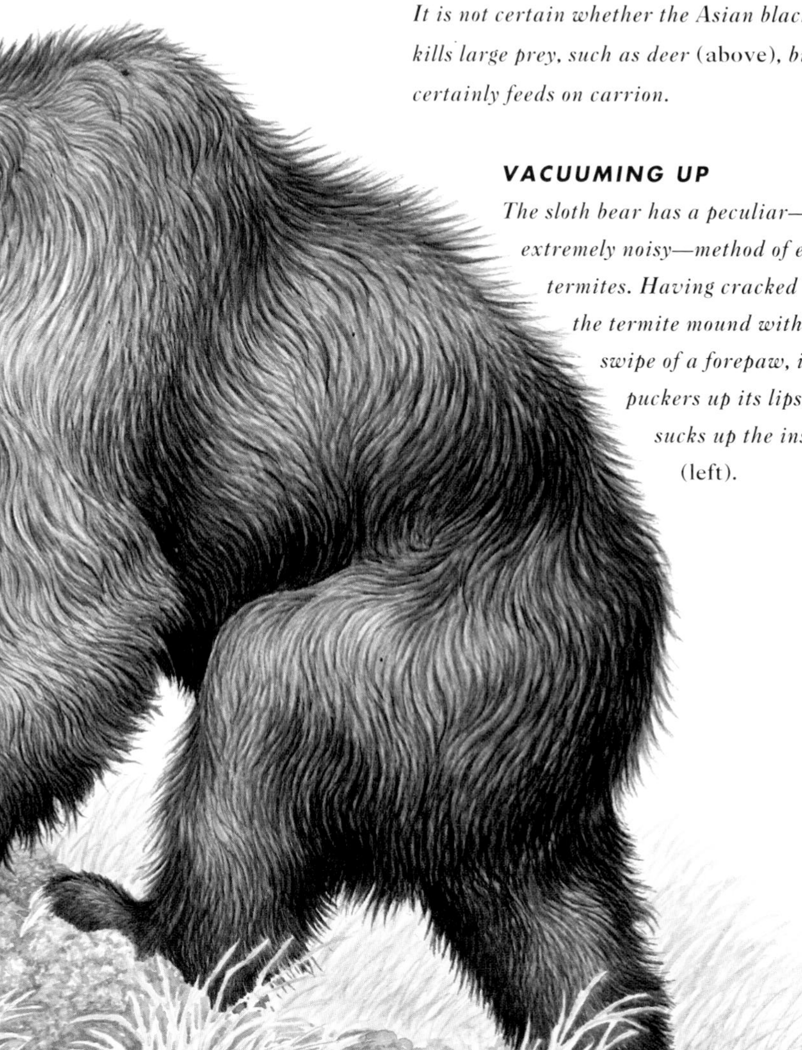

VACUUMING UP

The sloth bear has a peculiar—and extremely noisy—method of eating termites. Having cracked open the termite mound with a swipe of a forepaw, it puckers up its lips and sucks up the insects (left).

KEY FACTS

- **When an Asian black bear enters its winter dormancy, it is prevented from defecating by a plug of hair and vegetable material. To help it expel this in the spring when it emerges from its den, it claws the trunks of birch trees and licks up the oozing sap, which acts as a laxative.**

- **The eating habits of the spectacled bear, sun bear, and Asian black bear are highly important to the forest's continued growth and regeneration. As they move across the forest floor, they "sow" seeds of many fruits in their droppings, scattering them in new places far and wide. Also, when they tear at the branches of a fruit tree, far from damaging it, they are acting as natural "pruners," and usually the trees grow and crop the next year with renewed vigor.**

- **Although said to be mainly vegetarian, spectacled bears have an extremely varied diet that includes over 80 different recorded items. Among these are rabbits, mice, vicuña, llamas, deer, domestic cattle and their calves, birds, berries, 22 species of bromeliads, 11 species of cactus, 32 species of fruits, and food from 10 other plant families, including grasses, mosses, and orchid bulbs.**

The mainstay of its diet, however, is termites and ants, and the bear is specially adapted to attack these small insects. Having found a nest, the bear rips into it with its sickle-shaped claws. Putting its long muzzle close to the hole it has made, it blows fiercely to remove the dust and dirt, clenching its nostrils shut to keep out the dust. Then, with a powerful inhalation, it sucks up the insects, forming a perfect vacuum cleaner tube with its hollowed palate, mobile lips, and incisor gap. The impressive noise it makes while it does this can be heard about 650 ft (200 m) away.

The sloth bear tackles a bees' nest in similar fashion, having climbed into a tree—often to some height—to reach it. Having smashed into the nest, the bear hangs from a branch by its claws and dips its spare forepaw into the nest to scoop out the honey. Sloth bears have been heard crying with pain when stung by the angry bees, but it does not deter them; they will continue undaunted until they have eaten all the honeycomb. ■

LIFE CYCLE

Small bears breed at different times of the year depending on their location. The sun bear, for example, gives birth when fruit is abundant in the forest. In the northern parts of its range, the Asian black bear gives birth from late December to March, when it is tucked away for its winter sleep. Most births are subject to delayed implantation (see box); the sun bear, however, gestates for as little as 96 days, compared to seven to eight months in the Asian black bear, six to eight months in the spectacled bear, and six to seven months in the sloth bear.

Mating among sun and sloth bears tends to be noisy, with lots of hugging, mock fighting, barking, and growling. Sun bears form strong bonds in the wild, often throughout the year. Most other bears only leave their more solitary existence to breed, and often mate with a number of partners.

Birth occurs in a cave, among tree roots, or deep in the ground cover. One to three, but most usually two, young are born. They are tiny: Sun bear cubs weigh less than 8 oz (225 g) and are very fragile, with paper-thin, naked skin. The female bear licks them to encourage urination and defecation. At two months old, they begin to walk and are weaned two months later, although they will stay with the mother far longer.

Asian black bear cubs are about the same size, but within a month or so they can follow the mother about. Weaned at about three-and-a-half months old, they disperse about two years later. Some stay with the female even longer, for these bears have been seen with two sets of cubs.

Before giving birth, the female spectacled bear prepares a cozy "nest" among ground cover. Her cubs are heavy at 10.5–17.5 oz (300–500 g), but they are still helpless, and she has to encourage them to suckle. Their eyes open at three weeks old or more, and they start following the mother around soon after this. She keeps in constant touch with them, calling out to them with a high, singing sound. They respond with a whine if they are in distress, at which she comes running to their aid. These bears may leave their mother when only six months old.

The sloth bear stays with her tiny cubs in the den for one to two months after the birth. Later they will ride on her back, clinging tightly to her shaggy fur. The cubs soon establish which one rides on the shoulders and which sits on the lower back; if, for any reason, a cub climbs upon its mother and finds its "seat" already occupied, it becomes highly anxious

STRIFE BETWEEN SUITORS

Like all bears, Asian black bears are not used to dealing with company, and when two males track down the same female, they resort to an angry contest (above).

Illustrations Simon Turvey/Wildlife Art Agency

LOTS TO LEARN

The cubs grow rapidly, but they have much to learn about hunting and avoiding danger. It may be up to two years before they finally leave their mother (above).

FROM BIRTH TO DEATH

SUN BEAR

GESTATION: ABOUT 96 DAYS
WEIGHT AT BIRTH: 7.9 OZ (225 G)
FIRST WALKING: 2 MONTHS
INDEPENDENCE: 2–3 YEARS
SEXUAL MATURITY: 3 YEARS
LONGEVITY: 24 YEARS RECORDED

SLOTH BEAR

GESTATION: 6–7 MONTHS
WEIGHT AT BIRTH: 7.7 OZ (220 G)
EYES OPEN: 3 WEEKS
FIRST WALKING: 4–5 WEEKS
INDEPENDENCE: 2–3 YEARS
SEXUAL MATURITY: NOT KNOWN

SPECTACLED BEAR

GESTATION: 6.5–8.5 MONTHS
LITTER SIZE: 1–3, USUALLY 2 (SIMILAR IN OTHER SMALL BEARS)
WEIGHT AT BIRTH: 10.5–17.5 OZ (300–500 G)
EYES OPEN: 3–4 WEEKS
FIRST WALKING: 4–5 WEEKS
INDEPENDENCE: 6 MONTHS
SEXUAL MATURITY: 4 YEARS
LONGEVITY: 36 YEARS RECORDED IN CAPTIVITY; NOT KNOWN IN WILD

GROWING UP

The life of an Asian black bear

BORN BLIND

in a snug den, the bear cubs open their eyes after a week or so. They are a tiny fraction of their mother's size (above).

BEAR-BACK RIDERS

Asian bear cubs develop quickly, but they still need help in keeping up with their mother on food forays. For the first month at least, piggybacks are the most comfortable mode of transport (above).

PUTTING IT OFF

Delayed implantation—when the female's egg does not implant into the wall of the uterus until a few months after fertilization—is a survival mechanism for bears in cold climates. They usually mate in the spring. As bear babies are so tiny, the gestation period would actually be very short if the embryo development were to follow directly from mating. The babies would then be born in the autumn or early winter and become mobile and hungry when food is scarce and the weather cold. Instead, the delay permits the "real" gestation to occur over winter and the birth to occur in spring, when food is plentiful.

Although delayed implantation is less important to animals living in tropical areas, it still occurs in most small bears.

and fights to get to the familiar position. When nervous, they bury their heads in the mother's fur. They hitch rides until they are about one third the size of their mother—usually at one or two years old.

Male sloth bears are said to be particularly gentle to cubs, which is unusual among bears. In some species, the female has to protect them from their father and other males, who will readily kill them in order to get to the female. Some research suggests that male sloth bears assist with bringing up the cubs. The young will stay with the mother until they are between two and three years old. ■

Bear cubs, like their parents, are insatiably eager to investigate their surroundings (below).

Masahiro Iijima/Ardea

SMALL IS VULNERABLE

MOST BEAR SPECIES HAVE DRASTICALLY DECLINED IN NUMBER SINCE HUMANS HAVE ENCROACHED ON THEIR HABITATS. THE FOUR SMALL BEARS ARE AS MUCH AT RISK AS ANY AND COULD EASILY BECOME EXTINCT

Humankind has always shared the land with bears, for bears were roaming the world long before we evolved. For centuries, there were infinitely more bears than humans in the world, but even then it was likely that humans killed more bears than the other way round. Bears disappeared from the area now known as Denmark nearly 4,000 years ago, and although no one knows for certain what caused their demise, it is generally thought to have been attributable to humans in some way.

Throughout their association, humans have revered the bear, often at the same time as persecuting it. The spectacled bear of South America, said by some authorities to be the rarest species of bear in the world today, has been treated like a god in some places and destroyed on sight in others as a purveyor of evil. In Thailand, the sun bear is kept as a pet by devout Buddhists, who believe this will put them in good stead in the afterlife. At the same time, these bears are widely killed for their separate parts, which are believed to have healing and curing properties and which change hands, even today, for outrageously high sums of money.

STUDIES SUGGEST THAT IF MORE THAN TWO PERCENT OF THE FEMALE BEARS IN A LOCAL POPULATION ARE KILLED, THAT POPULATION WILL SUFFER A DECLINE

All four species of small bear have been hunted over the centuries for their fur, fat, and meat, as well as for sport. In South America, meat of the spectacled bear once fed the railway workers; the fat is said to have curative properties for conditions as varied as rheumatism and blindness, while the bones, when ground, are thought to provide strength and virility. Even the blood, if drunk while still warm, is said to be a tonic. These sorts of beliefs persist in most regions where the small bears are found, and they are extremely hard to change. In places where small bear cubs are prized as cuddly pets, such as in Thailand and other parts of Southeast Asia, their owners know that they will find a ready market for the animals when they grow too big.

HABITAT DESTRUCTION

Insidious though these practices and reasons for killing bears appear to us, there are other, more far-reaching ways in which humans have affected and

Masahiro Iijima/Ardea

Animal traps, like this vicious bamboo spike pit in Nepal, are still used illegally to trap bears (above).

THEN & NOW

This map shows the current distribution of the Asian black bear.

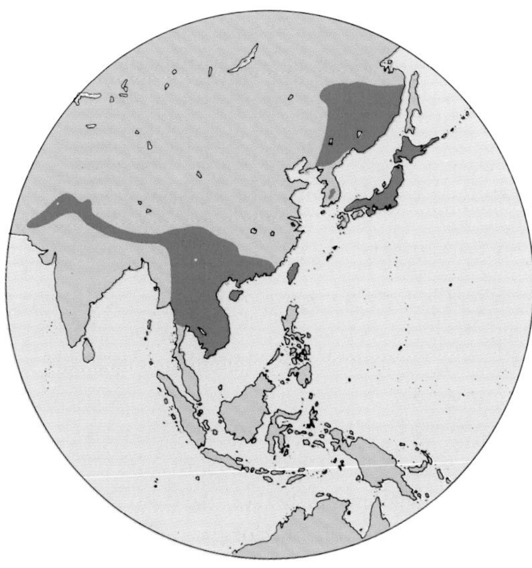

ASIAN BLACK BEAR

Although the Asian black bear enjoys the widest distribution of all the small bears, its future is in no way secure. It is declining all over its range wherever it encounters humans, and in Bangladesh it is almost extinct. The cause of most of its troubles is simply the massive increase in the human population. Its wooded habitats are slashed to make room for crops. To make matters worse, the bear raids these for food—usually with fatal results.

continue to affect the future of all small bears. The chief among these is in the destruction of the bears' habitats, forcing them into ever smaller, more fragmented areas. This sets up its own vicious circle, for as the bears find themselves with a reduced environment in which to live, they inevitably come into closer contact, and thus conflict, with humans. Such conflicts will almost always end in confrontations in which humans are bound to win.

By and large, bears are creatures of the woods and forests, straying out into fertile valleys where the rich soils produce plenty of fruit and berries upon which they glut. The story of the continued destruction of forest and woodland is well known, and it is particularly prevalent in the regions inhabitated by small bears. In many of these areas, the native human populations are poor, and by hacking

Andy Rouse/NHPA

Taiwan still turns a blind eye to a thriving bear-parts trade; this sun bear is awaiting export (left).

their way into the jungle, they are able to clear small areas that will sustain them and their families for a while. Unfortunately, their primitive farming practices soon make the land barren, and they are forced to move on, destroying more land—and therefore bear territory—as they go.

Of course, there are also forest clearances on much larger and more organized scales in many areas, where the land is needed to construct hydroelectric projects, to clear roads through, to build new cities, or simply to supply the world's demands for timber. One way or another, in tropical Asia, it has been estimated that close to 70 percent of original wildlife habitat has been destroyed in recent decades, and the destruction continues. In South America, the figures are probably worse.

Bears are particularly vulnerable to the alteration or loss of their habitat. If they were true carnivores—eating only, or even mainly, the flesh of other animals—they could probably survive in

> BECAUSE BEARS NATURALLY LIVE AT LOW DENSITIES, THEY SUFFER WHEN THEIR WOODLANDS ARE BROKEN UP

much smaller areas than they habitually need. The fact that they have become omnivorous and able to survive in variable habitats has undoubtedly led to their success, up until now. But, with the mainstay of their diet being fruit, berries, and other forms of vegetation, by and large they need a fairly big area over which to roam, sharing with few other bears. Females do not bear young until they are a few years old; they seldom produce more than two in a litter and they do not give birth again until these cubs are sufficiently mature to fend for themselves in the wild—a period that may be as long as three years. Thus a population does not renew itself quickly, in the way of small, fast breeders such as rodents, for example.

POPULATION FRAGMENTATION

The effect of habitat destruction is highly significant to these animals. Populations get forced into smaller areas where it is simply impossible for them to survive in large numbers, so the populations become smaller or disappear altogether. There is little or no chance for a population to renew itself, particularly as this takes years. Populations become fragmented, thus reducing the chance of bears finding new mates, since they cannot cross the new boundaries erected by man. Again, this will have an effect on resident populations, forcing inbreeding and a weakening of later generations.

When bears are deprived of sufficient natural

Andy Rouse/NHPA

ENDANGERED SPECIES

THE TRADE IN BEAR PARTS

That bear body parts are credited with medicinal powers may seem bizarre to us in the West, but it is nevertheless so deep-rooted in the culture of many Asian and South American peoples that bears continue not only to be caught and killed for their various parts but also to be bred and kept in captivity for this express purpose.

Much of the bear is valued: The fur and hide have obvious uses in providing warm clothing or rugs. The fat is said to have all manner of properties, from treating colds, baldness, and skin complaints, such as ringworm and blackheads, to "strengthening" the mind and promoting long life. On a more practical level, it can be used as lamp oil. Bones are ground down and used as a cure for rheumatism, among other things, and blood is drunk as a tonic and antidote to nervousness. The spinal cord, when rubbed on a scalp, is rumored to promote hair growth and prevent scalp disorders, while claws and teeth act as good-luck charms and amulets.

Many people credit the meat with good eating, but the most highly prized—and therefore expensive—edible delicacy, at least in China, is the bear's paw. The Chinese have placed a high value on this part of the bear for centuries, eating it not just for its apparently delicious taste, but because it is also supposed to be an antidote for rheumatism and provide strength of mind and body. Overall, however, the

CONSERVATION MEASURES

- The World Wide Fund for Nature (WWF) and other conservation organizations have been trying to halt the illegal trade in bear parts. Traders often claim the parts belong to American black bears or brown bears, when in fact they probably belong to Asian species.

- In 1991 the WWF opened additional offices in Malaysia and began training field investigators specifically to break the bear

most highly prized part, and the organ for which bears are killed illegally the world over, is the gallbladder. Many bears have been discovered slaughtered, left entirely intact except for this organ, which has been ripped out. According to traditional medicine, there is little that a bear's gallbladder cannot improve, and these organs change hands for huge sums of money. In the 1980s a single gallbladder from an illegally killed Asian black bear sold at a public auction in Korea for $64,000—this, even after the culprit had been caught and punished for his misdeed!

BEARS IN DANGER

THE CHART BELOW SHOWS HOW THE IUCN CURRENTLY CLASSIFIES THE STATUS OF THE FOUR SMALL BEAR SPECIES:

SPECTACLED BEAR	VULNERABLE
ASIAN BLACK BEAR	VULNERABLE
SUN BEAR	VULNERABLE
SLOTH BEAR	VULNERABLE

VULNERABLE INDICATES THAT THE ANIMAL IS LIKELY TO MOVE INTO THE ENDANGERED CATEGORY UNLESS STEPS ARE TAKEN TO IMPROVE ITS STATUS.

Masahiro Iijima/Ardea

THE ASIAN BLACK BEAR'S GALLBLADDER IS ALMOST AS COSTLY AS CHINESE WHITE HEROIN.

trade, with particular regard to the sun bear. In North Borneo at this time, a survey found only nine sun bears, all of them in captivity.

● Bear gallbladder has actually proven in tests to be medicinally effective; the active chemical was isolated by scientists in 1927 and can now be manufactured synthetically. Sadly, however, the modern drug is not deemed desirable by Chinese doctors.

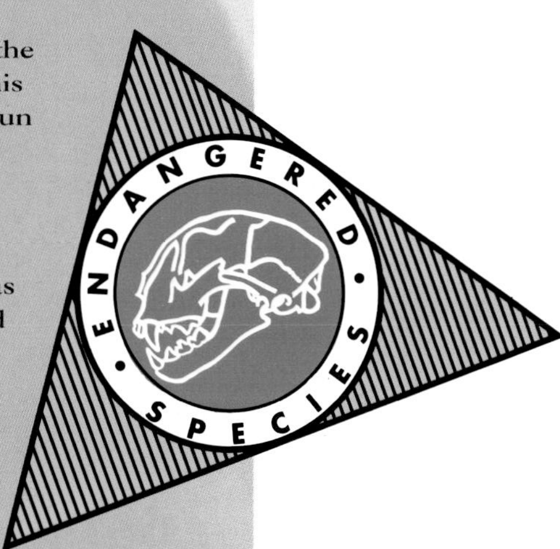

growing food, they readily turn to what is being "supplied" by humans. So they plunder orchards for fruit and crop fields for corn—even occasionally gardens for vegetables! They rip open beehives and take domestic animals as easy prey.

Farmers and foresters inevitably brand bears a nuisance and have no qualms about killing them, even though these species are given legal protection in many areas. Local people find the laws easy to ignore if a bear is apparently threatening their livelihood, and such protective laws are notoriously difficult to enforce over wide areas. If they escape the guns and traps of farmers and hunters, the bears may well go on to raid garbage cans, picking over the remains of food in these and eating other substances, which are not actually edible—even to bears. Many bears have died as a result of eating garbage.

What makes the plight of the small bears all the more acute is the nature of the areas they inhabit. Most bears are secretive and will live, if possible, in remote spots. The study of bears in the wild is difficult anywhere, but is made even more difficult where the small bears are concerned, for they tend to live in countries that either do not have money to spend on the study of bears or consider it less important than providing for the human population. So even if their needs were taken into consideration, lack of knowledge about their numbers and whereabouts could lead to wrong decisions and poor management.

The spectacled bear has certainly suffered a dramatic loss of habitat, mainly through people pushing further into its homelands to open up areas for agriculture. As a result, its populations have become fragmented, and deprivation of important food sources has led to conflict with local people as bears wander into cultivated areas and start competing for food. Peru was once a stronghold of the spectacled bear; not only has it fallen afoul of landowners and farmers in many parts of this country, but it is also

ALONGSIDE MAN

RELUCTANT ENTERTAINER

Since prehistoric times, the history of bears and humankind has been inextricably intertwined. Wherever bears have occurred, humans have been involved with them, usually hunting them but often catching them and keeping them as pets or exploiting them in some way. Throughout the ages and all over the world, bears crop up in mythology and literature. At some stage humans recognized the "entertainment" potential of bears; in Roman times they were adversaries for gladiators and dogs at public fights and spectacles, while the obscene sport of bearbaiting—in which a bear that was either restrained by a chain or had already been disabled, usually by blinding, was tormented with sticks and dogs—was carried on in European countries for centuries.

Humans also realized that they could exploit a bear's ability not merely to stand up on its hind legs but also to shuffle along. Bears have been popular as circus entertainers, probably since circuses began, and "dancing" bears—where the hapless beasts are led around, often by a ring inserted through the broken sinus bones of the nose—were once a common sight through much of eastern Europe and India. Sloth bears are still fairly common as street entertainers in India, even though it is illegal to own a bear caught in the wild in that country.

The sun bear is among the least studied of all bears, although it is a popular pet in its native Thailand. Its habitat continues to be destroyed in large measure for cash-crop agriculture, subsistence farming, and timber harvesting, resulting in the same habitat fragmentation and inevitable conflict with people as it shares their homeland, raids their crops, and preys on their livestock.

The sloth bear's more specialized diet of termites brings it less into conflict with humans than the other species. However, it does come into competition with local villagers in India as it is fond of a particular flower, the *mohwa*, which blooms in the spring and which villagers ferment to make an alcoholic beverage. The sloth bear's inclination to feed also on cultivated sugarcane, corn, and yams deepens this conflict in some areas.

The sloth bear's homeland on the Indian subcontinent is also beset by a human population explosion, and the forests of India and Sri Lanka fell to the chainsaw some while ago. The sloth bear's habitat has been much reduced, pushing the species into isolated areas and subjecting it to the problems of natural regeneration. In the main, however, the sloth bear is less likely than other bears to share its habitat with humans, and so has withdrawn deeper into the few areas of natural habitat left to it. ■

widely hunted for sport and killed for its meat, which is considered a delicacy, as well as for its skin and fat. Only in Ecuador, where the wilderness has yet to yield to agriculture, does the bear have a stronghold today. It also survives in various national parks in Peru, Colombia, and Venezuela.

The Asian black bear once had a distribution that was second in extent only to the brown bear. Unfortunately, however, it lives in a part of the world which has seen the greatest human population explosion in recent decades, and inevitably the bear has suffered. It is blamed—and killed—for preying on domestic animals in some areas, but it is even more vilified for the damage it apparently does to trees, plundering their harvest and ripping off branches of oak, beech, cherry, and dogwood trees. It also tears at the bark to get at the cambium—a practice that often kills the trees.

In Japan, this bear has a liking for cedars and cypress—trees that are considered valuable. This, combined with the fact that it is much feared as a killer itself and is valued both as a sport target and for its body parts, has led to some 3,000 bears being killed annually. It has become extinct in parts of Japan, as well as in Pakistan, China, and Korea.

Even today, when bears are rare, they continue to be humbled in tricks such as this.

David Hosking/Frank Lane Picture Agency

INTO THE FUTURE

The future for the small bears looks bleak. Their habitats are still being eroded, often in areas where funding for wildlife reseach has a low priority. In the case of the sun bear, so little is known about its lifestyle that conservationists simply do not know where to begin.

As long as bear parts continue to be sought after for medicinal purposes in Asia, people will defy legislation and kill them, for the prices they command are too tempting. Some 8,000 bears are farmed in China for their bile, under the pretense that it takes the pressure off the wild bears. This is a fallacy: Bears are not bred to be released back into the wild, their use in the medical trade is perpetuated instead of attempts being made to find other remedies, and their habits are not scientifically studied. Ranched wildlife products often create a conduit for illegal products from the species' wild relatives.

The sloth bear fares well in game parks and reserves such as the Royal Chitwan National Park in Nepal. Established in the mid-1970s, Chitwan probably had as its main aim the preservation of tigers. but sloth bears thrived so well there that, in 1990, they underwent radio-tracking research in Chitwan—the first time these bears had been so closely studied.

The rare spectacled bear may benefit from the fact that some, at least, of its habitat is in remote mountain regions. But if it is to survive, not only does it need protection in national parks, but safe natural "corridors" must be established between its isolated populations. This would allow the bears to mix more freely and avoid the risk of inbreeding.

There is an urgent need for education. Children in many Southeast Asian regions view bears as animals to be kept as pets until they grow too big, at which point they are sold to those who trade in their various parts. This is the accepted way of life for bears in many people's minds, and will continue to be so—unless the experts help to educate the less well informed. ■

PREDICTION

URGENT ACTION NEEDED

As large mammals with a price on their head in their homelands, small bears will continue to decline unless the destruction of their habitats is halted, the trade in animal parts is brought to an end, and the public is educated about their plight.

A CAPTIVE SPECTACLE

Spectacled bears, along with other bears, have been kept in zoos since the beginning of the 20th century. In times gone by, bears were kept in appalling conditions, and, unfortunately, little has improved over the years. In recent years, zoos have begun to provide bears with enclosures that make their lives more natural and less stressful. They are realizing, too, that bears are naturally inquisitive animals that need constant mental stimulation. Nevertheless, the number of spectacled bears kept successfully in captivity has risen steadily during the 20th century, an increase attributable recently to the Species Survival Plan (SSP).

This program was established by Americans in 1980 and aims to include some 200 species by the end of the 20th century. The idea is for zoos around the world to cooperate with one another to propagate species at risk in the wild. The spectacled bear became included in the SSP in 1989, joining such animals as Siberian and Sumatran tigers, the okapi, and the gorilla. Although it may not be possible to release animals bred in captivity back into the wild, the information learned about reproduction, behavior, and diet as well as genetic makeup can be used to help those animals that are still living free in their natural habitats. Captive animals also function as "wildlife ambassadors" to over 600 million visitors annually worldwide.

Illustration Barry Croucher/Wildlife Art Agency

BEAVERS

RELATIONS

Beavers are squirrel-like rodents of the suborder Sciuromorpha, within the rodent order. Other members of the suborder include:

TREE SQUIRRELS

FLYING SQUIRRELS

PRAIRIE DOGS

WOODCHUCK

POCKET GOPHERS

POCKET MICE

SPRINGHARE

Wendy Shattil & Bob Rozinski/Oxford Scientific Films

True beavers and mountain beavers belong to the order Rodentia, along with nearly 2,000 other species. The mountain beaver and beavers are no more closely related to one another than to any other of the almost 400 species in the suborder of squirrel-like rodents.

ORDER

Rodentia (rodents)

SUBORDER

Sciuromorpha (squirrel-like rodents)

FAMILY

Castoridae

GENUS

Castor

SPECIES

canadensis (Canadian, or North American, beaver)

fiber (European beaver)

FAMILY

Aplodontidae

GENUS

Aplodontia

SPECIES

rufa (mountain beaver)

MASTER BUILDERS

THE BEAVER'S DRAB APPEARANCE BELIES THE FACT THAT IT IS, INDEED, ONE OF NATURE'S FINEST ENGINEERS. IT WAS DAMMING AND DIVERTING RIVERS LONG, LONG BEFORE HUMANS HARNESSED THE POWER OF WATER

"In the beginning, the earth was covered with waters, in which the muskrat, the otter, and the beaver dwelt. They dived down into the waters and raised up the mud, from which the great spirit Manitou created the earth. The mountains, waterfalls, and caves were the work of beavers, which were as big as giants."

These words from a North American Indian fable illustrate how humans have always admired the beaver for its feats of engineering. The lodges and dams of the North American, or Canadian, beaver, *Castor canadensis,* are among the most remarkable constructions in the animal kingdom. The European beaver, *Castor fiber,* has the same building skills, but uses them only when conditions are unsuitable for burrowing. These two species are the only members of the true beaver family, Castoridae. Many zoologists consider them to be the same species, but the North American beaver is generally darker in color and has shorter nasal bones in its skull.

The mountain beaver (below) *is in fact neither a true mountain-dweller nor really a beaver.*

Pat & Tom Leeson/Oxford Scientific Films

Related to the two true beavers only through its placement in the suborder Sciuromorpha is the mountain beaver. Considered to be among the most primitive of living rodents because of the nature of its eye sockets and its teeth formula, this small animal looks more like a marmot or a woodchuck than like the other beavers.

All beavers are contained in the group known as the squirrel-like rodents, the Sciuromorpha (ski-yor-o-MOR-fah). The true beavers are the giants of this group; in fact, the European beaver is Europe's largest rodent, while the North American beaver is beaten in size only by the South American capybara.

Beaver beginnings

The three groups of rodents—squirrel-like, mouselike, and cavylike—began their evolution during the Eocene epoch (54–38 million years ago). The first ancestors of the true beavers emerged early in the Oligocene epoch (38–26 million years ago) in North America and Europe. These ancient beavers spent less time in water than their modern descendants. *Steneofiber* was a European beaver that lived during the early Miocene epoch (25–5 million years ago). One of its contemporaries, *Palaeocastor,* inhabited the dry, sandy uplands of middle America. It had slightly longer legs and a much chunkier body than today's beavers.

During the course of evolution, beavers gradually adapted to suit a more aquatic lifestyle. Around two million years ago, giant beavers roamed in both North America and Europe. The giant American species was the size of an American black bear; it lived near water and had large webbed feet, indicating an ability to swim well. However, it probably did not

A sleek torpedo in the water, the beaver appears as an ungainly and bedraggled creature on land (left).

Hans Reinhard/Bruce Coleman Ltd.

fell trees as modern beavers do. Incidentally, the brains of the giant beavers were no larger than those of today's beavers, which evolved in Europe sometime within the last seven million years. They crossed to North America, where they evolved separately from the European beaver into today's North American beaver.

The mountain beaver is now restricted to a small strip of North America's Pacific coast, but its ancestors once radiated from America to populate Asia and Europe as well. The earliest species lived about forty million years ago in America; today's mountain beaver occurred within the last two million years only in America and is the sole survivor of a long and varied line of ancestral species.

Beavers Today

Swimming is as natural to the beaver as it is to a seal. Propulsion comes mainly from the hind legs, with their broad, fully webbed feet, while the broad, oval, paddle-shaped tail serves both as a rudder and as a source of speed when required. Valves close over the nostrils and ears while underwater, and the tiny eyes are guarded by a translucent membrane. The fur has two layers; a dense, soft undercoat traps an insulating layer of air, on top of which lie long, oily guard hairs. The hairs mat together over the underfur, which

A PRICELESS HARVEST

Like many animals, the beaver possesses a pair of anal glands, the greasy secretions of which give off a distinctive musky odor. As far as the beaver is concerned, the function of this secretion, known as castoreum, is to mark territory in order to advertise its presence or sexual condition to other beavers that are passing by. However, for centuries humans have prized the secretion for use in the perfume industry and also for quasi-medical or pharmaceutical remedies. Various tribes and people in countries inhabited by beavers have varyingly attributed castoreum with aphrodisiac powers as well as being a cure for conditions ranging from frostbite to hysteria. In days gone by, the fur trappers would smear sticks with castoreum and use them to bait traps to attract and catch beavers.

stays virtually dry and prevents the skin from ever getting wet. This keeps the beaver warm in its often cold environment, but the animal is aided in this, too, by a thick layer of fat under the skin.

A beaver often needs to gnaw or carry branches underwater. It can seal its mouth by closing its lips behind its incisors, and, as an extra precaution, it can block the passage to its pharynx with its tongue.

Like most rodents, the beaver has a good sense of smell, but this is of little use underwater, where its nostrils are closed to keep water out. Instead, there are sensory whiskers on its snout that help it find its way in particularly murky water. However, the whiskers are not as developed as those of the mountain beaver, which uses them to navigate in the dark tunnels of its underground world.

Living an almost entirely subterranean lifestyle, the mountain beaver is equipped with few of the true beaver's adaptations, although it does have a similar coat arrangement of a thick underfur topped with guard hairs, which in this case are quite sparse. The fur is short and colored a reddish or grayish brown—usually a little paler on the undersides. The mountain beaver has a dumpy, thickset body and a blunt head with small ears and eyes. Each foot has five toes, with those of the forefeet being used for grasping food items as well as for digging. ■

B/W illustrations Ruth Grewcock

EUROPEAN BEAVER

Castor fiber
(KASS-tor FY-ber)

The largest of all European rodents, it is found mainly in northern Europe and Eurasia, having been successfully reintroduced in many areas. Those in the more southerly parts of the range are generally paler in color than northern individuals.

MOUNTAIN BEAVER

Aplodontia rufa (ap-lo-DON-ti-a ROO-fa)

Known also as the sewellel, this sole member of its family is not a true beaver. It looks like a woodchuck, except that its tail is virtually nonexistent.

The claws on its forefeet are particularly long and strong for digging, and the first toe is specially flattened to serve as a grooming aid. The family name means "rootless teeth," and refers to the simple molars.

SPRINGHARE

SCALY-TAILED SQUIRRELS

POCKET MICE

POCKET GOPHER

MOUSELIKE RODENTS

THE RODENTS' FAMILY TREE

The suborder Sciuromorpha, squirrel-like rodents, comprises seven families including those of the true beavers and the mountain beaver. Also in this group are the squirrels, scaly-tailed squirrels, pocket gophers, pocket mice, and the springhare. The suborder Myomorpha, or mouselike rodents, comprises nearly 1,200 species in five families, whereas there are fewer than 200 species within the suborder Hystricomorpha, or cavy and porcupinelike rodents.

CANADIAN BEAVER

Castor canadensis
(KASS-tor can-ah-DEN-sys)

Probably the best known of the true beavers, this animal is widespread in Canada and the United States and has been introduced to parts of Scandinavia and Europe. In appearance, it probably most resembles the muskrat and coypu, although it is bigger than both these rodents, neither of which possesses the beaver's unique tail.

SQUIRREL

QUIRREL-LIKE RODENTS

CAVYLIKE RODENTS

ANCESTORS

STENEOFIBER

Steneofiber **(sten-i-oh-FY-ber) was one of the prehistoric beavers that lived in Europe in the early Miocene period, which began 25 million years ago. A chunky animal, similar in size to a muskrat, it possessed none of the aquatic adaptations of today's true beavers. However, clearly it did possess the chisel-like incisors that are a characteristic of all rodents, for it used these together with its claws to dig its deep burrows, scooping the loose soil away with the feet and finally pushing it aside with the blunt head. Abundant remains of this animal have been found in limestone deposits in St. Gerand-le-Puy in France.**

Color illustrations Evi Antoniou

ANATOMY: THE CANADIAN BEAVER

THE FACIAL FEATURES

are all small. The ears and nostrils are protected underwater by valves that close to keep out the water, and the eyes are protected by a translucent "third eyelid."

With a head-and-body length of 35–47 in (89–119 cm), the Canadian beaver (above center) is generally a little larger than the European beaver, which tends to vary slightly in size according to location. In the rodent world, the Canadian beaver is second in size only to the capybara. However, a mature male beaver may weigh as much as a capybara. The mountain beaver (above right) is considerably smaller, reaching a maximum length of 18 in (46 cm) and a top weight of 3 lb (1.4 kg).

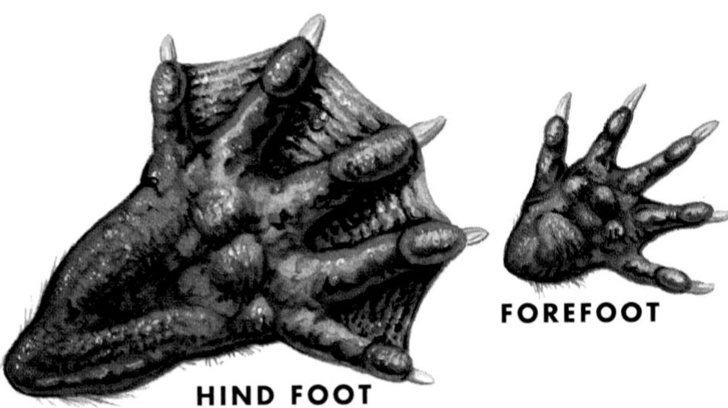

TEETH

Lower and upper jaws each have a pair of chisel-like incisors, which are covered on their front surfaces with an extremely hard enamel. The inner part of each tooth is softer, so as the beaver gnaws at bark, the teeth are both worn and sharpened. The action of each pair of teeth against the other pair also helps to keep them sharp. The long roots of these teeth curve far back inside the bones of the skull and jaw; they have open roots so that they grow continuously, the upper pair over the lower pair.

FOREFEET

The forefeet are considerably smaller than the hind feet, but remarkably dexterous. The beaver uses them to pick up and hold branches as it gnaws them, to dig its canals, and to scoop up mud from the bottom of the pond or lake. It also uses them to extract waterproofing oil from its sebaceous glands before rubbing its forefeet over its fur. All the front toes have claws.

X-RAY

CANADIAN BEAVER SKELETON

In all rodents, the elbow is so jointed as to allow free motion of the forearm. The beaver's shoulder blades are comparatively small, as its forelimbs are not needed to carry the animal's weight.

small shoulder blades

fully articulating elbow

long and robust hind limbs

SKULLS

The bone structure is heavy, with broad, flat anchorages for the larg[e] masseter muscles: These are responsible for the gnawing action typical of beavers and other rodents, achieved by closing the lower jaw and pulling it forward.

X-ray illustration Elisabeth Smith

THE BODY

is compact and heavy. The beaver forms a sleek shape in the water, diving and swimming with grace and ease. A special respiratory and cardiovascular system enables large amounts of oxygen to be stored in the lungs, blood, and muscles; this enables the beaver to dive deep and stay underwater for up to 15 minutes if necessary.

THE FUR

is made up of two distinct layers; long guard hairs grow over a softer underfur. Both of these are remarkably dense—there are about 77,400 hair filaments per square inch (12,000 per square centimeter) on the back and almost double this number on the belly. The beaver constantly anoints the guard hairs with an oily secretion from sebaceous glands on its underside to waterproof them.

THE TAIL

may measure 10–18 in (25–46 cm) long and 4–5 in (10–13 cm) wide. It is covered with thickened scaly skin; unlike true scales, they do not overlap, allowing for great flexibility. The tail acts as a rudder in the water and as a balancing prop on dry land. It can also be used to radiate excess heat from the body, and it stores fat for when food is scarce.

THE HIND FEET

are broad and fully webbed between the toes, improving the beaver's swimming skill. The claws on the first and second toes are cleft and are used in grooming the fur.

FACT FILE:

THE CANADIAN BEAVER

CLASSIFICATION

GENUS: *CASTOR*

SPECIES: *CANADENSIS*

SIZE

HEAD-BODY LENGTH: 35–47 IN (89–119 CM)

TAIL: 10–18 IN (25–46 CM)

WEIGHT: 45–60 LB (20.3–27 KG);

OCCASIONALLY UP TO 66 LB (30 KG)

WEIGHT AT BIRTH: APPROX 1 LB (450 G)

COLORATION

RICH, GLOSSY, DARK BROWN WITH SLIGHTLY PALER UNDERPARTS. NO MARKINGS

FEATURES

THICKSET, ROUNDED BODY

VERY SMALL EARS AND EYES

SMALL FORELIMBS, WITH DEXTEROUS PAWS

LONGER AND STRONGER HIND LIMBS, WITH MUCH LARGER, FULLY WEBBED HIND FEET

OVAL, HORIZONTALLY FLATTENED TAIL, COVERED WITH SCALY SKIN

CANADIAN BEAVER SKULL

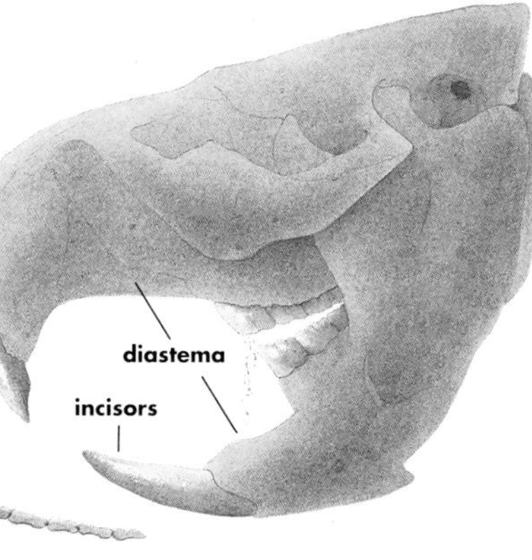

TEETH

The huge incisors dominate the muzzle area. In the absence of canines, the incisors and molars are separated by a gap called the diastema. The beaver, like many other rodents, can draw its lips into the diastema when gnawing, to keep debris out of its throat. The molars have efficient grinding surfaces for processing tough food.

EUROPEAN BEAVER SKULL

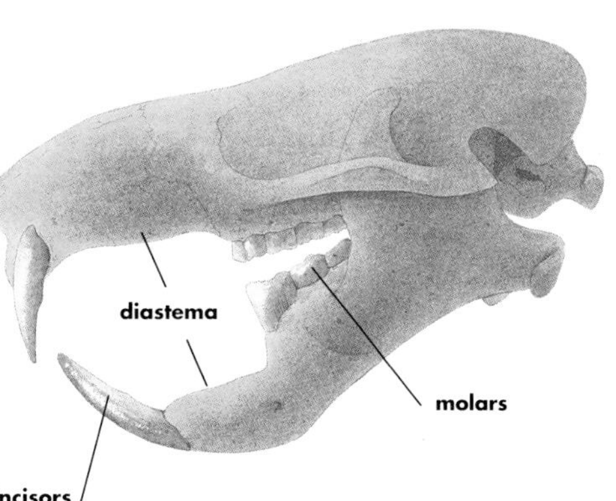

MOUNTAIN BEAVER SKULL

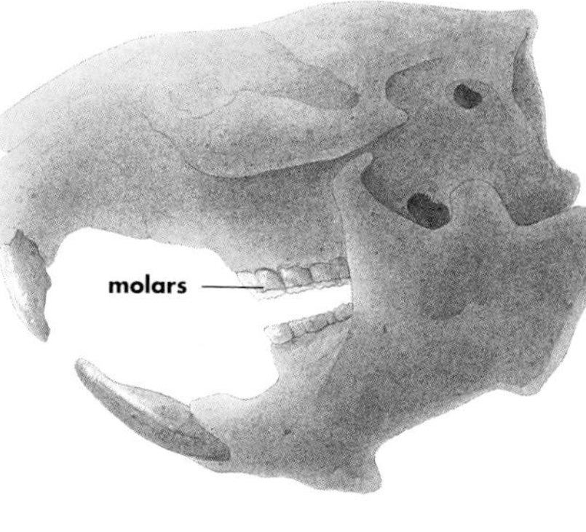

Main illustration Rachel Lockwood/Wildlife Art Agency

KING OF THE WATERWAYS

IN ITS TAILOR-MADE, MOATED CASTLE THE BEAVER IS KING. LARGELY UNCHALLENGED BY PREDATORS AND TOLERATING FEW INTRUDERS, IT IS A SOCIABLE ANIMAL ALWAYS FOUND WITHIN A SMALL FAMILY GROUP

The expression "as busy as a beaver" gives a clue to this animal's industrious lifestyle, which reaches a peak in the spring and autumn. In the spring, the beaver repairs its home after the ravages of winter, while in the autumn it is gathering and storing food to last the family through the hard months ahead. The beaver does not hibernate through winter, although the ice and snow cover in its northerly ranges makes for less activity at this time.

Other occupations of the busy beaver include tree-felling, dam-building, lodge or burrow construction, and canal excavation—along with regular repairs to all these structures. Time in the burrow or lodge is passed mainly in sleeping, although the beaver is also a prodigious groomer. Sitting with its tail jutting forward between its hind legs, it rakes through its fur with the split nails on the hind feet and then daubs it with gland secretions. The beaver generally ventures outside in the early evening, but in remote areas it may be active by day, too.

SLEEK AND SLIPSTREAMED

Beavers feel most at home in the water, and from an early age they swim and dive with ease. Averaging some 5–6 mph (8–10 km/h), they can cover over half a mile (almost a kilometer) underwater without surfacing. A beaver usually slips so gently into its pond that scarcely a ripple breaks the surface. If alarmed, however, it will crash-dive with a loud splash, often alerting other beavers to the danger with a "warning dive." This involves taking a shallow plunge while slapping the tail flat on the water with a loud smack before surfacing and diving again noisily. Any disturbance—a raccoon or human near the water's edge—will bring this response from a beaver. Other beavers respond by hurrying to the safety of the water if they are on land or by moving to deeper water if they have been paddling about in the shallows.

Despite its love of water, the beaver spends a fair amount of time on land, where it forages and gathers most of its building materials. Compared to its antics in the water, its actions on land are slow and clumsy; sitting back frequently on its haunches to sniff the air cautiously, the beaver moves in a pigeon-toed waddle, shuffling along on all fours. Usually its nose is low to the ground and its hindquarters high in the air. At the slightest threat it races for the nearest water in an ungainly hopping gallop.

BURROWING BEAVER

The mountain beaver, too, is active throughout the year, and, although mainly nocturnal, it may go about its business during the day. Its "business,"

A young sapling like this (right) *is no match for the beaver's incisors: It will be felled within minutes.*

L. Lee Rue/Frank Lane Picture Agency

The beaver waterproofs its "overcoat" of guard hairs by anointing it with oily secretions (above).

Although its natural buoyancy works against it, the beaver is a powerful swimmer with plenty of stamina to cope with winters under the ice (below).

Tom McHugh/Oxford Scientific Films

however, is conducted mainly underground—it really only comes out of its extensive burrow to gather food, much of which it then takes back below ground to eat.

One reason why the mountain beaver spends so much time in its burrow is that it lacks any truly efficient biological equipment to regulate its body heat, so it has to live in an environment that provides stable temperature and moisture. It has equal difficulty in conserving fat and moisture, so it needs to eat and take in water constantly, preventing it from hibernating in the winter or taking long, torpid sleeps in the summer. ■

CUTTING IT FINE!

Tree-felling is an important part of the beaver's activity, providing it with food and building materials. While it commonly goes for trees of 6 in (15 cm) in diameter, it has been known to topple stalwarts of 39 in (1 m) in diameter. The beaver gnaws around the trunk, making deep grooves and spitting out the wood chips as the typical hourglass form takes shape around the tree. While it works, the beaver supports itself on its hindquarters and broad tail, its forelegs resting against the base of the tree. As the tree begins to fall, the beaver generally scampers out of the way, but stories of it never being caught under a falling tree are not true. Beavers are frequently killed by falling trees.

Hans Reinhard/Bruce Coleman Ltd.

HABITATS

True beavers are creatures of the Northern Hemisphere. In America, the Canadian beaver was originally found in just about all the forested areas from the far north south to northern Mexico. Over the centuries it has been so extensively trapped that by the early 1900s it had actually disappeared from much of its former range. Deforestation activities led to still further disappearances.

The story is not as gloomy as it may sound, however. There have been many reintroductions of the beaver in Canada and the United States, and the animals have taken to their surroundings rapidly and successfully, so that today they have recolonized many of their former haunts. Their current range covers most of North America, except for much of Florida, large tracts of southern California, and Nevada. They have even been introduced into Argentina, although it is uncertain whether this will prove to be a long-term success.

The European beaver has suffered much the same fate—that of extensive hunting and trapping and also loss of habitat through the march of civilization. At one stage it was found throughout the forested areas of Europe and Asia, including Great Britain—absent only from the Mediterranean zone and Japan. It is now extinct over much of this former range and survives only in isolated pockets in Norway, France, Germany, Poland, and parts of Russia. In the form of the Canadian beaver it has also been successfully introduced into Sweden, Finland, Switzerland, and Austria. Once established in an area, beavers generally have a high survival rate, the chief threat to their existence having always been humans.

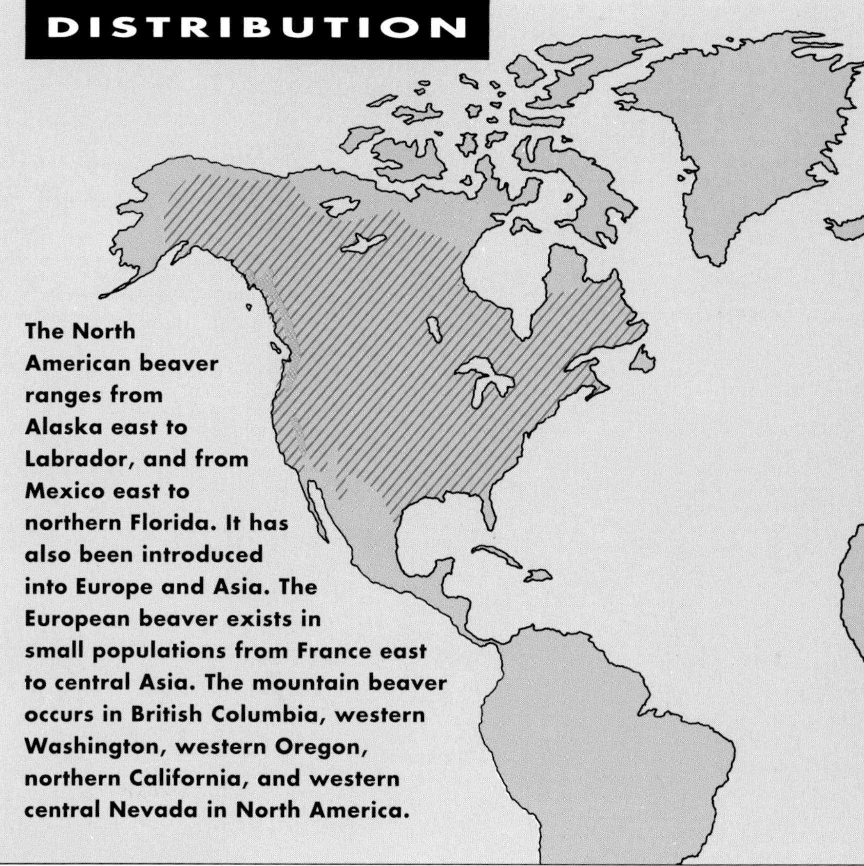

The North American beaver ranges from Alaska east to Labrador, and from Mexico east to northern Florida. It has also been introduced into Europe and Asia. The European beaver exists in small populations from France east to central Asia. The mountain beaver occurs in British Columbia, western Washington, western Oregon, northern California, and western central Nevada in North America.

Both the Canadian and European beavers favor the same kind of habitat—the most important requirement being reasonable expanses of water. This may be provided by rivers, streams, marshes, lakes, ponds—even reservoirs and deep, water-filled ditches. Left to their own devices, beavers seem to prefer wooded areas, and they have been found in forests at altitudes of more than 11,155 ft (3,400 m) in North America.

NATURE'S LANDSCAPERS

Beavers are unique in the mammal kingdom for shaping their environment. No other mammal apart from humans controls, influences, and ultimately

Jen & Des Bartlett/Survival Anglia

Beavers can be hard to spot in the wild. Often it is just a few ripples that betray their presence (left).

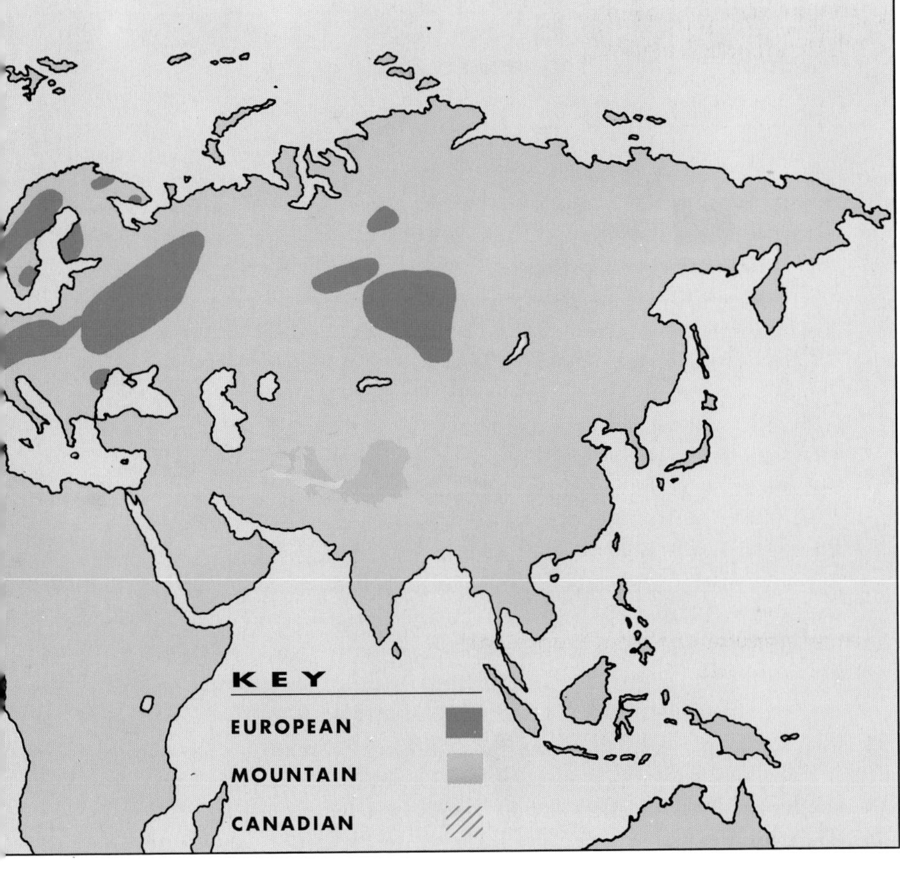

A MISLEADING NAME

Everything about the mountain beaver's name is deceptive. It is not, as we have seen, a true beaver, nor is it particularly found in mountainous environments. Although it may be found at elevations of up to 7,220 ft (2,200 m), it is more common at lower levels. In fact, it will never be found above the tree line, for forests and thickets are its natural home. In addition, because of its need for constant moisture, it is generally found near streams in areas where the rainfall is heavy.

Despite these constraints, the mountain beaver is faring better today than at any point during the last three centuries. Yet considering its capacity for survival, its distribution is remarkably limited: It is found only down North America's Pacific coast. This confusing animal might have earned the "beaver" part of its name through its habit of diverting small streams into its underground tunnels.

changes its habitat to the extent the beaver does. It achieves this mainly by building dams across rivers and streams to provide an area of still, deep water where it may build a lodge to house its family safely. Many of these dams have been in place for years, kept in good repair by generations of beavers. They vary in span from just 39 in (1 m) or so to more than 2,000 ft (609 m), and their design differs according to the flow of water and how the beaver wants to direct it. For example, when heavy rainfall raises the water level, the beaver knows to construct spillways at each end of the dam to insure that its lodge does not also become flooded.

Once a pond of sufficient depth has been created, a beaver digs out a network of canals radiating from it. These extend its safe food-gathering range—time spent in the water carries the minimal risk from land-based predators, such as the wolf, coyote, lynx, and bobcat. They also provide it with an easy way of getting food and building materials back to the pond where it wants them, by floating them down these newly constructed waterways.

Generations of beavers may also add to the dams and create more canals. Often the canals will have a series of smaller, "secondary" dams built to act like

Rushes (right) *are a favorite food. Much of the beaver's diet doubles as building material, too.*

Janos Jurka/Bruce Coleman Ltd.

locks to overcome the problem of sloping ground. These may well be accompanied by a mud slide, again fashioned by the beaver itself and enabling it to slip easily into the water of the canal.

Beaver meadows

In addition to diverting and creating new waterways, the damming of rivers and streams inevitably leads to a change in the immediate environment. Floods are commonplace, and many trees, particularly conifers, will not be able to tolerate the new wet conditions around their roots. They die, to be replaced either by softwoods, such as willows and poplars, which can more easily survive the boggy growing conditions, or by low shrubs. Eventually the marshy areas dry out, leaving newly created "beaver meadows."

These accomplished feats of hydroengineering are most frequently associated with the Canadian beaver. Beavers in Europe and Asia have similar skills, but they exercise them less frequently. This results in part from their persecution; beavers that survived in the wild generally did so in wide, deep rivers with high banks, where they were hidden and often inaccessible. There was no further need to build a safe, moated lodge, as it was quicker, less laborious, and far less conspicuous to burrow into the bank. Now that beavers are protected in Europe and Asia, they have started to colonize areas of shallower water, where they need to build dams.

The mountain beaver inhabits the extensive coniferous forests on North America's Pacific coast. Living within the safety of the soil, it can adapt to a range of altitudes, from sea level to the upper tree line on mountain slopes. It does, however, depend on a plentiful supply of food, in the form of leafy vegetation. This restricts it to areas where rainfall is medium to high and winters are fairly mild. ■

FOCUS ON

Labrador

Labrador, in the extreme eastern part of Canada, is a largely barren tundra that comprises the mainland part of Newfoundland Province. A land of boreal forests, Labrador is characterized by a chilly, inhospitable climate. Its interior is a saucer-shaped plateau averaging 1,470 ft (450 m) above sea level, cut across by large rivers. Some 50 percent of the terrain supports little more than mossy outgrowths and marshy bogs, but forests of both deciduous and coniferous trees cover about 87,000 sq mi (225,000 sq km) in total.

At the extreme northeastern part of Newfoundland Province are the Torngat Mountains; their highest peak, Mt. Caubvick, rises to a height of 5,420 ft (1,652 m). The Torngats flank a shoreline that is locked in ice for most of the long winter. The biggest river in the province is the Churchill, which rises in the west, dropping down to Lake Melville, which extends more than 80 mi (130 km) inland from the coast. Huge volumes of water flow over the Churchill Falls, which are more than twice the height of Niagara. The area has been developed into a large hydropower complex that centers on the vast Smallwood Reservoir in the northwest.

Labrador contains a maze of lakes and rivers supporting deciduous trees such as aspen, birch, and willow; this makes it ideal country for the North American beaver.

Mickey Gibson/Oxford Scientific Films

TEMPERATURE AND RAINFALL

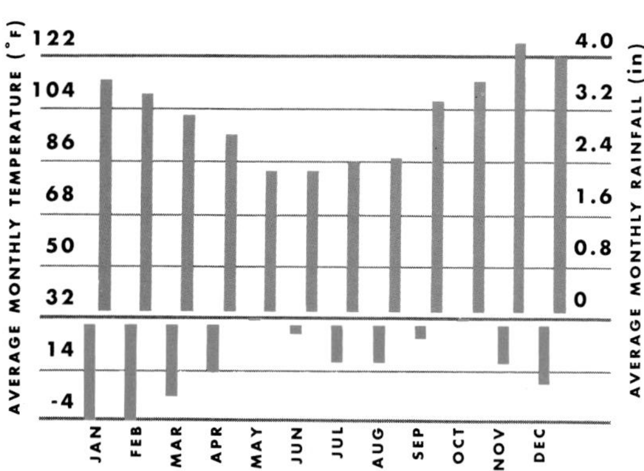

TEMPERATURE

RAINFALL

Most of Labrador has a harsh climate with long, icy winters, although the interior is much warmer than the coast. Rainfall varies with the region, generally being lighter in the south, but snowfall may be as much as 150 in (3.8 m).

NEIGHBORS

This cold region supports far fewer species of wildlife than warmer, more southerly areas. Many of the resident mammals are fully furred, and reptiles are entirely absent.

AMERICAN BLACK BEAR

This North American bear is faring so successfully that it has been designated a big-game animal.

BLACK-LEGGED KITTIWAKE

A highly social seabird, the kittiwake breeds in noisy, bustling colonies beside the coastal inlets and lakes.

Neighbor illustrations: Arctic hare, Joanne Cowne; all others, Peter Bull

ENEMIES

WOLVERINE

MODERATELY DANGEROUS

One of the most powerful mammals for its size, this mustelid is known in Labrador as the "beaver-eater."

WOLF

MODERATELY DANGEROUS

Beavers are easy prey for this practiced hunter of the north.

LABRADOR

Labrador lies in the northeastern corner of Canada. Its northern tip, dominated by the Torngat range, stands sentinel over the Hudson Strait. To the northeast across the Labrador Sea lies the southern tip of Greenland, which, at 60° North, lies on a latitude with Oslo and the Shetland Islands.

Enemy illustrations: Wolverine, Peter Bull; wolf, Dale Evans/Wildlife Art Agency

ARCTIC HARE

The coat of this large hare changes to white in the winter, providing perfect camouflage in the snow.

LAKE TROUT

In the oxygenated waters of northern rivers and lakes, the lake trout can grow to a phenomenal size.

PUFFIN

The horny covering of the puffin's brilliant bill peels off in the autumn, leaving a duller one in its place.

WOOD LOUSE

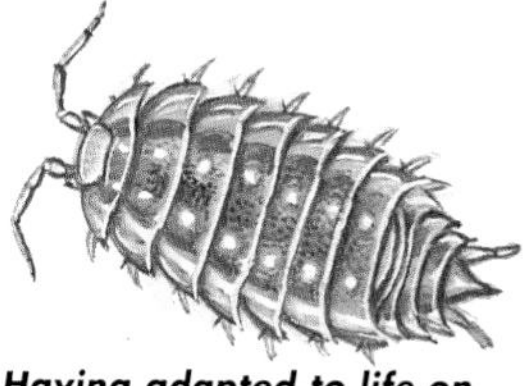

Having adapted to life on land, these crustaceans thrive in damp places and eat decaying organic matter.

SNIPE

This wader is often seen beside freshwater lakes, ponds, and marshes, and is a popular game bird.

TERRITORY

One reason for the success of beavers in the wild is that they live in close-knit units. These comprise a mated pair with their young of two years—generally no more than about eight to ten animals. Young beavers usually leave the family at two years old, when another new litter is born.

Each group occupies a home range, which varies greatly in size and shape according to the location. If it flanks a stream, it tends to be long and narrow; whereas around a pond or small lake it may be circular or rectangular. It may include a few small ponds linked by beaver-dug canals. Always it contains an area of dry land—the main source of food and building materials. Generally a quite small area may be used exclusively by one group, while a larger surrounding area is accessible to a number of groups.

Group defense

The core of the territory—the lodge or burrow, the surrounding water, and the key area on the bank or shoreline—is fiercely defended by all the family, particularly the male. First of all the area is marked with pungent secretions of castoreum mixed with urine. Often, beavers heap mounds of earth along the shore and the territorial boundaries, which they then anoint with scent. Should a stranger daub one with its scent, the residents react aggressively by hissing and slapping their tails before rebuilding and reanointing the mound. Such intrusions into the territory often provoke outright fighting, but the resident beavers usually precede hostilities by hissing, growling, and lunging at the intruder, tail aquiver and teeth snapping. This is often enough to scare the stranger off without bloodshed. After an initial encounter, neighboring animals of different species, such as raccoons, are usually tolerated.

All for one and one for all?

Although constructional repairs and foraging are often said to be group activities, many experts claim that this is an illusion and that each family member is actually caring only for itself. Certainly, beavers seem generally to collect food on their own, almost enjoying a quiet break away from the fairly crowded conditions in the lodge or burrow. Tree-felling is often, but not always, a solitary occupation.

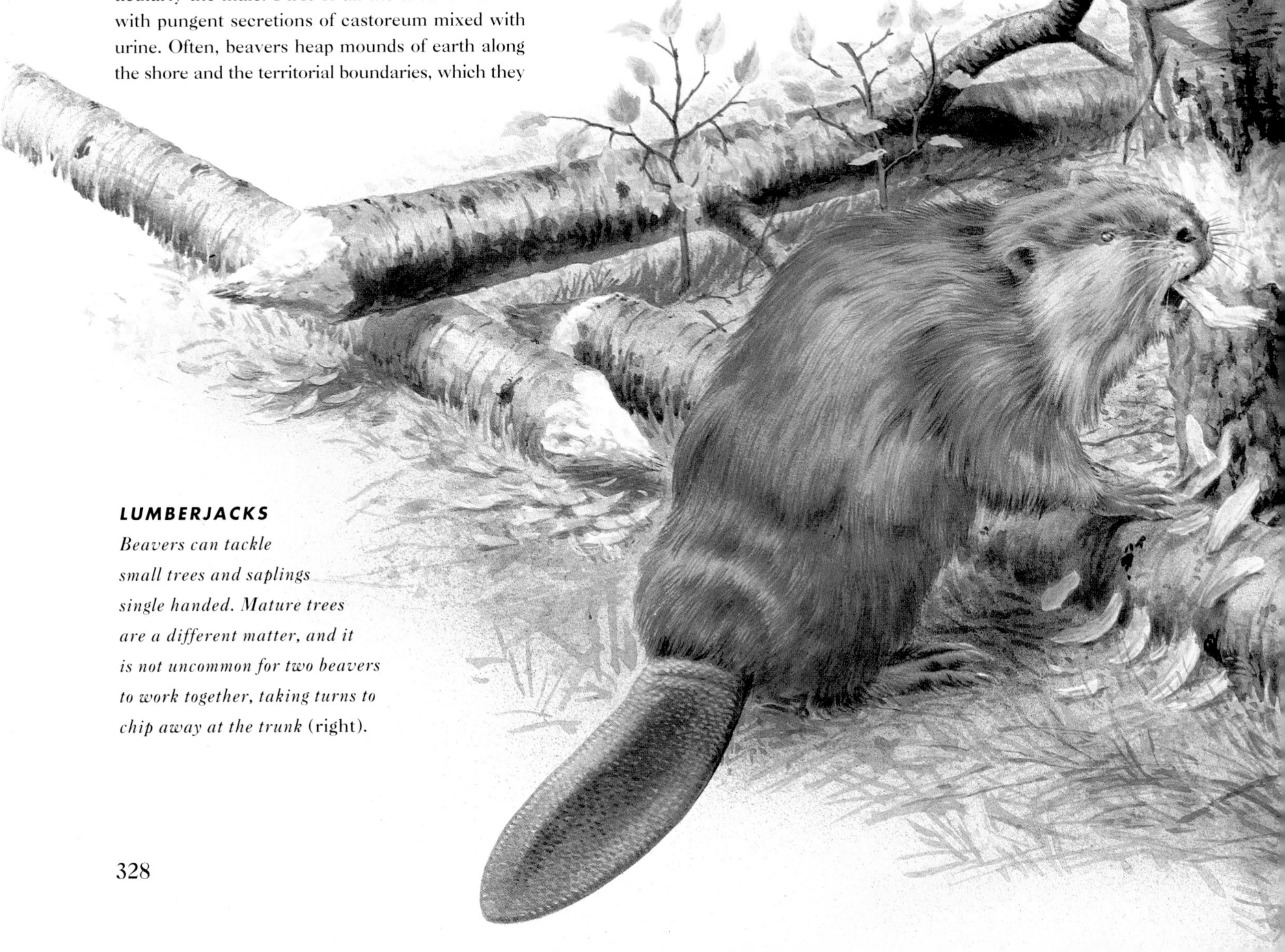

LUMBERJACKS

Beavers can tackle small trees and saplings single handed. Mature trees are a different matter, and it is not uncommon for two beavers to work together, taking turns to chip away at the trunk (right).

The beaver can carry surprisingly large boughs in its mouth, trapping the burden behind its long, stout incisors (right). *Some pieces it eats, some it takes below water to a larder, while others it uses to reinforce a dam or lodge.*

Mark Newman/Frank Lane Picture Agency

in SIGHT

SELF-SUFFICIENCY

True to form, the mountain beaver differs from the true beavers in its social structure; it has none. It is not wholly solitary, for often these animals may be found sharing a burrow. Usually this simply means that the burrowing quality of the land and the existing food conditions are such that they can sustain several animals, or a vagrant animal may pause for a day or two in the burrow of another. More usually, the mountain beaver defends its nest, uttering shrill noises and grating its incisors to warn off any intruder. It does occupy a home range, but this is a very small area—100 ft (30 m) or so from the burrow—which provides it with all its needs.

In winter, visits to the shore become rare. While beavers have been known to fell trees when the snow lies thick, once the pond or lake has iced over completely, they generally stay in the lodge or swim about below the ice. In the lodge the temperature remains constant and warmer than the air outside. The light level also remains constant, and without the obvious signs of dusk and dawn to alert them, many beavers extend their "day" to a 26- or 29-hour period. In effect, this means they spend fewer days under the ice during the winter months. ■

Illustration Robin Boutell/Wildlife Art Agency

LODGE BUILDING

The structures built by beavers appear so complex that it seems they must have been created with intelligent planning and forethought—but this is not the case. Almost all the beaver's building activity stems from innate behavior.

In areas where the riverbanks are high, beavers often dig deeply to make a burrow, tunneling some 33 ft (10 m) back into the earth. The entrance is usually below water level. Where their habitats lack such conveniently high banks, however, beavers are obliged to build lodges and dams.

THE LODGE

A lodge needs to be weatherproof and, as far as possible, out of reach of predators. Although it is usually built close to the shore, it ends up in the middle of a newly created lake where the beavers have dammed the stretch of water. To build this dome of mud and sticks, the beaver jams sticks and branches into the riverbed, reinforcing these with mud scooped up in its paws. Soon the construction shows above the surface of the water.

When the construction is high enough, a chamber, little more than beaver height, is dug out in the center of the mound to form the dry living quarters. The floor, which is above the water level, is lined with wood chips to improve drainage. Usually, there are two entrances to the living chamber, set beneath the surface of the pond.

THE DAM

At sites where the water is too shallow to deter predators, the beaver also builds a dam. It lays a foundation of mud and stones across the river, usually collected from the bed with its forepaws. Into this the beaver fixes small branches, later adding logs and more mud and stones to raise up a barrier. Flotsam in the river helps to seal the cracks, too.

The construction and regular maintenance of a dam is more than a lifetime's work for a beaver. Generations of beavers will attend the same dam and occupy the same lodge, constantly adding to both constructions. A lodge may rise 6.5 ft (2 m) above the surface of the water and have a diameter at its base of more than 39 ft (12 m), while beaver dams in excess of 1,970 ft (600 m) long are by no means uncommon.

David Hosking/Frank Lane Picture Agency

This dam at Grand Teton National Park in Wyoming testifies to the efforts of generations of beavers (above).

in SIGHT

LIVING QUARTERS

The mountain beaver digs out its burrows in firm, but moist, soil. They comprise a labyrinthine system of tunnels focused on a well-drained, domed nest chamber lined with dried vegetation. Smaller chambers or blind tunnels are dug to store food, feces, and food waste. The mountain beaver works on its burrow industriously, cleaning existing tunnels and digging new ones. Most tunnels are 6–8 in (15–20 cm) across, and if they become flooded by heavy rain, the mountain beaver simply swims along them. Unused sections often provide sanctuary for other animals, such as ground squirrels, deer mice, and rabbits.

The beaver's tree-felling skills are instrumental in providing building materials. The usual size of a tree felled is 2–6 in (5–15 cm) in diameter and one such will require less than five minutes of gnawing before it topples. The beaver then strips off the branches and gnaws the trunk into manageable sections, which it either drags, pushes, or carries in its incisors to the water, steering it toward whichever construction is most needy. Occasionally, a beaver will waddle to the water on its hind legs, holding a bundle of small twigs and vegetation in its arms.

Most maintenance work takes place in the spring and autumn—either repairing the ravages of the winter or insuring that everything is as secure and watertight as it can be for the months ahead. Mud and sticks are slapped onto the outside of the lodge until the walls may be up to 39 inches (1 m) thick; in winter, this mud will freeze to provide extra insulation. Although all members of a family group take part in both construction and repair work, the adult female is the most active. ■

AT HOME

Gathering boughs from the bank and mud from the riverbed, beavers build a safe lodge for their family (below). *The artificial lake raised by damming the flow helps to keep lynxes and bobcats at bay.*

John Morris/Wildlife Art Agency

FOOD AND FEEDING

The beaver eats plant matter, and, like many rodents, its digestion has adapted to cope with large quantities of woody material: It consumes about one-fifth of its own weight in food every day.

A beaver's diet varies through the seasons. In the spring and summer, much of its food is found on dry land, where the animal nibbles away at succulent or herbaceous plants, often plucking just their leaves. Herbs, ferns, and grasses are all on the menu, as are the starchy tubers and roots of myrtle and cattail—even thistles—together with their buds and shoots. Inevitably, beavers feast on water plants whenever possible, and they seem to favor those on which there is plenty of plant life. The young shoots of water lilies are a great favorite.

In the autumn, beavers turn their attention to woody plants and trees, feeding on the twigs, bark, and cambium—the layer of cells below the bark. Willow, alder, birch, and aspen are popular, whereas conifers are the least favorite. The beaver bites off branches before nipping them into 12 in (30 cm) lengths. Then it holds one of these in its paws, much as we would hold a corn on the cob, turning it as it nibbles off first the leaves and then the bark.

PREPARING FOR WINTER

Although beavers do feed a lot in the autumn, they still need a daily intake through the winter months, since they do not hibernate. Often they slip from their lodges and scamper over the deep snow in search of food; heavy snowfalls that elevate the ground level explain the high gnawmarks observed on trees in the spring.

Through the harshest winter months, however, the surface of the pond is frozen solid and the beaver cannot get to land to search for food. Once again, it must make contingency plans for such eventualities. This it does in two ways.

The most common method is to store food under the water near the lodge exits. This is another reason why autumn is such a busy time for beavers; they fell small trees, especially aspen, and tow the pieces into the water. Drawing near to the lodge, the beaver dives into the water and pushes the branches into the pond bed, anchoring them in the mud. The water acts as a refrigerator, keeping the timber at a constant temperature that actually preserves the

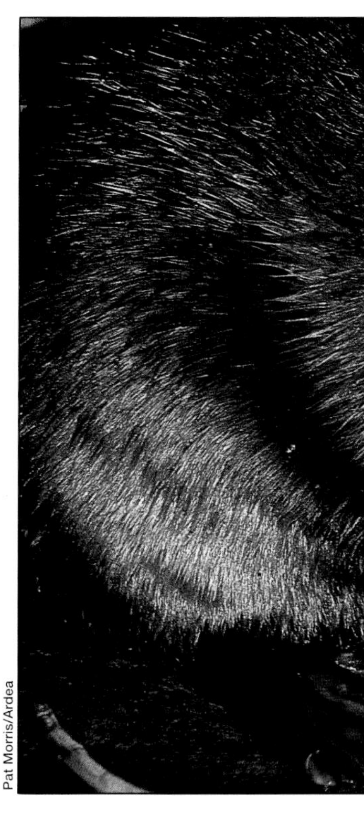

When tackling tough vegetation, the beaver chews its food painstakingly before swallowing (right).

Pat Morris/Ardea

FOOD

Although able to digest the toughest tree fiber, beavers adjust their diet to take full advantage of the lush spring growth of herbs and water plants. Sticks and branches form the basis of the food larders beneath the ice.

BIRCH

WILLOW

Food illustrations Ruth Grewcock

HOARDER
What the mountain beaver cannot eat at once, it takes back to the burrow to store for later (above).

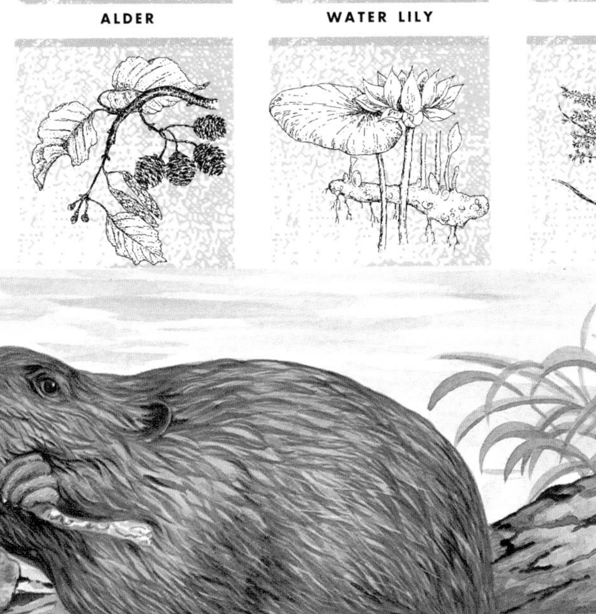

LILY FEAST
Succulent water plants (above) *are not available all year round, so beavers gorge on these and on lush ground cover in spring and summer.*

nutritional value—at its highest in the autumn, when the most nutrients are stored under the bark.

The advantage of this winter food store under the ice is that the animals do not have to leave the comparatively warm waters—compared, that is, to the outside temperature, which will be well below freezing, particularly at nighttime, when the beaver is traditionally active.

In some instances, however, even when the pond surface is frozen over, these ingenious animals find a way to get ashore to look for food. In various locations, it has been discovered that beavers have dug canals into the pond bed. These extend to the edge of the pond and beyond into the bank, from which the beavers can burrow up through the earth and then through the snow, into the world above to search for food. ■

KEY FACTS

- **An adult beaver eats an estimated 8,800 lb (4,000 kg) of woody material each year.**
- **Some 300 species of plant, shrub, bush, and tree are known to provide food for beavers.**
- **A beaver can process about 30 percent of the cellulose and 44 percent of the protein it eats into usable energy.**
- **A family group of beavers may gather and store a winter larder of some 2,825 cu ft (79 cu m) of branches under the ice.**

Main illustration Wendy Bramall/Wildlife Art Agency

LIFE CYCLE

Adult beavers usually pair for life. Mating, which takes place in the water, occurs in January or February in both species of true beaver.

After a gestation period of 100–110 days, three or four young are born, although there may be up to six in the European and up to eight in the Canadian beaver. The female gives birth in the lodge and the young, known as kits, are highly precocious when born. Fully furred, with eyes open and teeth already cut, they can swim within a few hours of birth, although their dense fur and light body weight make them too buoyant to dive. Also, their glands have not yet begun to secrete the oily substance needed to render their coats waterproof at this stage, and so their mother anoints them with secretions from her own sebaceous glands by simply rubbing her fur against theirs.

In fact, young beavers often show a marked reluctance to enter the water initially, in spite of the fact that they will soon be more at home here than on dry land. Quite often, when the kits are about one week old, the mother has to pick

LIVELY LITTER

The kits are fully furred at birth, with their eyes open. Although eager to investigate their snug surroundings, they still lack the courage to take a plunge (above).

DRIVEN FROM HOME

Beavers form close family bonds, and the young adults are reluctant to leave. The parents have to bully the young into departing (right), *since they themselves must start preparing for the next litter.*

Jen & Des Bartlett/Bruce Coleman Ltd.

Illustrations Robin Budden/Wildlife Art Agency

The adults spend an inordinate amount of time caring for their young. Although much of a beaver's skill is based upon pure instinct, there is still a great deal to be learned by copying from elders and betters (left).

GROWING UP

The life of a Canadian beaver

WATERPROOFING

It takes a while before the kits' sebaceous glands start to function. To prepare them for the water, the female rubs her own oily secretions against their coats (above).

WATER BABIES

The first encounters with the lake and the shore can be somewhat traumatic for the kits, accustomed as they are to the cozy fug of the lodge. It is left to their mother to take a firm hand in launching them bodily into the water, and onto dry land (above).

them up in her forearms and throw them into the tunnel from the lodge to make them take their first swim. This seems to trigger the sebaceous glands into operation, and before long the young animals are diving and playing in the water at every opportunity.

A FAMILY RESPONSIBILITY

The kits suckle from the mother until they are at least six weeks old, and sometimes for up to three months. Before they are fully weaned, however, they have begun to take solid food, brought to them by all other family members, particularly the male. In fact, in the first week or so after the birth, solid food is brought to the female as well so that she does not have to leave her kits at all at this time. This is one of the few times where the family acknowledges a pecking order, with the female taking the dominant position. She spends quite some time grooming herself while in the lodge, leaving her babies in a heap on one side of the chamber. As soon as she moves over to them, they greet her with high-pitched squeaks, anxious to suckle. She has only four teats, so if there are more kits than this, they have to wait their turn, which they do with great impatience.

All members of the family assist in looking after the kits, and the adult male has a strong sense of paternal care, which is unusual in a rodent. Should one of the babies fall into one or another of the floor entrances before it is ready to dive, the father will often be the one to rescue it, nudging it back to the safety of the living chamber.

When the kits have their first foray onto dry land, it is often in the arms of the mother, who may walk erect, holding one in her forepaws. Sometimes she also gives them a ride on land on her tail. If they get tired on their early swimming forays, she is generally close by to give them a lift through the water on her broad back. Autumn, when the kits begin learning to feed on bark, is a difficult time and the mortality rate is often quite high. If they survive their first year, however, they have a fair chance of living a good ten years or more.

INDEPENDENCE

The kits stay with their parents for up to two years. Although this seems like a long time, they have a lot to learn, for they must be skilled in the ways of building if they are to survive on their own. This they learn by watching their parents and older siblings at work and eventually joining in. Sexual maturity is reached as the animals approach two years old, although they are unlikely to mate until a year or more later. Around this time the parents become aggressive toward their young, finally pushing them out altogether. They rarely disperse far from parental territory—perhaps only some 10 miles (16 km) or so—but it has been known for a beaver to establish a new territory more than 62 miles (100 km) away. ■

FROM BIRTH TO DEATH

TRUE BEAVERS

GESTATION: 100–110 DAYS
LITTER SIZE: 1–8 IN CANADIAN, 1–6 IN EUROPEAN
LITTERS PER YEAR: 1
WEIGHT AT BIRTH: 1 LB (450 G)
WEANING: 6–12 WEEKS
SEXUAL MATURITY: 18–24 MONTHS
LONGEVITY: AT LEAST 10 YEARS IN THE WILD; UP TO 35 IN CAPTIVITY

MOUNTAIN BEAVER

GESTATION: 28–30 DAYS
LITTER SIZE: 3–5
LITTERS PER YEAR: 1
WEANING: 6–8 WEEKS
SEXUAL MATURITY: 2 YEARS
LONGEVITY: 5–10 YEARS

PELTS THAT MADE HISTORY

THE BEAVER HAS HAD A PROFOUND EFFECT ON HUMANS THROUGH THE AGES. NOT ONLY HAS IT RESHAPED THEIR ENVIRONMENT IN SOME AREAS; IT HAS ALSO ENGENDERED EXPLORATION AND INFLUENCED ECONOMIES

It would seem that humans have recognized the beaver's importance ever since prehistoric times. The animal's clumsiness on land has made it an easy target; Stone Age humans hunted it and used its incisors as scraping tools. Beaver bones dating from the Bronze Age show that beavers were used in sacrifice and as funeral offerings.

The Inuits and Indians of North America have long enjoyed a relationship with the beaver that shares their often hostile environment. The beaver provided them with meat to eat and warm furs to protect against the bitter cold. The killing of beavers by these people was originally done purely for these reasons; in addition, they only took mature animals. In this way, humans and beaver coexisted.

UPSETTING THE BALANCE

But all this changed when white settlers invaded North America. During the 18th century, demand for beaver fur was nearly insatiable and the animals were trapped in droves—so much so that by the late 1700s, the Canadian beaver had already been completely eradicated in parts of the eastern United States.

The demand for beaver pelts led white explorers and trappers to push further into remote northern areas, incidentally opening up the land to settlers as they traveled. North American Indians were soon being encouraged to kill beavers in greater numbers, no longer simply for their own requirements but in order to trade. Pelts were exported in huge numbers to Europe—England in particular. So valuable did beaver pelts become that wars were even fought over them; one reason for the French and Indian War of 1754–1763 was access to beaver country.

By the 19th century, a beaver pelt was rated the single most valuable commodity in much of North America. White trappers and fur companies were totally unscrupulous, their only concern and motive being profit. Not only did they exploit beavers, but they also exploited the North American Indians, pushing them to travel into new areas to meet the demand for beaver pelts.

Probably the most famous company to trade in beaver pelts was the Hudson's Bay Company, formed in 1670. Between 1853 and 1877 it marketed nearly three million pelts—an average of 125,000 a year. In 1904–1905, the cull soared to three times this figure, representing a revenue of $2,300,000. The furs were in constant demand for coats, trims, and hats, which were the height of fashion in Europe and the eastern United States. Some of America's greatest financial empires and real-estate holdings were founded on the profits made from the sale of beaver pelts.

The cull of 1904–1905 is all the more amazing for the fact that by the early 1900s it was estimated that beaver numbers were not only drastically reduced

Derek Karp/NHPA

Beavers such as this (above) *have been released in Poland in a bid to repopulate the country's rivers.*

L. Lee Rue/Bruce Coleman Ltd.

THEN & NOW

This map shows the former and current distribution of the European beaver

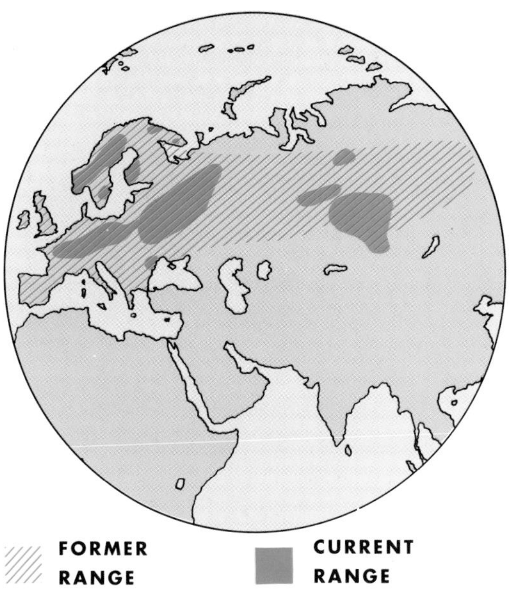

The European beaver was once common in rivers and forests across northern Europe and deep into northern Asia. Populations have suffered severe fragmentation and depletion, although recent reintroduction programs seem to have been successful.

but populations were restricted to isolated areas; in truth, the animal had completely disappeared from much of its original range.

The story was much the same for the European beaver. Across its range, it has been hunted for its fur, flesh, and castoreum. In the 16th and 17th centuries, beavers were killed more for this supposedly health-giving secretion than for their fur.

The Fish That Wasn't

The flesh of beaver had a key significance from an early date in the monasteries of Europe, for it was designated "fish" and could therefore be eaten during times of fasting when meat was forbidden. By 950, the Benedictines decreed that "beaver, otter, and wild duck, with either fur or feathers, that eat fish, is eaten again as fish." Rich monasteries paid handsomely for beaver flesh, and the fact that the beaver does not eat fish did not seem to matter!

Clothes made from beaver fur—hats, waistcoats, gloves, and other apparel—were popular in Europe

The Canadian beaver is secure, but will probably never recover its original status.

from early on in the Middle Ages. Beavers were caught in traps or hunted by dogs; they had become extinct in Spain by as early as the 6th century, in Britain by the 12th century, in Italy by the 16th century, in Sweden by the beginning of the 19th century, and in Finland by the late 19th century. In the 1400s in Prussia, the bounty tariff set for a beaver was twice that of the otter, and in the 16th century a beaver pelt had the same value as that of a bear.

By the 1920s, the European beaver was surviving only in parts of Russia and Poland, along a stretch of the Elbe River in Germany, in the Camargue delta of southern France, and in a virtually inaccessible part of southeastern Norway.

In some areas beavers have been killed because they have been considered a pest. Certainly they do attack and destroy trees, although it has generally been recognized that the species they favor have little value as timber. Their landscaping activities are not always appreciated by humans. When beavers get to work, cattle pastures may become more suitable for fish and waterfowl.

There is, of course, a reverse argument claiming that beavers are actually beneficial to the ecology of a region. Their dams can regulate water courses, slow down the drainage of river basins, prevent flooding or land silting up in torrential downpours, raise the level of the water table, and also equalize the flow of water so that it is conserved in times of shortage or drought. Plant and animal life benefit—trout will often colonize the ponds formed upstream of a dam, supported by the larvae of insects and by the tiny animals exposed in the mud used in beaver constructions. Water plants flourish, and all sorts of birds and animals will come to the area to drink. Ultimately these new ponds silt up, forming marshes and, eventually, fertile meadows suitable for grazing or cultivation where once the land was barren or marshy.

In truth, the mountain beaver does more damage to trees than the true beavers. Young conifers provide this animal with both food and nest material; new plantations of Douglas fir in parts of the Pacific Northwest have suffered considerable damage, the resulting loss of timber estimated at several million dollars. Within its restricted range, however, it seems to be abundant, although some subspecies may be endangered. Its numbers are not always easy to judge; its shy nature and subterranean lifestyle mean that it can actually be quite abundant in an area where it is thought to be absent. ■

ALONGSIDE MAN

SACRED PROTECTOR

Although the North American Indians and Inuits killed the beaver for fur and food, they nevertheless treated it with more respect than the white settlers did. The North American Indians, in particular, revered it. In order to appease its spirit, they begged forgiveness of the animal when it was killed, and before leaving for the hunt, the hunters would say a prayer which promised to treat the beaver with respect. The beaver was central to their world and they credited it with "shaping the earth, the mountain chains, the waterfalls, and the caverns." After eating beaver flesh, the Indians would place the bones on a sacred altar. Parts of the beaver, in particular the teeth, have been treated as amulets by many European cultures, too. Early Romans prized beaver incisors as amulets—a tradition that persisted in Italy through the ensuing centuries.

BEAVERS IN DANGER

THE FOLLOWING SUBSPECIES ARE LISTED IN THE *RED DATA BOOK*:

POINT ARENA MOUNTAIN BEAVER	INDETERMINATE
POINT REYES MOUNTAIN BEAVER	INDETERMINATE
BROAD-TAIL BEAVER (MEXICO)	ENDANGERED
RIO GRANDE BEAVER (MEXICO)	ENDANGERED
MONGOLIAN BEAVER	ENDANGERED

A. Andrews/Survival Anglia

These trees have been flooded and drowned by the waters rising behind a beaver dam.

INTO THE FUTURE

By the beginning of the 20th century, beavers had become extinct in much of their former habitats in both North America and Eurasia. The need to stop the slaughter was realized in some areas before this; in the state of Maine, for example, legislation to protect the beaver was passed in 1866. In France, beavers have been protected since 1905.

However, far more positive steps have been taken in the 20th century with regard to the beaver. It has been extensively reintroduced both in North America and Europe, mainly in recognition of its unique value in establishing suitable environments for other wildlife. Today it is present over most of its former range in North America. It survives, albeit often in isolated populations, in some 34 states. In these areas, culling is carefully regulated and beavers have been released into some of their old haunts. In the 15 states where they were once found but had become extinct, they have been reintroduced or encouraged to move from nearby areas.

The depletion of the beaver in Europe was, if anything, even more comprehensive than in North America, and although it has been quite widely reintroduced, its range is considerably reduced from earlier times. The first country to take action was Sweden, importing beavers from Norway to populate its rivers and lakes. Since then, beavers have been released into suitable areas in Finland, Poland, Switzerland, and Austria, while the populations that have managed to survive in Germany, France, and Russia have been strengthened. Plans have been considered to reintroduce them into Belgium and the Netherlands, but these have yet to be ratified.

Interestingly, it is often the Canadian beaver that has been used in the reintroduction programs in Europe, partly because it breeds more successfully than its European counterpart. Certainly it tends to have larger litters. ■

PREDICTION

SAFE BUT SCARCER

In its heyday there were an estimated 60–400 million beavers in North America. There are now thought to be between 6 and 12 million, and, while numbers seem to be stable, the species is unlikely to recover its original density.

BEAVER CONTROL TODAY

Beavers have proved that they can rapidly establish themselves when reintroduced to suitable habitat; such programs have been so successful by and large that beavers are now managed over much of their range. This allows for culling and there is still some demand for the fur, meat, and castoreum, although all of these are used far less than in former times. Since the 1950s some 200,000–600,000 pelts have been taken annually in Canada, although the price has dropped from an average value of around $24 per pelt in the 1970s to about $7.50 in the 1980s. During the 1970s in the United States some 100,000–200,000 were harvested each year. This number is far lower in Europe, where the beaver is probably not so well established. On average, fewer than 1,000 pelts are harvested annually in the Scandinavian countries, with Russia producing a few more than this.

THE PEST FACTOR

Inevitably with the gradual spread of the beaver in the 20th century, it has been viewed in some areas as a pest. Crops and timber have been damaged by flooding caused by beaver activity, and the dams also block the upstream run of spawning salmon in certain areas. In some places where this has occurred, the authorities have dealt with the problem in sensitive ways. On Vancouver Island, for example, Fisheries Service personnel dynamited dams that blocked the salmon's run. By the time the beavers had rebuilt their dams, the salmon were safely on their way.

Illustration Carol Roberts

CAMELS

RELATIONS

Camels and llamas are members of the order of even-toed ungulates, or Artiodactyla. Other members of the order include:

PIGS & PECCARIES

HIPPOPOTAMUSES

DEER

MUSK DEER

WILD CATTLE

ANTELOPES

GIRAFFES & OKAPI

SHEEP & GOATS

L. Lee Rue/Bruce Coleman Ltd.

Camels, llamas, and their relatives are all even-toed, hoofed mammals and members of the Camelidae family. This family is broken down into three genera containing a total of six species.

ORDER
Artiodactyla (even-toed hoofed mammals)

FAMILY
Camelidae

CAMEL GENUS
Camelus

BACTRIAN CAMEL SPECIES
bactrianus

DROMEDARY SPECIES
dromedarius

LLAMA, ALPACA, GUANACO GENUS
Lama

LLAMA SPECIES
glama

ALPACA SPECIES
pacos

GUANACO SPECIES
guanicoe

VICUÑA GENUS
Vicugna

SPECIES
vicugna

ONE HUMP OR TWO?

FROM THE TOP OF ITS FAT-BEARING HUMP TO THE TIPS OF ITS SOFT, PADDED FEET, THE CAMEL IS THE ULTIMATE DESERT DWELLER

Camels walk easily through swirling sandstorms, their nostrils shut and eyes protected by long lashes. They can also go for long periods without food or drink, thanks to the fat stores in their humps and their remarkable ability to conserve water.

There are six members of the camel family—or camelids—in the world today. The Old World members of the family are the Bactrian, or two-humped, camel, which is found from Soviet Central Asia to Mongolia, and the dromedary, or one-humped, camel, which is found throughout the Arabian region and is sometimes known as the Arabian camel. The remaining four species—the llama, the guanaco, the alpaca, and the vicuña—are known as lamoids or cameloids. They inhabit the mountainous regions of the South American continent and, lacking humps, look very different from their Old World cousins.

Of the lamoids, only the vicuña and guanaco are

The Old World camels look quite similar—though dromedaries (above) *have one hump instead of two—while the New World lamoids, such as the vicuñas* (right), *are smaller and have no humps.*

found in the wild, mainly in protected areas. Many zoologists believe that the llama and the alpaca are domesticated descendants of the guanaco, selectively bred over the centuries for the characteristics human beings valued—primarily an ability to carry loads in the case of the llama and to produce fine wool in the case of the alpaca.

A SIGNIFICANT CHANGE

Camelids are ungulates—members of a group of large, plant-eating animals that have hooves rather than claws. The ungulates are further divided into the odd-toed ungulates, such as the horse and the rhinoceros, and the even-toed ungulates, such as the camel and the deer.

During the course of their evolution, successive camelids adapted to the habitats in which they lived. Probably the most significant change was the adaptation of their feet, from having four toes to just two. In fact, the toes are actually bound together with skin and the "hooves" are actually nails at the end of the digits. Underneath there is a soft elastic pad that supports the animal's weight as it walks.

WALKING ON SAND

In the Old World, camels are mainly found in desert areas, and this padded sole is ideal for walking over soft sand. The feet of the South American species are similar, although the toes are less closely bound together and the nails are comparatively larger.

With feet that are not as wide as those of the camels and pads that are more flexible, they are better adapted for walking on the rocky trails, loose gravel, and soft earth that abound in their mountainous and often stony environment.

An ungainly gait

A feature of all the members of the camel family is their characteristic swinging pace known as the rack, which is produced by moving the front and hind legs on one side together. Although it is quite ungainly to watch and uncomfortable for a rider—at least until he or she is used to it—it is extremely efficient for traversing open habitats, particularly when the animal takes long strides. The gaits of the guanaco and vicuña tend to be more graceful than that of the camels.

Camels look very much alike, apart from the fact that the dromedary has one hump in the middle of its back, while the Bactrian has two—one over the shoulders and one over the hindquarters. The humps are used to store the energy-rich fats that enable the camel to go for long periods without food. Both camels are large animals, with long legs and

WHITE CAMELS

Cyril Isy-Schwart/The Image Bank

Some dromedaries are entirely white. In northern Saudi Arabia, Jordan, Syria, and Iraq, these white breeds are the most favored for their superb soft fur, and, in these countries, owning all-white herds is a mark of much prestige.

In the past, white camels were the object of raids and counterraids. They still fetch the highest prices at the camel market and are frequently given as gifts.

short tails. The fairly large head with its aloof expression is carried high on the long, curved neck.

All the lamoids, on the other hand, are much smaller. The llama is the largest and heaviest, while the vicuña and guanaco are much more delicate in appearance, with the long, slender legs, long necks, and short tails of their Old World relatives. Their faces are much finer in their features, with widely set eyes and narrow, pointed ears.

North American roots

The first camels evolved in North America about 75 million years ago. By 40 million years ago *Poebrotherium* (pee-bro-THEE-ree-um)—which was about the size of a goat and had a head like a zebra's—had evolved. Later ancestors increased in size, and, by about 12 million years ago, an animal known as *Procamelus* (pro-KAM-a-lus) had emerged. It looked similar to today's vicuña, with long, thin legs, upright ears, and a pointed snout. Its feet were splayed, ending in two toes, and the animal walked on the soft foot pad underneath.

THE FIRST CAMELS WERE SCARCELY BIGGER THAN RABBITS AND HAD FOUR TOES ON EACH FOOT

By 3 million years ago, camels had invaded South America and became adapted to grazing on the steppes at high altitudes, just as they do today. At the same time, *Titanotylopus* (tie-TAN-o-tie-low-pus), the biggest camel ever, lived in North America. It stood some 11.5 feet (3.5 meters) high at the shoulders. All North American camels were to die out later, during the ice ages, though not before the ancestors of today's camels had migrated to Eurasia and North Africa over the land bridges that once connected these continents. ■

Bactrian camel

Camelus bactrianus (KAM-a-luss bak-tree-AH-nuss)

Distinguished by its two humps, the Bactrian camel has a long, woolly coat that is uniform in color, but may be a light or dark brown. Though shorter and usually paler in summer, the hair is always longer on the throat, shoulders, and humps.

Dromedary

Camelus dromedarius (KAM-a-luss drom-a-DARR-ee-uss)

The dromedary, or one-humped camel, also known as the Arabian camel, has a much shorter coat than the Bactrian, as it lives in a hotter climate. Its coat color varies, to merge in with the sandy soil of its environment

Camel

Pigs

Hippos

Peccaries

Bovids

Chevrotain

Even-toed ungulates

Illustrations Ruth Grewcock

THE CAMEL'S FAMILY TREE

The Old World camels evolved quite separately from the New World lamoids, although they had a common ancestor. Some scientists believe that the dromedary evolved from the Bactrian camel, while many consider the llama and alpaca to be the domesticated descendants of the guanaco. The vicuña is a close relative and may also have been used in the breeding of the alpaca.

LLAMA

Lama glama (LAM-ah GLAM-ah)

Much stockier in appearance than the other lamoids, the llama has a long, shaggy coat that may be uniform in color or spotted and speckled with light and dark brown patches. The neck is much thicker than the other species.

ALPACA

Lama pacos (LAM-ah PAK-oss)

This species is characterized by its hair, which is longer even than the llama's and much finer.

GUANACO

Lama guanicoe (LAM-ah GWAN-ik-o)

The guanaco has a drooping upper lip with a deep cleft. The sole of its foot is also divided in two.

VICUÑA

Vicugna vicugna (vie-CUE-na vie-CUE-na)

The smallest and most graceful of the lamoids. Its coat is long and wooly, particularly on the sides, and is usually a rich cinnamon color on the back.

Illustrations Alan Male/Linden Artists

ANATOMY: THE CAMEL

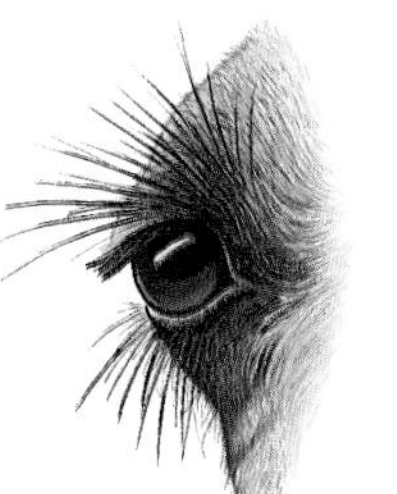

BACTRIAN CAMEL

LLAMA

DROMEDARY

The largest lamoid, the llama, weighs in at up to 340 lb (154 kg), while the dromedary can weigh up to 1,350 lb (613 kg). The Bactrian, though shorter than the dromedary, tips the scales at over 1,575 lb (715 kg).

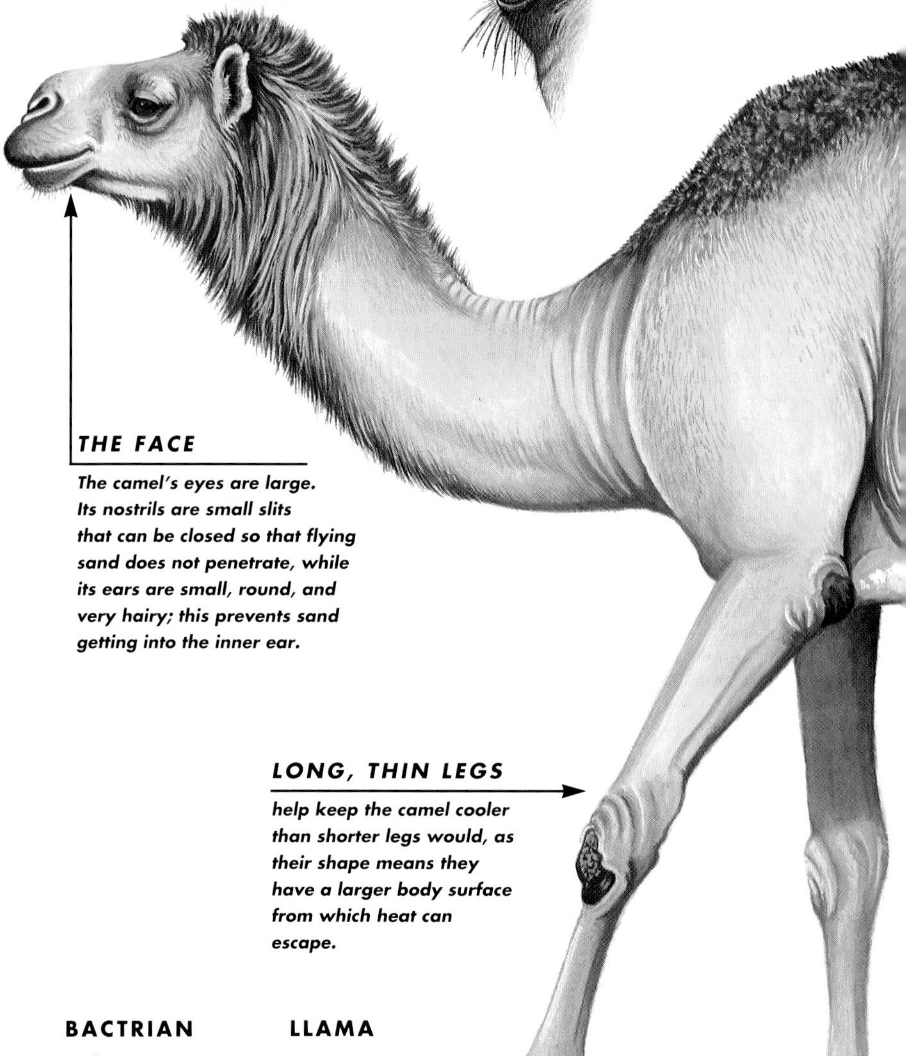

Long, thick eyelashes (left) protect the camel's eyes from the blowing sand and glaring sun of the desert.

THE FACE

The camel's eyes are large. Its nostrils are small slits that can be closed so that flying sand does not penetrate, while its ears are small, round, and very hairy; this prevents sand getting into the inner ear.

DROMEDARY

BACTRIAN CAMEL

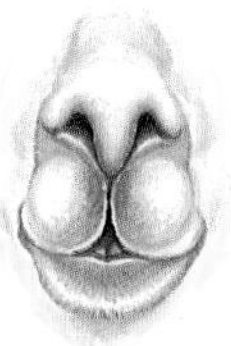

LLAMA

Camelids have sloping muzzles with deeply cleft upper lips that overhang the lower lips. The dromedary has grooves running from each nostril to the upper lip, allowing moisture from the nostrils to be caught in the mouth.

LONG, THIN LEGS

help keep the camel cooler than shorter legs would, as their shape means they have a larger body surface from which heat can escape.

DROMEDARY BACTRIAN LLAMA

Both dromedary and Bactrian camel have broad footpads on which they walk, while llamas have two smaller pads with strong nails on each foot; they walk on the edges of the nails.

Illustrations Kim Thompson

X-RAY

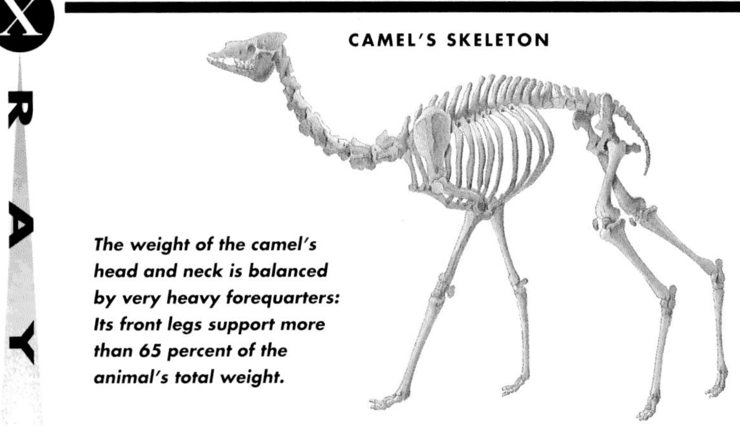

The weight of the camel's head and neck is balanced by very heavy forequarters: Its front legs support more than 65 percent of the animal's total weight.

As camels evolved, the two long foot bones fused into one, the cannon bone.

Present-day camels have two toes with very long bones on each foot. Because of this, they have increased strides and so can run faster.

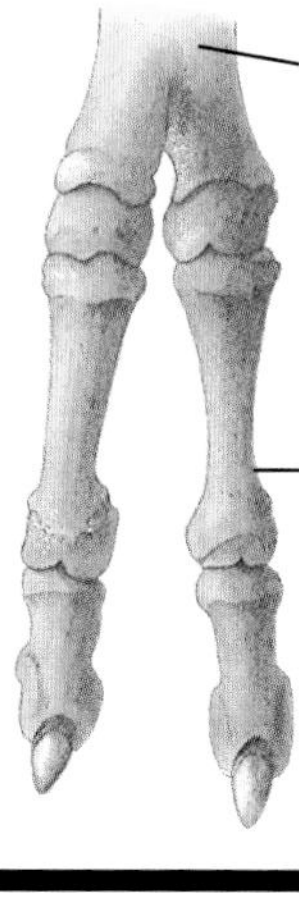

cannon bone

toe

CAMEL'S FOOT

X-ray illustrations Elisabeth Smith

FACT FILE:

THE DROMEDARY

CLASSIFICATION

GENUS: *CAMELUS*

SPECIES: *DROMEDARIUS*

SIZE

HEAD–BODY LENGTH: UP TO 10 FT (3M)

SHOULDER HEIGHT: 8 FT (2.4 M)

HEIGHT TO HUMP: UP TO 7.5 FT (2.3 M)

TAIL LENGTH: 14–22 IN (36–56 CM)

WEIGHT: 990–1,350 LB (450–613 KG)

WEIGHT AT BIRTH: 80 LB (36 KG)

COLORATION

USUALLY UNIFORM BEIGE OR PALE BROWN WITH SLIGHTLY LIGHTER UNDERSIDES; SOME ANIMALS ARE ENTIRELY BLACK OR WHITE.

FEATURES

VERY LONG LEGS

LONG, CURVED NECK

LOFTY HEAD CARRIAGE

ONE HUMP ON BACK

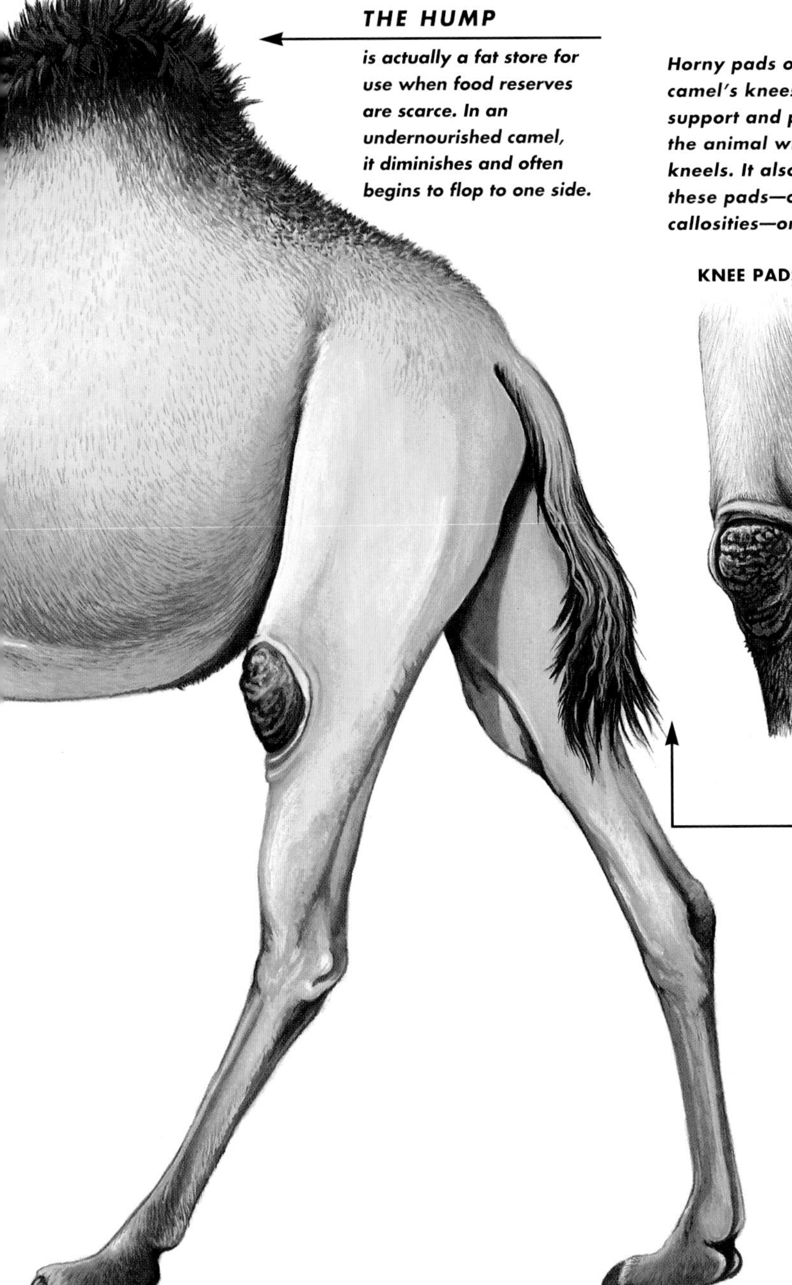

THE HUMP

is actually a fat store for use when food reserves are scarce. In an undernourished camel, it diminishes and often begins to flop to one side.

Horny pads on the camel's knees (below) support and protect the animal when it kneels. It also has these pads—or callosities—on its chest.

KNEE PADS

THE TAIL

is thick and fairly long, with a long tuft of hair at its end.

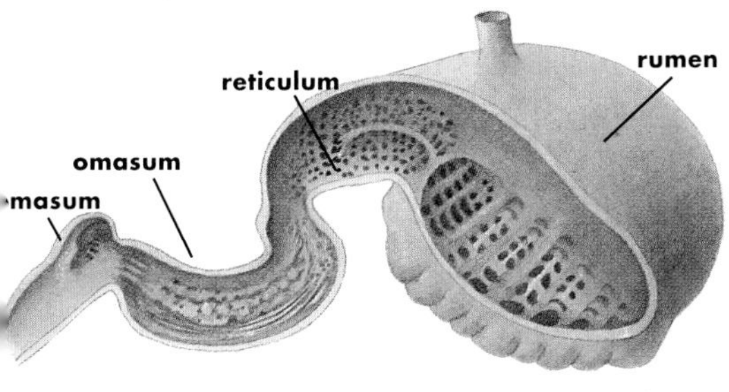

The camel's stomach has four chambers (above). As food is broken down in the rumen, reticulum, and omasum, it releases protein that is digested in the abomasum. Digestive glands are found in sacs lining the rumen walls.

CAMEL'S SKULL

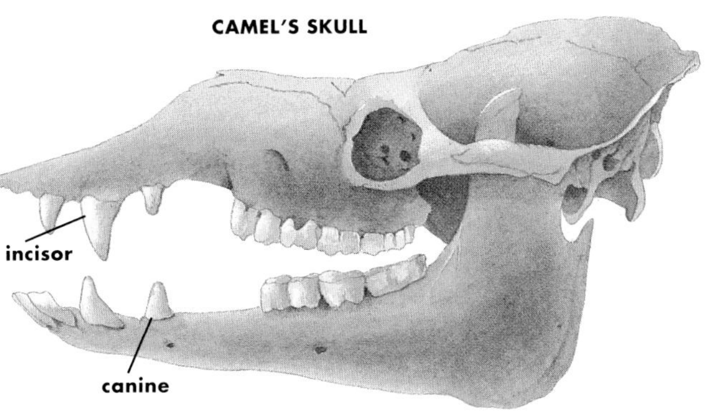

Members of the camel family have elongated skulls with very deep eye sockets. Unlike other ruminants—animals that chew the cud—camels have upper incisors. Young animals have three pairs, but in adults this is reduced to just one. They also have upper canine teeth, again possessed by few other ruminants.

SHIPS OF THE DESERT

FROM THE BLEAK WASTES OF ASIA'S GOBI DESERT TO THE ARID, HIGH-ALTITUDE STEPPES OF THE ANDES, CAMELS AND LLAMAS HAVE BECOME WELL ADAPTED TO LIFE IN INHOSPITABLE ENVIRONMENTS

Scientists concerned with studying camels in the wild are presented with a major problem: Only the vicuña and guanaco, both of South America, exist in a truly wild state. Even the small population of Bactrian camels found in the Gobi Desert is felt by many experts to be descended from feral stock (domesticated animals that have escaped back into the wild) rather than truly wild animals.

The very fact that four species have become domesticated over such wide-ranging areas may, however, tell us a little about their behavioral patterns. Over the centuries, as many as 15 species of ungulate have been domesticated—more than in any other group of mammals—and all these species share a number of common features, most important their lack of territorial behavior.

> THE FACT THAT SO MANY CAMEL SPECIES HAVE BECOME DOMESTICATED SUGGESTS THAT FEW OF THEM ARE TERRITORIAL BY NATURE

Males of the lamoid species that have proved hardest to domesticate—the vicuña and the guanaco—are relatively territorial and are prepared to defend their space. This probably explains why they have resisted human domination.

INTIMIDATING BEHAVIOR

Interestingly, the domesticated llamas and alpacas grazing freely in areas also occupied by vicuñas and guanacos seem able to intimidate the wild species. A single alpaca has been observed charging repeatedly at a band of vicuñas, driving them away from the choicest grazing. Similarly, vicuñas have been seen beating a hasty retreat from llamas.

All camels and llamas display a remarkable ability to adapt to harsh environments. In desert habitats, water is at a premium. Animals that live there must either be able to tolerate a high level of dehydration or avoid exposing themselves to soaring daytime temperatures—either by becoming active at night or by spending the hottest daylight hours under cover or in the shade.

HEAT SEEKER

Camels seem never to seek shade—indeed, they generally rest in the full glare and heat of the sun—and they are diurnal, or active by day. Instead, they have adapted in various ways to tolerate high degrees of heat. They are able to withstand great fluctuations in body temperature—over a range of 13°F (7°C)—with no ill effects. Human beings, on the other hand, experience problems if their

Co Rentmeester/The Image Bank

Raymond Tercafs/Jacana

The South American vicuña (right) *is one of only two truly wild species of camelid. The dromedary* (above) *is, given the chance, a prodigious drinker.*

WHY DO CAMELS AND LLAMAS SPIT?

Rod Salm/Planet Earth Pictures

The camel's bad-tempered reputation is further enhanced by a tendency to spit. This is made worse by the fact that its aim is deadly accurate, straight into the face of the recipient. This habit may seem unpleasant, but it is purely a defensive one. For example, a female llama may spit to ward off a prospective male.

temperature varies by as much as 2°F (1°C).

The South American species face equally challenging problems, because of the high altitudes at which they live. Humans would need to go through a period of acclimatization to cope with the lack of oxygen. Llamas are already adapted to cope with this situation, as their blood contains a high proportion of red blood cells, which make more efficient use of the limited oxygen available.

Fast on their feet

Many ungulates are fleet of foot, a necessary characteristic since they have few other means of defense. Even the ungainly Bactrian camel can reach speeds of 40 mph (65 km/h). In some areas, two types of dromedary are bred—one a heavy beast of burden that can carry a load of 440 pounds (200 kilograms) over a distance of 40 miles (65 kilometers) in a day, the other a much lighter animal that can go three times that distance.

A vicuña is capable of 30 mph (48 km/h) over the rough terrain found at elevations of 15,000 feet (4,572 meters), while llamas carry loads of up to 132 pounds (60 kilograms) for 18 miles (29 kilometers) on hazardous mountain tracks without rest. ■

HABITATS

Despite originating on the rich and fertile grasslands of prehistoric North America, the ancestors of today's camels were successful in challenging new and unforgiving habitats. All the surviving camel and llama species now inhabit such environments.

THE BACTRIAN CAMEL'S NATURAL HOME IS THE GOBI DESERT—A WILD, DESOLATE LANDSCAPE WHERE ONLY THE HARDIEST OF CREATURES SURVIVE

The Bactrian camel is found throughout dry steppe and semidesert zones from central Asia to Mongolia, but its true home is the Gobi Desert, in the foothills of central Asia's Altai Mountains. In winter, when the ground is covered in snow, hordes of camels congregate along the rivers, but then move back to the deserts as the snow melts.

MADE FOR THE DESERT

The dromedary has been domesticated for too long for it to have a true native environment. However, its physical characteristics make it indisputably an animal of hot, arid lands. Indeed, for centuries it has lived in the desert regions of southwest Asia and North Africa.

The dromedary's supreme abilities as a desert dweller and beast of burden led to its introduction into the remote arid areas of Australia and Central America, where it played an important role in the early exploration of those regions' interiors. In both places, camels soon escaped to begin a feral existence in the wild, and large herds of dromedaries are still found in parts of Australia.

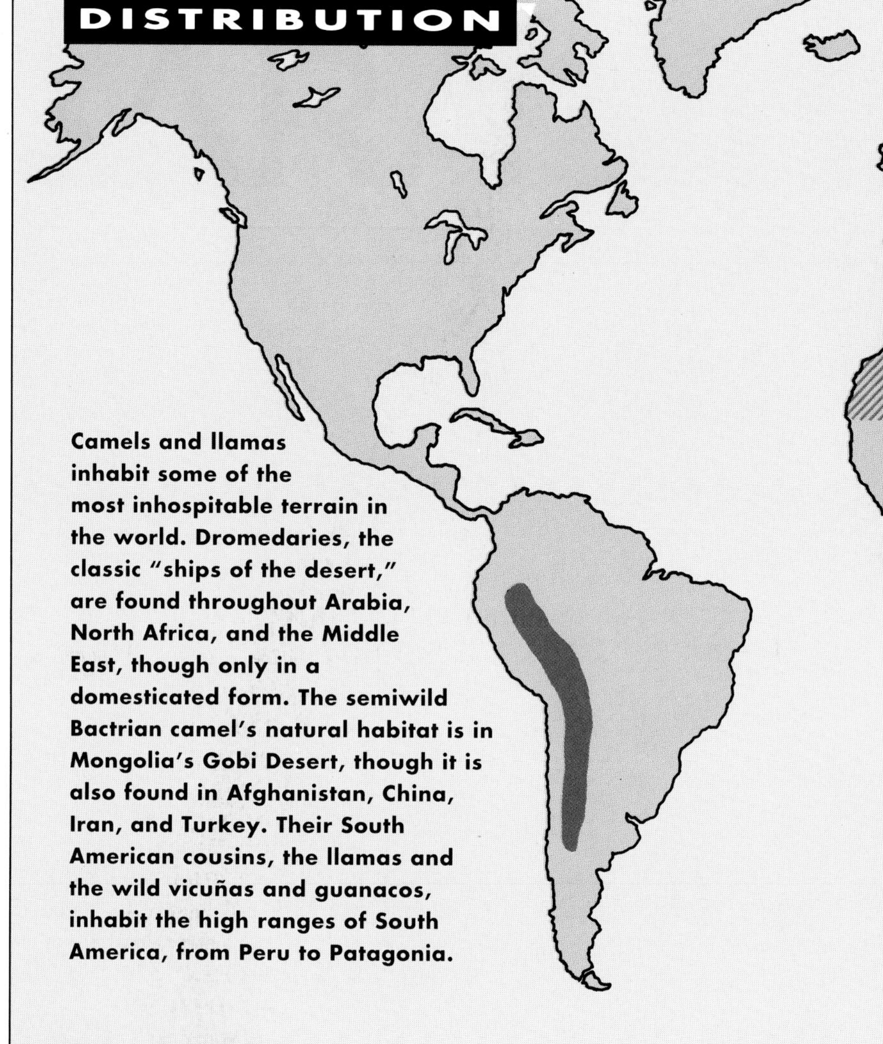

Camels and llamas inhabit some of the most inhospitable terrain in the world. Dromedaries, the classic "ships of the desert," are found throughout Arabia, North Africa, and the Middle East, though only in a domesticated form. The semiwild Bactrian camel's natural habitat is in Mongolia's Gobi Desert, though it is also found in Afghanistan, China, Iran, and Turkey. Their South American cousins, the llamas and the wild vicuñas and guanacos, inhabit the high ranges of South America, from Peru to Patagonia.

HIGH UP IN THE ANDES

The South American lamoids have adapted to similar habitats—arid and mountainous—in the high plains of the Andes Mountains. Compared to Africa, the continent of South America has a remarkably small diversity of grazing animals—in fact, the guanaco is the dominant large South American herbivore.

J. Kugler/Telegraph Colour Library

Desert caravan: In a scene unchanged for thousands of years, dromedaries, supremely adapted to the hardships of the desert, make their way across the shifting sands of Arabia.

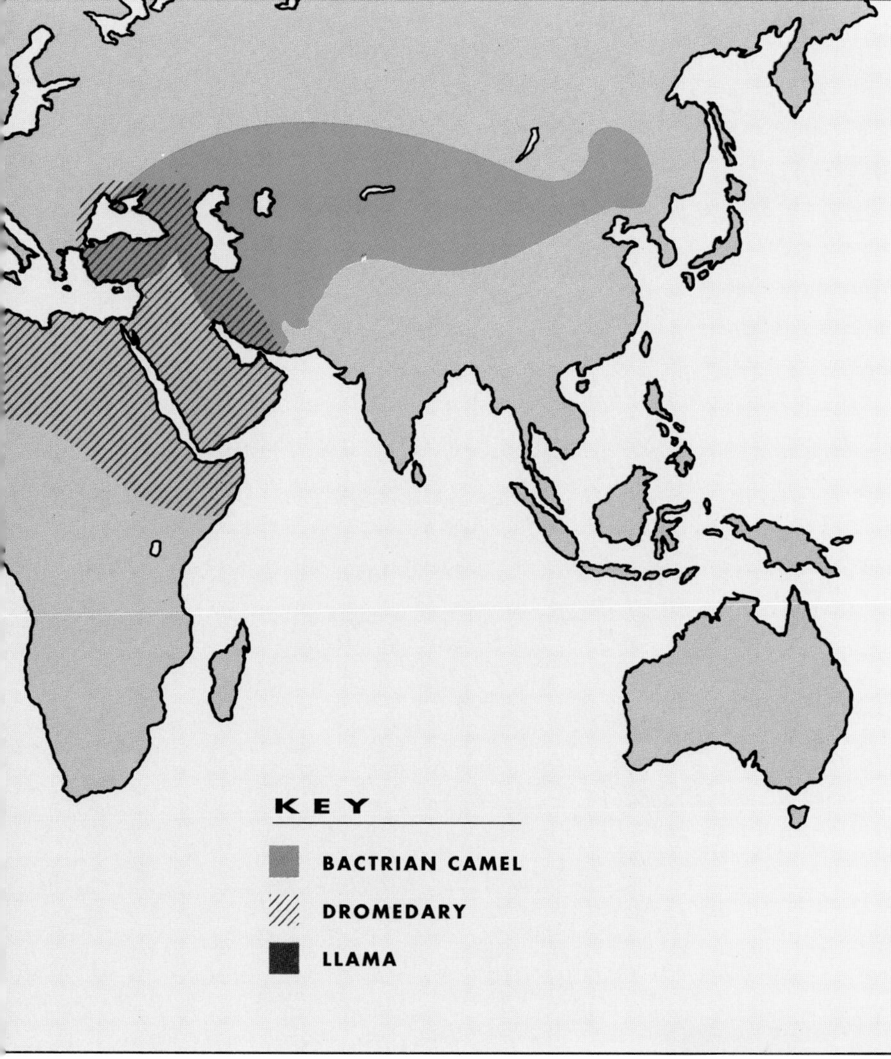

KEY FACTS

- All camels are at home in water and are able to swim, although the Bactrian camel and the dromedary have rarely been observed doing so.
- Camels seem to have an innate ability to detect distant rainfall and green pastures and will often travel long distances to find them.
- The domestication of the Peruvian llama is thought to have taken place some 5,000 years ago in the area to the west of Lake Titicaca.

J. Kugler/Telegraph Colour Library

Today, the guanaco is the most widely distributed lamoid, found throughout the Andes from Peru to the southern tip of Patagonia, though its numbers have been greatly reduced.

It has shown itself to be capable of living in various habitats, from deserts and plains to forests (its padded feet can cope with soft sand, stony ground, or snow), and from sea level to altitudes of over 13,000 feet (3,962 meters).

ONE-TENTH OF THE WORLD'S WILD GUANACOS ARE FOUND ON AN ISLAND THE SIZE OF DENMARK, LOCATED AT THE TIP OF SOUTH AMERICA

One of its strongholds is the island of Isla Grande in Tierra del Fuego, at the southern tip of South America. It has been estimated that about one-tenth of all the world's wild guanacos are found here, in an area about the size of Denmark, with the greatest numbers on the west of the island, where

W. E. Townsend Jr./Bruce Coleman Ltd.

Dromedaries (above) *were introduced to Australia in the 19th century as transport for the early settlers. The animals adapted well to their new habitat, and feral populations remain there today.*

Llamas (left) *congregate on a plateau in the Peruvian Andes. They are often found at altitudes exceeding 10,000 feet (3,048 meters).*

huge ranches seem to offer protection from hunters.

Different populations of guanacos vary in their habitat requirements. Some family groups will occupy a specific area all year-round, while others migrate between winter and summer ranges to avoid snow or drought.

Guanacos are much more inquisitive than vicuñas, a characteristic that draws them to examine anything unusual, and they will run quickly over rough terrain to examine the source of their interest.

There is evidence that guanacos have long been at home in harsh conditions. In 1830, Charles Darwin found a number of guanaco bones in a low ravine and came to the conclusion that they shared communal cemeteries. This theory has now been discounted, as it is believed that the guanacos huddled together in large numbers in order to escape the cold generated by the surrounding snow. Unfortunately, groups of them became trapped there and died in the ice.

The vicuña, a native of the central Andes, is generally found at even higher elevations than the guanaco—in its wild state, it is perfectly at home as high as 18,865 feet (5,750 meters). The environment at these heights consists of rough grasslands and plains, and the daily range in temperatures can vary by as much as 18°F (10°C).

A natural hazard for all the Andes lamoids is lightning, which strikes regularly at such high elevations. Each year it claims the lives of many hundreds of animals: sheep, cows, and goats as well as llamas, vicuñas, and guanacos. ■

LARGE NUMBERS OF GUANACOS WENT TO THEIR DEATHS HUDDLED TOGETHER IN A VAIN ATTEMPT TO ESCAPE FROM THE EFFECTS OF THE BITING COLD

FOCUS ON

THE GOBI DESERT

Although the popular image of deserts is that of heat and sand, deserts are actually defined by their lack of rainfall—generally less than 10 inches (25 centimeters) a year. While it is true that most desert regions are found in the tropics, some are located in the world's colder regions. The Gobi Desert, which stretches from the mountains of southern Mongolia toward northern China, is one such region.

It is as bleak a place as any on earth: Small mountain ranges occur across its vast wastes, and the flatter areas are covered in tiny stones, known locally as *gobi*, from which it gets its name.

Temperatures in the Gobi Desert can vary from a summer midday heat of 110°F (43°C) to a winter cold of -40°F (-40°C), when the ground remains covered in snow for long periods. Always scarce, rainfall varies from year to year, so there is never a time when fresh plant growth can be assured.

For centuries, the Gobi has been home to one of the world's most primitive horses, the Mongolian wild horse, also known as Przhevalski's horse. Other large animals that were once common are the saiga herds and the gray wolf, the latter a predator on the more docile grazing animals and once the most widespread member of the dog family. Today its range is greatly restricted.

DESERT TEMPERATURES

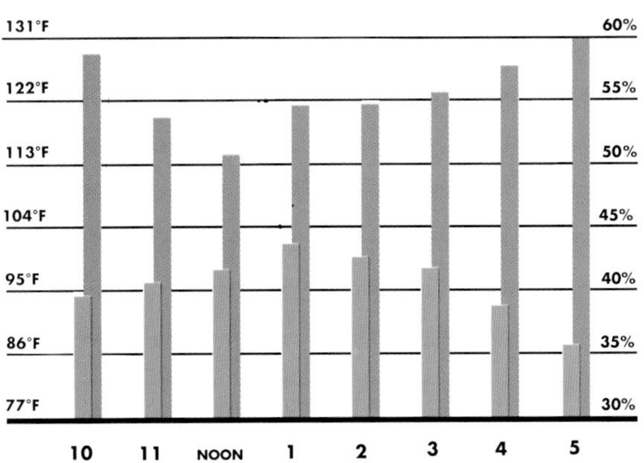

TEMPERATURE

HUMIDITY

Desert temperatures reach their peak at midday. Consequently, many desert animals are nocturnal, taking advantage of the relatively high humidity and very cool temperatures caused by the lack of cloud cover.

NEIGHBORS

Only the hardiest of creatures can survive the rigors of life in the Gobi Desert. Huge extremes in temperature and a critical lack of vegetation have led to a range of unusual adaptations.

LONG-EARED JERBOA

A nocturnal animal, the prolific jerboa moves swiftly through the desert propelled by its powerful back legs.

DESERT LOCUST

This insect migrates in huge flocks over vast distances. The male "sings" by rubbing its legs against its wings.

Illustrations Peter Bull

ENEMIES

MODERATELY DANGEROUS

WOLF

Packs of wolves, though rarer than they once were, may attack elderly or infirm camels.

THE GOBI DESERT

Set in the middle of Asia, the world's largest con-tinent, the Gobi Desert is simply too far from the sea for rain-bearing winds to reach it with any frequency.

What little moisture there is falls as rain when it reaches the Himalayas to the southwest or the Chinese ranges to the northeast. Because of this "rain shadow" caused by the tall mountains, there is little rain left by the time winds reach the desert.

Guido Alberto Rossi/The Image Bank

EAGLE OWL

The largest of all owls, the eagle owl is distinguished by its brightly colored eyes. It hunts small mammals.

LEBERTINE VIPER

This nocturnal viper lies in wait for rodents and lizards, which it bites with its poisonous, hollow teeth.

DESERT HEDGEHOG

Lighter and faster than its European relative, the desert hedgehog moves swiftly in pursuit of insects.

ONAGER

Capable of speeds up to 40 mph (65 km/h), this wild ass can go for up to three days without drinking.

MONITOR LIZARD

This large, aggressive lizard feeds on birds, rodents, and other lizards, which it swallows whole.

FOOD AND FEEDING

François Gohier/Ardea

Division of labor: Some vicuñas keep a lookout for predators as fellow herd members graze on a rocky Andean outcrop. Vicuñas often lick stones and rocks that are rich in salt and other valuable minerals.

All the camel family members are herbivores, animals that feed on a diet made up almost exclusively of vegetable matter such as grasses, herbs, and other foliage. They are also browsers or grazers, sometimes both. Browsers are animals that pluck leaves off trees or shrubs, while grazers crop low-growing grasses and herbs.

Like cows and sheep, camelids are ruminants, animals that regurgitate vegetable matter to be chewed and digested as much as possible in order to gain the maximum nutritional benefits.

Chamber works

Ruminants have a varying number of digestion chambers or stomachs; members of the camel family have four. They get their name from the first of these chambers, which is known as the rumen.

Camelids crop their food by seizing it between their long, forward-pointing lower incisors and tough upper gums, then tearing it away. The food passes directly down to the rumen.

This system of feeding and digestion is an evolutionary adaptation. Much of the food in the camelids' environment is low in protein—an essential nutrient in the diet of any animal. This means that the animal must eat and digest a considerable amount of food to obtain the necessary protein.

Useful saliva

Chewing the food twice allows a greater surface area of the food to be exposed to the action of the digestive juices, which are able to break down cellulose into useful and essential nutrients. Greater exposure to saliva also helps to neutralize the fatty acids that are produced as the

HEROIC DRINKING *efforts allow tired, thirsty camels to regain their body weight quickly. Dromedaries can drink as much as 30 gallons (136 liters) at one time.*

Illustrations Andie Peck/Wildlife Art Agency

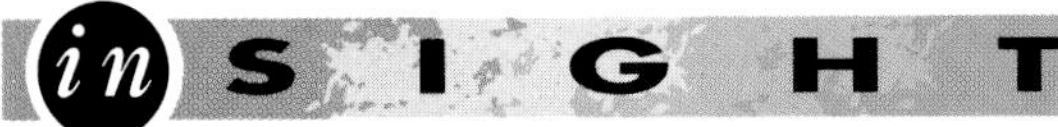

WATER CONSERVATION IN CAMELS

AIR TEMPERATURE — CAMEL BODY TEMP. — HUMAN BODY TEMP.

TEMPERATURE: 113°F, 104°F, 95°F, 86°F, 77°F, 68°F

DAYS 1 2 3 4

Camels have a distinct advantage over humans when it comes to conserving water. Able to withstand a high body temperature, camels have little need to lose heat—and precious fluid—through sweating. This is helped further by their ability to lower their temperatures during the cold desert nights, which means it takes longer for them to heat up the next day. Humans, by contrast, retain more heat because they have more fat and, consequently, need to sweat more.

digestive juices in the rumen get to work.

The Old World camels in particular face a diet of desert plants that are hard, dry, and tough; many have strong, alkaline flavors. In fact, camels thrive on salty plants that are rejected by many other desert dwellers and actively seek out plants that grow in salty or alkaline soil.

CAMELS MAKE THE MOST OF THE DRY, TOUGH VEGETATION THAT THE DESERT OFFERS, THRIVING ON SALTY PLANTS UNTOUCHED BY OTHER ANIMALS

Camels will browse and graze virtually any vegetation they can find, their thick lips seemingly immune to sharp prickles. When times are really hard, they will pick over carcasses. Their humps indicate how well fed they are; contrary to popular myth, these are reserves of fat, not water. When animals are undernourished, the humps become noticeably smaller and less rigid.

DIVIDED LAND

Vicuñas are strictly grazers, feeding mainly on low-growing plants. Their territories are divided in two: one area specifically for feeding, the other for sleeping. Young animals often lie down to graze, tucking their legs neatly under their body. Grazing continues throughout the day, with half-hour rests every couple of hours, but the last few hours of the afternoon are spent continually eating—the best forage, it seems, is saved until last.

The guanaco is both a grazer and a browser, which is why it is also found in shrub lands and forests, as well as grasslands. ■

The dromedary's long neck means it can reach vegetation almost 11.5 ft (3.5 m) above the ground. Here a dromedary feeds on an acacia bush.

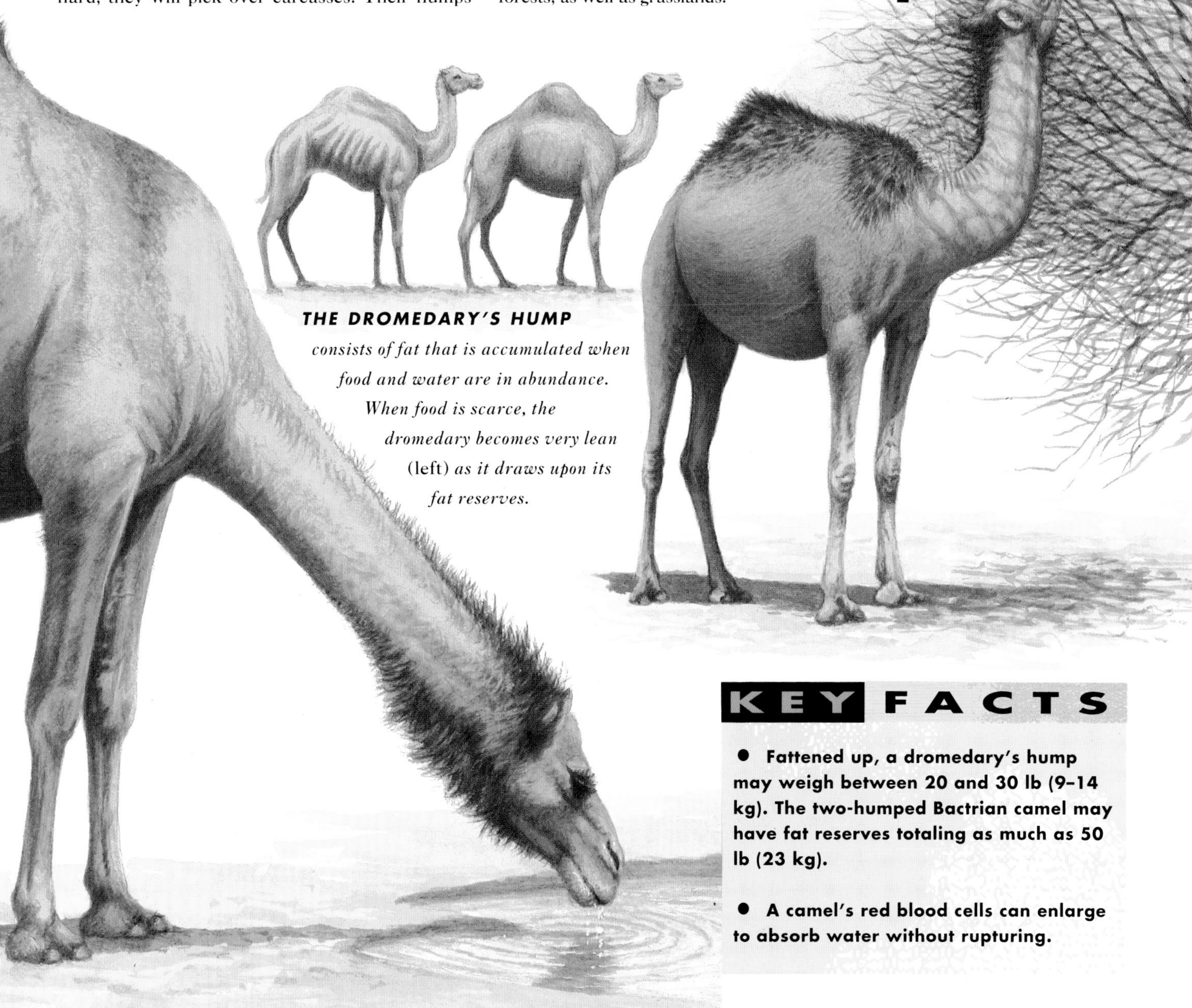

***THE DROMEDARY'S HUMP** consists of fat that is accumulated when food and water are in abundance. When food is scarce, the dromedary becomes very lean* (left) *as it draws upon its fat reserves.*

KEY FACTS

- **Fattened up, a dromedary's hump may weigh between 20 and 30 lb (9–14 kg). The two-humped Bactrian camel may have fat reserves totaling as much as 50 lb (23 kg).**
- **A camel's red blood cells can enlarge to absorb water without rupturing.**

SOCIAL STRUCTURE

Because the Old World camels have been domesticated for so long—records suggest they were first domesticated in Arabia about 3,000 years ago—it has proved difficult to study the true nature of their social relationships, though it is thought that the behavior of the semiwild Bactrian camels of the Gobi Desert is probably very close indeed to that of a wild camel.

These camels roam the arid wastes in groups consisting of one or two males with between three and five females and their young. Males defend the females against intruding males, beginning with intimidating displays in which each one urinates,

BECAUSE THEY REMAIN UNDOMESTICATED, THE VICUÑA AND THE GUANACO HAVE LOST NONE OF THEIR NATURAL SOCIAL INSTINCTS

defecates, and makes a noise by slapping its tail against its hindquarters. A fight will ensue if neither animal backs down.

It is to the wild lamoids of South America—the vicuña and guanaco—that we must turn for the greatest insights into the social structure of the camelids, since, free from domestication, they have lost none of their natural social instincts.

THE HIGH LIFE

The little vicuña is one of the few hoofed animals in the world to occupy and actively defend separate sleeping and feeding territories all year-round. Its chosen habitat, high up in the Andes, means that each family group, or "harem," feeds, sleeps, mates, and gives birth largely free from the interference of other mammals.

The size of a territory depends on the amount and quality of grazing, but the single dominant male is at pains to choose territories where the grazing is as good as it can be. Territories are marked with large piles of dung that are visited, sniffed at, and constantly added to by members of the group.

Border disputes are not uncommon among dominant males. When males charge at each other, they draw up their front legs at the last second and slam their chests together with great impact, while seeking to gash each other's necks with their teeth.

At all times, the male keeps a close eye on his females. If he sees danger—vision is the best developed of all the senses—he lets out a screeching

HERDS OF MALE DROMEDARIES (right) *on their way to a common watering hole. Males usually tolerate each other's presence, though during the breeding season fights to the death are not uncommon.*

WHEN AT REST, *dromedaries face directly into the midday sun, their legs tucked under their body. This helps to keep the minimum of body surface exposed to the sun, reducing heat stress and so minimizing potential water loss.*

Illustrations Andie Peck/Wildlife Art Agency

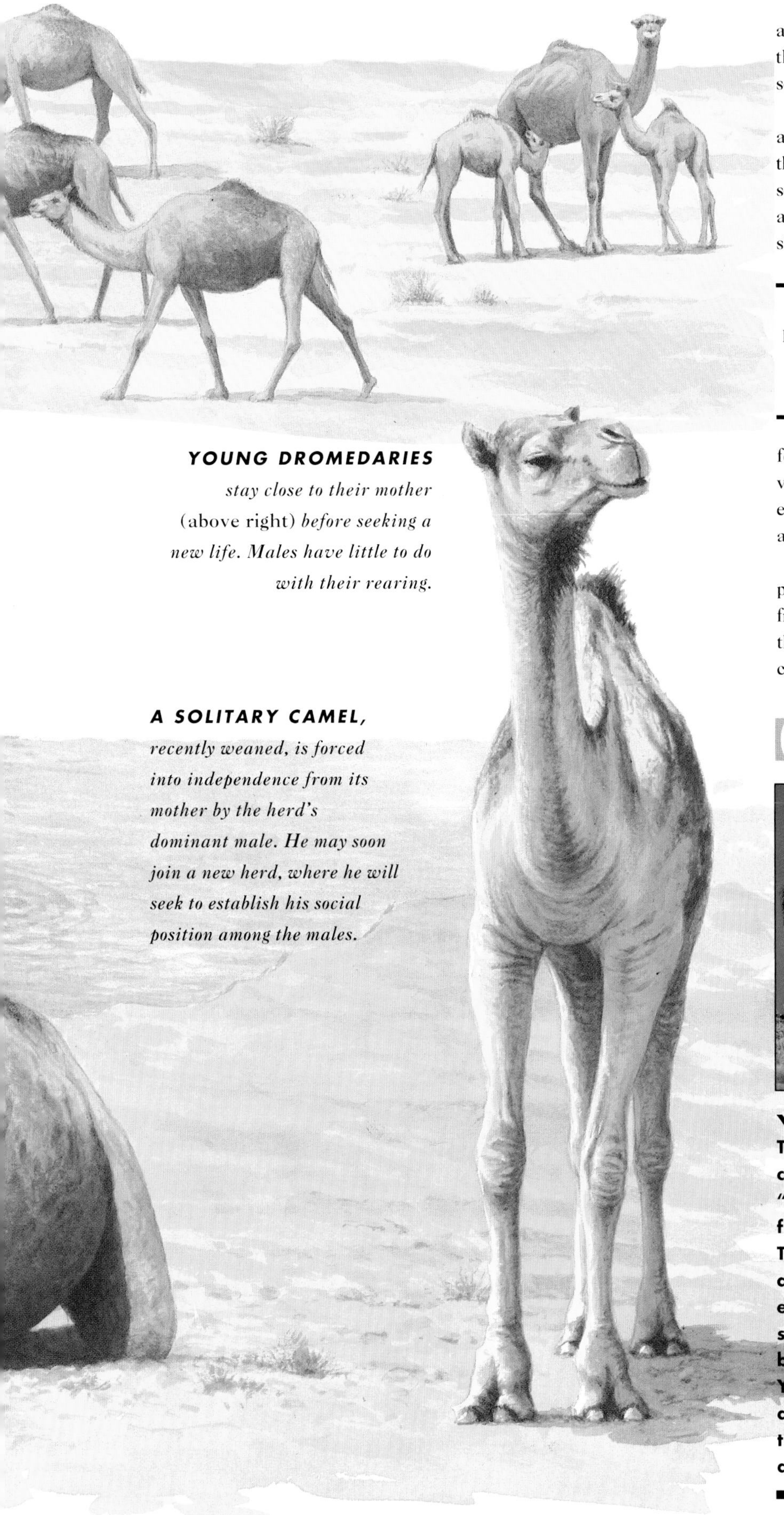

alarm call consisting of several whistles. He will then place himself between the females and the source of the danger.

Guanacos have a very similar social structure, although the dominant males are less aggressive than the vicuña, and the females wander in and out of social groups more freely. A male guanaco defending a territory and a band of females displays behavior similar to that of the vicuña, often watching over the

MALE GUANACOS KEEP A WATCHFUL EYE ON THEIR FEMALE BANDS, AND THEY WILL DEFEND THEM WITH VIOLENCE IF NECESSARY

females from a vantage point and warning them vocally of danger. If another group begins to encroach, he will get anxious, stiffening his body, arching his tail, and flicking his ears nervously.

If this is not enough to discourage the approaching intruder, the male will rear and kick his front feet high in the air, uttering loud cries. Often these territorial conflicts are resolved by a simple chase, but males will fight if need be. ■

YOUNG DROMEDARIES *stay close to their mother* (above right) *before seeking a new life. Males have little to do with their rearing.*

A SOLITARY CAMEL, *recently weaned, is forced into independence from its mother by the herd's dominant male. He may soon join a new herd, where he will seek to establish his social position among the males.*

ZEFA-Allstock

VICUÑA HAREMS

The basic social group of the vicuñas consists of a dominant male and his "harem"—somewhere between five and fifteen breeding females and their young. The male always grazes close to his females and is quick to chase off any intruders—even females from neighboring bands—that stray too close. By doing this, he controls both the size and behavior of the group. Young males and females are harshly driven out of the band, the males to form new harems, the females to find another harem ready to accept them.

LIFE CYCLE

The breeding season for vicuñas and guanacos can be a time of considerable aggression as males compete with one another for females. The dominant male of a vicuña herd has his work cut out: He is busy chasing after his females and anxious to catch them when they are receptive to mating; at the same time he is nervous about leaving the other females in the herd in case some trespassing male should try to steal them away.

Vicuñas mate in March and April, and, after a gestation period of 11 months, a single young is born. Within a matter of weeks of giving birth, the female will mate again, even though she is likely to go on suckling her young for 8 more months.

WITHIN A FEW WEEKS OF GIVING BIRTH, FEMALE VICUÑAS ARE READY TO MATE AGAIN

When camels and llamas mate, they generally do so lying down; females give birth standing up, and, unlike most mammals, they do not lick their newborn offspring. Most give birth to a single young—twins are very rare—that is well developed at birth. A vicuña foal, for instance, is able to stand and walk within 15 minutes of birth. It will stay close by its mother's side until it is at least 8 months old, leaving her only to play with the young of the other females in the herd.

The fact that vicuñas give birth each year, whereas most other lamoids give birth every other year, probably explains why the dominant males are so fierce in their protection of good grazing territories. This way they can be sure that there will be enough food for all the newborn young. It may also explain why the dominant male begins to chase young males out of the herd at 8 months old and females when they are no more than a year.

NERVOUS WITHDRAWAL

The guanaco's mating season is rather longer, taking place from November to February. The gestation period is between 11 and 12 months. After the female has given birth to her young—called *chulengo*—she is quite

JUST A FEW HOURS OLD, *the newborn camel is too weak to stand and is dependent upon its mother in every way.*

MATING *among camels is unusual for mammals, as the male mounts the female from behind when she is lying down.*

DISEASES OF THE DESERT

Camels can fall victim to a number of diseases that often spread quickly within a camel herd. One of the most dangerous and, unfortunately, common of these is jarrah, a form of mange. This spreads quickly, often attaining epidemic proportions, and brings death in little over a month if left untreated.

Another ailment is manhus, a disease of the lungs. Before the introduction of modern veterinary practice, this could have a mortality rate of 50 percent.

Like any other creatures inhabiting a difficult environment, camels suffer cuts and bruises from stones, rocks, and thorns, but these usually heal quite quickly.

GROWING UP

The life of a young Bactrian camel

THE MOTHER SUCKLES *the young foal on her rich milk. Females produce up to 1.59 gallons (6 liters) a day.*

YOUNG BACTRIAN CAMELS *trail behind their mother in search of food. Foals feed on easily digestible food such as tender grass.*

Illustrations Jo Cowne with thanks to Colin Fountain/Cotswold Wildlife Park

FROM BIRTH TO DEATH

BACTRIAN CAMEL
GESTATION: 13 MONTHS
LITTER SIZE: 1
BREEDING: MATING OCCURS IN JANUARY AND FEBRUARY
SEXUAL MATURITY: 5 YEARS
LONGEVITY: UP TO 50 YEARS

LLAMA
GESTATION: 10 MONTHS
LITTER SIZE: 1
BREEDING: SEASONAL; BETWEEN SPRING AND EARLY SUMMER
SEXUAL MATURITY: 1–2 YEARS
LONGEVITY: 20–25 YEARS

DROMEDARY
GESTATION: 12 MONTHS
LITTER SIZE: 1
BREEDING: SEASONAL
SEXUAL MATURITY: 5 YEARS
LONGEVITY: UP TO 50 YEARS

GUANACO
GESTATION: 11 MONTHS
LITTER SIZE: 1
BREEDING: NOVEMBER TO FEBRUARY
SEXUAL MATURITY: 6–12 MONTHS
LONGEVITY: 20–25 YEARS

nervous for a few weeks, withdrawing to the cover of the forest at the slightest hint of danger.

Guanacos are one of the few ungulates that nurse two generations of offspring simultaneously. This only occurs for a few weeks, however, before the dominant male chases off the previous year's offspring. The female will attempt, almost always in vain, to prevent him from doing so.

CAMEL COURTSHIP

Old World camels mate throughout the year, although births tend to coincide with the maximum plant growth in an area. These camels have a gland on the back of their necks which produces a secretion that seems to be sexually stimulating to both male and female. During courtship, the animals rub this secretion onto their own humps and also over their partner's, intertwining their necks as they rub their heads together.

> BIRTHS AMONG OLD WORLD CAMELS TEND TO COINCIDE WITH THE TIME OF OPTIMUM PLANT GROWTH

Males also possess a peculiar physical feature at the back of their mouths. Known as a *palu*, this can be inflated so that it extends outside the mouth like a pink rubber balloon. This is displayed when the male is sexually aroused.

Gestation in camels lasts between 12 and 13 months. Again, the single young is well developed and covered in fur at birth, and will move about freely by the end of its first day. Human owners usually wean a foal when it is about one year old, but it will not be fully grown for another four years.

Old World camels usually live longer than their South American counterparts. It is not unusual for a dromedary to reach 50 years of age, while it is unlikely that a lamoid will live even half as long. ■

BEASTS OF BURDEN

AS DOMESTICATED, SEMIWILD, OR WILD ANIMALS, MEMBERS OF THE CAMEL FAMILY ARE AT THE MERCY OF HUMANKIND—ONLY HUMANS HAVE THE POWER TO DECIDE THE FATE OF THE CAMELS

Throughout the centuries, humans have posed the biggest threat to the wild members of the camel family, particularly those living in South America. Now it is humans alone who can save these precious animals from sliding into oblivion.

HEAD COUNTS

Recent estimates have put the total number of camelids in the world at 21.5 million. The lamoids in South America make up nearly 8 million of this total, but more than 90 percent of these are totally domesticated llamas and alpacas.

Of the wild guanacos and vicuñas, guanacos are the more common—in fact, there are thought to be some six times as many as vicuñas. Although numbers have been greatly depleted from former times, the guanaco still remains the most widely distributed lamoid in South America.

OF ALL THE DROMEDARIES IN THE WORLD, A HUGE MAJORITY ARE DOMESTICATED OR SEMIWILD ANIMALS. THEIR FUTURE DEPENDS ON THE FORTUNES AND PRIORITIES OF HUMANS

Of the nearly 14 million camels in Africa and Asia, around 90 percent are dromedaries. These dromedaries have only ever been known in a semiwild or domesticated state, and, as such, they are still of vital importance to humans in these areas.

Domestication has always taken two forms: that by settled people who live off the land and keep herds of camels as livestock; and that by nomadic people whose life on the move means that they are almost wholly dependent on their camels for their survival. Nomads use camels for transporting supplies; they drink their milk; and, if times are very hard, they even know how to take blood and meat from the beasts without killing them.

The total number of Bactrian camels has dropped significantly. Right up until the 19th century, these camels were thought to be relatively widespread in the wild and also quite widely domesticated across their range. They are still used as beasts of burden in parts of Afghanistan, Iran, Turkey, and the former USSR, and, because they are popular in zoos and wildlife parks, their future is reasonably secure for the moment.

However, the Bactrian camel's future as a truly wild animal—if those still found in the Gobi Desert are indeed wild, and not the descendants of feral stock—is less certain, even though it is protected in various reserves. The International Union for the Conservation of Nature lists the Bactrian camel as vulnerable, but this might not be enough. It is

Tony Morrison/South American Pictures

Lamoids such as the guanaco (right) *have long been domesticated by humans. The vicuña produces wool that is particularly fine* (above).

François Gohier/Jacana

Though often set free to roam in the desert for several months, dromedaries are dependent on humans for their drinking water (below).

Jean Paul Ferrero/Jacana

thought that there may be only around 500 wild animals left, which may not be sufficient to ensure the continued survival of this race.

Long before the Spanish conquistadores invaded South America in the 16th century, the inhabitants of the Andes have made good use of the local vicuñas. Even before the time of the great Inca civilization, local people recognized the quality and value of the vicuña's wool, which is still considered by many to be the finest in the world.

THE INCAS—AN EARLY SOUTH AMERICAN CIVILIZATION—ROUNDED UP AND KILLED THOUSANDS OF VICUÑAS IN ORGANIZED HUNTS

The Indians of pre-Inca civilizations built special traps to hunt vicuñas, where the animals were rounded up and chased into a stone enclosure. Along the walls in the enclosure were small gaps, behind which the Indians had dug pits so that, as the animals tried to jump to freedom, they fell in the pits and broke their front legs. Such a trap was known as a "kill trap." Vicuñas were also rounded up and herded into pens called "live traps" where, one by one, they were caught, shorn of their wool, and then released back into the wild unharmed.

The Incas, too, organized enormous vicuña hunts, when thousands upon thousands of animals would be captured under the supervision of the royal leaders. Any sick, old, or inferior animals were killed, while the others were shorn and set free for another four years in order to allow their coats to regrow. The cloth woven from the wool was considered so precious that only members of the Inca royal family were allowed to wear it.

It was the arrival of the Spanish and their powerful weapons that changed the vicuña's history. Around one-and-a-half million vicuñas were suddenly faced with mass slaughter on a giant scale and stood very little chance. In 1825, South America's great liberator, Simón Bolívar, declared vicuña hunting illegal, but the wool was too valuable to local people who needed to feed and clothe their families and the ban could not be enforced. In the four centuries since the time of the Incas, it is

NEVER BEFORE HAD VICUÑAS FACED SUCH MASS SLAUGHTER AS WHEN THE SPANISH ARRIVED WITH THEIR POWERFUL WEAPONS FOR HUNTING

estimated that the numbers of vicuñas in the wild had fallen some 400,000, and, by the 1970s, just 10,000 animals remained.

Recognizing this decline, the IUCN placed the vicuña on the endangered list in 1969, and ensuing conservation agreements between Peru, Chile, Argentina, and Bolivia have given it full protection.

As always, however, protection laws are very difficult to enforce, and, if there is a demand for skins, people will always be prepared to run the risks of poaching. Large numbers of skins have apparently been smuggled through Paraguay—which has no vicuñas and, therefore, does not protect them—for sale to European markets. In the early 1970s, the United States and Britain banned the import of vicuña products.

SAFE HAVEN

Today, the vicuña is given full-scale protection in a 15,000-acre (6,070-hectare) reserve in Peru, known as the Pampa Galeras National Vicuña Preserve, where a third to a half of South America's entire vicuña population is free to roam and graze. To establish this, officials explained the purpose of the plan to numbers of herders, who willingly moved their sheep to other areas. Without the competition from other grazing herds, vicuña numbers there slowly began to increase. By 1981, the IUCN was able to change the status of the vicuña from endangered to vulnerable.

The Peruvian government has taken the protection of the vicuña extremely seriously and has funded various research projects with a view to conserving them as best it can. A number are kept at the National Cameloid Center where some have been interbred with domestic alpacas—the other

Victor Engebert/Colorific / Telegraph Colour Library

ENDANGERED ENVIRONMENT

GROWING TOURISM IN THE ANDES

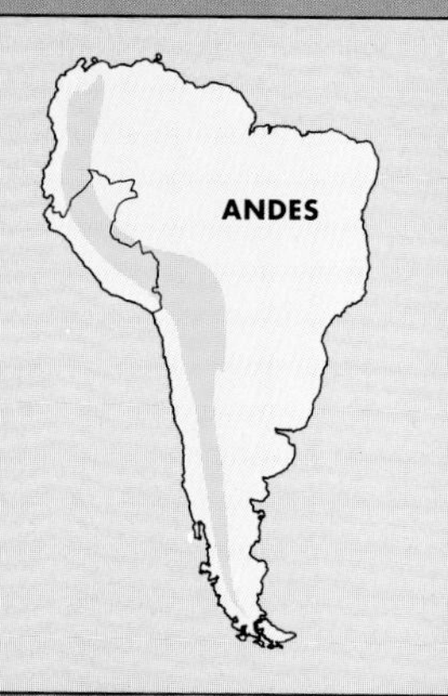

It is a well-known fact that tourism boosts a country's economy, particularly in isolated and rural areas. But the negative aspects sometimes carry equal weight.

The Andes range of mountains forms the backbone of the entire western side of the South American continent, running through a number of developing countries, such as Ecuador and Peru. The national parks in these countries, such as Sangay National Park in Ecuador, are drawing an increasing number of visitors every year, and this regular "traffic" is having a detrimental effect on previously unspoiled areas.

UNDER PRESSURE

When a national park exceeds its "carrying capacity"—that is, the number of visitors it can accommodate with high levels of satisfaction for visitors and few negative impacts on resources—the resulting damages are evaluated in ecological and esthetic terms.

Ecologically, pressure from too many visitors changes the behavior of the local wildlife—where numbers of animals may be reduced or nesting patterns are disrupted—as well as the environment. The

CONSERVATION MEASURES

- Since South American tourism is still a relatively new industry, it is difficult to evaluate how the environment is affected.

- The Ecuadorean Park Service and Fundacion Natura are putting a new national conservation plan together, proposing innovative and sustainable management strategies for Ecuadorian parks.

erosion of paths, the careless disposal of litter, and the pollution of streams are most often reported. Tree-cutting for firewood by hikers and by local people as a sellable resource is aggravating the problem of deforestation in the Andes.

For example, Podocarpus National Park contains a rich diversity of plant species that are unique to Ecuador. In fact, it is named after a species of tree that grows only there. As a result of growing tourism, however, park wardens are now trying to combat illegal forest-cutting by visitors. If it continues, some plant species may be lost to us forever.

Eventually, the damaging effects of tourism come full circle as a beauty spot's esthetic image is destroyed, and, because it is no longer attractive, the tourists go elsewhere.

Andrew Ward/Life File

LLAMAS GRAZE PEACEFULLY NEAR THE RUINS OF THE ANCIENT CITY OF MACHU PICCHU.

About one-half of all the parks have yet to implement management plans, as official funding is inadequate.

- A park's ecological balance may be better maintained using new management methods such as encouraging wet- or off-season visitors, providing adequate information, and designating hiking trails and viewing areas.

ENDANGERED ENVIRONMENT

CAMELS IN DANGER

THE CHART BELOW SHOWS HOW THE INTERNATIONAL UNION FOR THE CONSERVATION OF NATURE (IUCN) CLASSIFIES THE STATUS OF CAMELS AND LLAMOIDS:

BACTRIAN CAMEL	VULNERABLE
VICUÑA	VULNERABLE

VULNERABLE INDICATES THAT THE ANIMAL IS LIKELY TO MOVE INTO THE ENDANGERED CATEGORY IF THINGS CONTINUE AS THEY ARE. *ENDANGERED* MEANS THAT THE ANIMAL IS IN DANGER OF EXTINCTION AND ITS SURVIVAL IS UNLIKELY UNLESS STEPS ARE TAKEN TO SAVE IT.

G. K. Brown/Ardea

fine wool-bearing lamoid. The paca-vicuñas, as they are known, grow wool that is much longer than the vicuña's and almost as fine. In 1973 paca-vicuña fleece was five times as valuable as cashmere.

Like that of the vicuña, the guanaco's history is the history of its Andean range. To the local tribes of early civilizations it was vital, providing them with meat, wool and hides, sinews, and also images for their mythology and folklore. And, as in the case of the vicuña, it is thought that guanacos roamed in their tens of thousands when the Spanish arrived, and, though their persecution began later, they too were eventually brought to the edge of extinction, but for different reasons.

ROUGH AND TOUGH

Guanacos had long been hunted for their meat but not for their wool—the soft underfur is very valuable, but separating it from the coarse outer guard hairs is a time-consuming business. Young guanacos were, however, taken from their mothers for their soft, cinnamon-colored pelts.

The fate of the guanaco proved to be not in the hands of the hunters but in the hands of the ranchers who had begun to farm the land. Fences interrupted the animals' traditional movements, and many guanacos died entangled in wire; many more were shot by ranchers who saw them as potential competitors for the grazing land they had earmarked for their livestock.

By the end of the 1970s, the total guanaco population across its entire range was estimated to be between 50,000 and 100,000 and on the decline. To boost dwindling numbers, protected preserves were formed in Chile and Peru, but not initially in Argentina, from where thousands of pelts were said

ALONGSIDE MAN

INCA LINKS

Llamas were of vital importance to the Incas—natives of Peru whose civilization dated from A.D. 1200 and who ultimately ruled all along the Andean range. As beasts of burden, llamas were the transport of military conquests as well as of the workers in the fields.

When an Inca ruler named his heir, the priests would sacrifice a llama and "read" the entrails to see if the appointed heir would be a good leader.

Pure white llamas were sacrificed to Mother Earth in return for good crops, a practice that was continued by local tribes way into the 20th century. Each family was allowed to own ten llamas, and a llama fetus buried under a house was said to bring good luck.

Brian Henderson/Bruce Coleman Ltd.

For many centuries, llamas have played a vital role in the everyday lives of the Andean people.

to have been exported at this time.

However, Argentina now also offers protection; experience has taught that there can be a return through tourism and the controlled sale of meat and wool products. The total guanaco population has increased significantly since the slump in figures in the late 1970s, although it is doubtful that it is still increasing today.

In nations where the economy is either developing or undergoing serious problems, such as in South American countries, there is always a problem with implementing conservation measures. In the case of the guanaco, the high profits to be gained from trade in the animals, combined with the remoteness of the populations and the scarcity of funds for the protection programs, have hampered conservation efforts. Any conservation effort can really only survive if it is seen to have a return benefit to the people and the economy.

Like the dromedary, the llama and alpaca are animals that, as far as we know, have only ever existed as domesticated creatures. The llama's prime use to the early civilizations was the same as it is to the people living in remote areas of the Andes today—as a beast of burden. The wool its coat produces is too coarse for anything but the roughest goods and has mostly been used to make carpets and rugs.

IT IS POSSIBLE THAT THE ALPACA WILL SOON REPLACE THE LLAMA AS THE MOST IMPORTANT DOMESTIC LAMOID IN THE ANDES

All beasts of burden in the world today face competition from the modern four-wheel-drive vehicles. However, these still do not pose a real threat to the llama in many of its habitats, as they are not appropriate to the way of life of the people, nor could they afford them. Although there may be a dwindling of numbers along its range, the llama in no way currently faces any real threat to its survival.

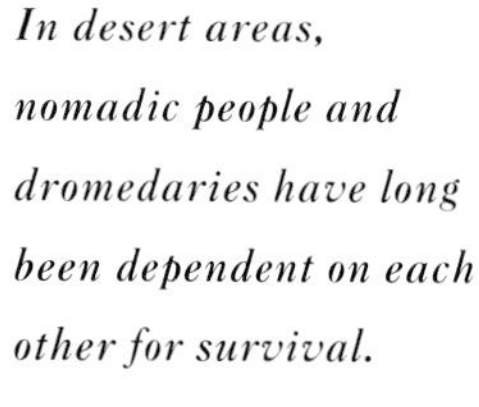

In desert areas, nomadic people and dromedaries have long been dependent on each other for survival.

Kevin Rushby/Bruce Coleman Ltd.

A VITAL RESOURCE

The fact that the llama's rough coat was of no use for clothes may well have been what led to the breeding of the alpaca. This way people could get fine wool and cloth without having to hunt wild vicuñas. Some sources say that the alpaca, still bred for its wool and also more and more extensively used to cross with the vicuña, is beginning to replace the llama as the most important domestic lamoid in the Andes in the 20th century. ■

INTO THE FUTURE

Enlightened conservation measures in the last 20 or so years seem likely to have saved South America's wild lamoids from extinction, and numbers of both the vicuña and the guanaco in the wild and semidomestication seem stable.

The interesting aspect for the future lies in the continued domestication and far-reaching ranges of the llama and alpaca, which are increasingly found in countries far away from those of their origin.

PREDICTION

THE BACTRIAN CAMEL

The Bactrian camel may die out in the wild in its Gobi Desert environment because too few numbers exist there to breed a healthy population for the future. If this occurs, however, it will still survive as a species in protected preserves and wildlife parks.

Many people who keep llamas make use of their carrying ability. It is not uncommon to encounter hikers on forest trails leading a llama that is carrying a tent, sleeping bags, and provisions for a couple of days' outdoor adventure.

The alpaca's future as a domesticated animal outside of its natural environment is slightly different. Here the hope is to breed these animals, like sheep, for their wool, and, in this regard, there is said to be a worldwide alpaca revival. The alpaca is the only fiber-producing animal left in the world with its full range of natural colors; sheep and goats, for example, have mainly been bred as white, whereas the alpaca's color range runs through the spectrum from white to black, encompassing every shade of gray, brown, cream, and fawn.

The problem facing current breeders is collecting sufficient wool, as modern processing machines require vast amounts at a time and, outside their home country, there are still not enough animals in any one place to produce this. Though export licenses have been granted from Chile that allow the export of 300 animals a year, several countries are waiting in line for their share of the precious animals.

With regard to the foreseeable future at least, dromedaries and Bactrian camels are likely to continue to do service as domesticated animals in areas where they have long been found. ■

WORLDWIDE SUPPORT

To highlight the interest in camelids that has occurred in the last several years, the International Llama Association (ILA), located in Denver, Colorado, now has over 2,200 members. ILA has been dedicated to advancing the well-being of llamas and the interests of llama enthusiasts since 1980. The association's main purpose is to educate the public on how to care, breed, and raise llamas and other camelids. ILA offers social and educational opportunities while promoting research, appropriate government policy, and informed public opinion. It is a responsive association that encourages innovative, equitable, and ethical practices that contribute to the long-term expansion and stability of the llama.

LLAMAS AS PETS

In the United States, llamas are increasingly common as pets, and, provided they are handled kindly and correctly, they will become very friendly. For example, a llama should be led by a halter, not herded from behind, since this frightens the animal and makes it defensive. Many people prefer to keep llamas rather than sheep, because as they are more attractive and entertaining animals.

Many people breed llamas for show, and, with training, they can even be taught to jump. Llama owners put them through their paces at local shows known as "llamaramas."

Illustration Peter Bull

CAPYBARAS

RELATIONS

Capybaras and coypu belong to the suborder Caviomorpha, or cavylike rodents. Other members of the suborder include:

PORCUPINES

CAVIES

HUTIAS

PACARANA

CHINCHILLAS

SPINY RATS

TUCO-TUCO

Mike Wilkes/Aquila

Capybaras and coypus are rodents, the most widespread order of mammals, which includes gnawing animals such as mice, rats, and squirrels. The capybara is the only species of the Hydrochaeridae family, and the coypu is the single species of the Myocastoridae family.

ORDER

Rodentia (rodents)

SUBORDER

Caviomorpha (cavylike rodents)

SUPERFAMILY

Cavoidea

FAMILY

Hydrochaeridae

SPECIES

Hydrochaeris hydrochaeris (capybara)

SUPERFAMILY

Octodontoidea

FAMILY

Myocastoridae

SPECIES

Myocastor coypus (coypu)

SUPER RODENTS

KNOWN ALSO AS WATER HOGS AND SWAMP BEAVERS, THE CAPYBARA AND COYPU ARE IN FACT COUSINS OF THE CAVIES AND BELONG TO THE MOST WIDESPREAD GROUP OF MAMMALS—THE RODENTS

The late morning sun creeps into the South American sky, and heat waves begin to blur the horizon beyond the far side of the lake. On the grassy shore a dozen stocky capybaras move ponderously about, their slow gait broken by an occasional trot. The purrs of the young join the soft clicks and whimpers of the adults. Then a sudden bark cuts across this murmur, sending the group leaping headlong into the water. A few minutes later, the reeds rustle and the water surface is gently parted. Isolated fragments—sniffing nostrils, a blunt snout—are the only traces of the group that had looked so cumbersome minutes ago back on land.

THE CURIOUS CAPYBARA

The capybara seems to have evolved simply to puzzle zoologists. It has the profile and semiaquatic habits of a hippopotamus and the gallop of a horse, but its Latin name suggests that it is a pig. Spanish missionaries of the 16th century, noting the capybara's affinity for water, classified it with fish as an acceptable food during the fast of Lent.

A closer inspection shows that the capybara is in fact a rodent—the largest in the world. It grazes among the dense vegetation around lakes, ponds, rivers, and marshes. With its two pairs of large incisors and large grinding molars, the capybara is able to eat even the toughest short grasses growing in these habitats.

The capybara is a native of the northern half of South America, east of the Andes. Its range covers tropical and semitropical zones, including some of the cooler areas south of the Tropic of Capricorn.

Amphibious Neighbor

South of the capybara's great range lives the coypu, another large rodent, which is even more at home in the water. It inhabits lakes and slow-moving rivers throughout temperate South America. The coypu lives in burrows dug in waterside banks and spends much of its time in the water, sometimes swimming for five minutes underwater in the search for food.

The coypu sometimes eats mollusks and other small shellfish, but it is primarily a vegetarian. Certain features make it an efficient eater. Good lung capacity and webbed hind feet enable it to swim for long periods underwater; that time is spent gnawing away at the tough stems of reeds and other aquatic plants with its large orange incisors. Much of the coarse fiber that the coypu eats would be indigestible to other animals. Special bacteria in its digestive tract slowly break down this fiber, rendering it digestible.

Adrian Warren/Ardea

Frank Schneidermeyer/Oxford Scientific Films

The capybara has a distinctive profile (above), *with a large, broad head and squared-off snout.*

The coypu (below) *has large orange incisors that it uses to gnaw away at water weeds and grasses.*

R. Revels/Natural Science Photos

Coypus often build nestlike platforms away from shore. There they sit on their haunches, gnawing away at a pawful of stems and roots or grooming themselves. The soft, gray-brown underfur of the coypu is known as nutria. This acts as insulation against the cold, and also possesses superb water-repellent properties. Coypus are fastidious about keeping this dense fur combed and clean; they lubricate it, too, with a secretion from glands located at either side of the mouth.

Nutria's excellent qualities could easily have driven the coypu to extinction. Esteemed by the European fashion trade as early as the 17th century, the luxuriant fur was exported in ever-increasing quantities. South American traders feared, however, that overexploitation would wipe out the coypu early in the 19th century. It was only the establishment a hundred years later of coypu breeding farms—first in South America and then closer to the eventual markets for nutria—that greatly reduced exploitation of natural populations.

Both capybaras and coypus are caviomorphs (CAY-vee-o-morfs), one of the three principal divisions used by zoologists to classify rodents. Members of this suborder roughly resemble the

Although not totally amphibious like the coypu, the capybara does lead a semiaquatic lifestyle.

most familiar species, the guinea pig. In the case of the capybara, the resemblance is obvious. With other caviomorphs, such as the coypu, the link has more to do with dental arrangements and the shape of certain channels in the skull.

Ancient Island-Hoppers

Caviomorphs appeared abruptly in the Oligocene epoch, between 40 and 25 million years ago. South America at that time was still an island continent, and the early caviomorphs are believed to have originated in North America and then "island-hopped" across the Caribbean Sea to South America. North American fossil evidence of these animals ends at around the same time, suggesting that caviomorphs there fell victim to predators or were squeezed out of their environment by rival mammals.

The newcomers to South America filled ecological niches that in other continents were occupied by nonrodents such as deer and goats. Huge species evolved, typified by the dinomyids (die-no-MIE-ids), meaning "terrible mice." Telicomys (tel-i-CO-mis), which resembled the modern capybaras, reached approximately 3.5 feet (1 meter) in height—the size of a small rhinoceros.

Three million years ago, a land bridge formed between the Americas, ushering in a two-way flow of mammal traffic between the land masses. The porcupine was the only caviomorph to colonize North America, and many of its larger relatives died out at the same time. The reason for these extinctions is still a mystery, although the arrival of new predators must have played a part. None of the caviomorphs developed aggressive behavior, but a close look at the modern capybara and coypu shows how they survived while other species died out. ■

Ancestors

Room to Expand

With no natural South American rivals, many early caviomorphs evolved into very large species during the Tertiary period (ending about 3 million years ago). Some were as big as bears or small rhinos. *Eumegamys* (yoo-mi-GAH-mis), which lived in the Pliocene epoch (10 million to 3 million years ago) had a skull close to 2 ft (61 cm) long and a bulk comparable to that of a wild boar. *Protohydrochaeris* (pro-to-hie-dro-KIE-ris), which flourished at the same time, closely resembled the modern capybara, but weighed up to 1,000 lb (454 kg).

Color illustrations Richard Tibbitts

B/W illustrations Ruth Grewcock

The Capybara's & Coypu's Family Tree

Capybaras and coypus are both members of the suborder Caviomorpha (cay-vee-o-MORF-a), which describes rodents that resemble the cavy (guinea pig) and other members of the family Caviidae (CAV-ee-id-ie). Some caviomorphs, such as cane rats and rock rats, live in Africa, but most are native to South America or the West Indies.

Coypu

Myocastor coypus

(mie-o-CAST-or KOI-pus)

The amphibious coypu, like the capybara, is the only species in its family but is closely related to a number of terrestrial and tree-dwelling West Indian species. Its body shape and long, bare tail make it look like a giant rat, but it is more closely related to the guinea pig.

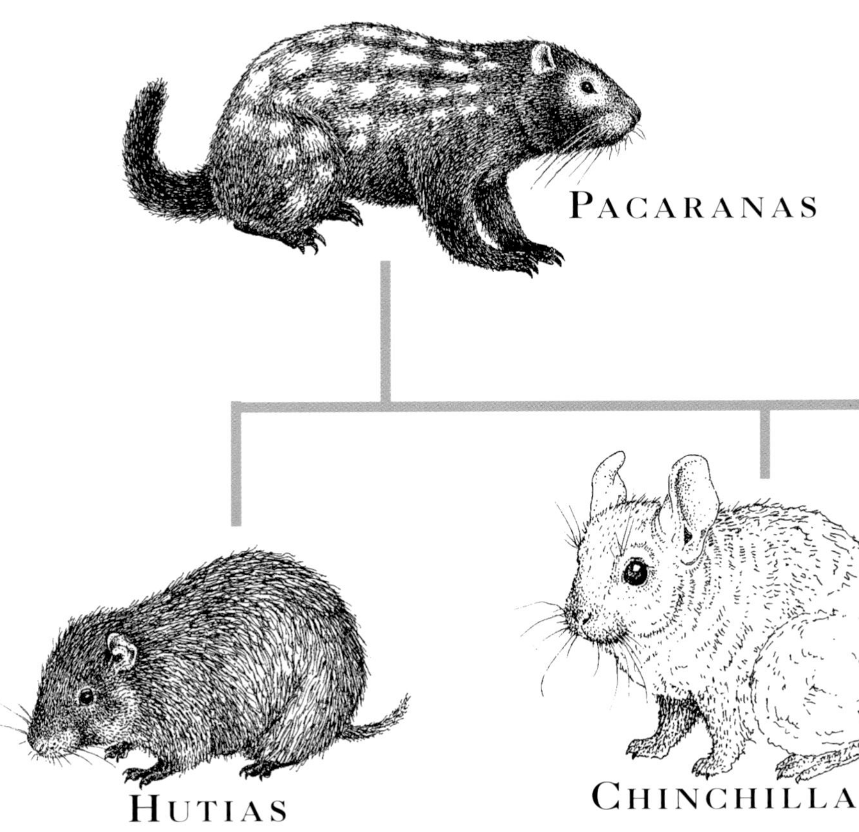

CAPYBARA

(*Hydrochaeris hydrochaeris*)
(*hie-dro-KIE-ris hie-dro-KIE-ris*)

The capybara is the largest rodent in the world but is the direct descendant of even larger species that were twice as long and eight times as heavy. With its squat, stocky build and semiaquatic habits, the capybara has often been described as a "miniature hippopotamus."

ROCK RAT

CANE RAT

NEW WORLD SPECIES

OLD WORLD SPECIES

CAVYLIKE RODENTS

SQUIRREL-LIKE RODENTS

MOUSELIKE RODENTS

ALL RODENTS

ANATOMY: THE

CAPYBARA

The capybara (above left) is the world's largest living rodent, approximately the size of a large dog. The coypu (above right) is a robust rodent that weighs up to 22 lb (10 kg).

THE MORRILLO GLAND

is a feature of adult male capybaras. It is a dark, mound-shaped scent gland on the upper surface of the snout. It produces a white secretion that serves as a scent marker.

FRONT AND HIND FEET

The undersides of coypu feet are hairless. Its hind feet have webbed membranes between all the digits except the fourth and fifth. This arrangement allows for burrowing with the forefeet and swimming with the hind feet. A capybara has four digits on the forefeet and three on the hind feet. Short, webbed membranes connect the digits on all four feet, and each digit has a short, hooflike nail.

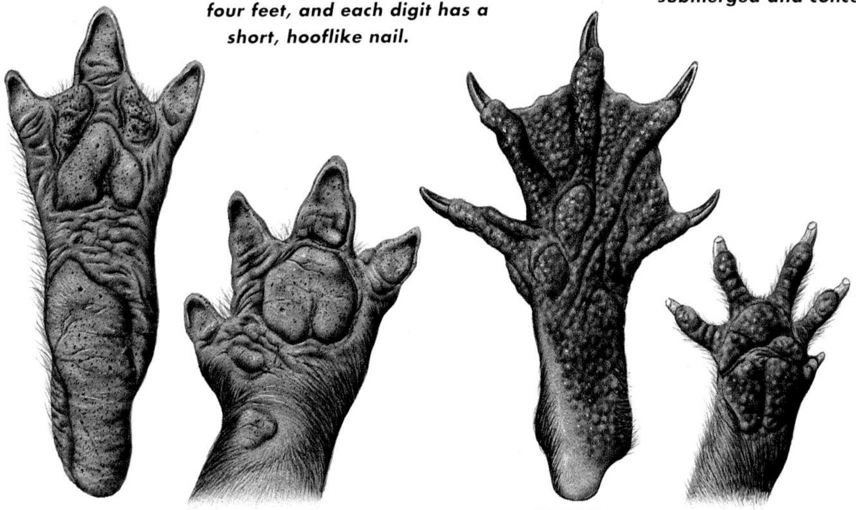

THE EYES

are set high on a capybara's snout, enabling it to see above the water surface while the rest of its body is submerged and concealed.

HIND FORE
CAPYBARA

HIND FORE
COYPU

X-RAY

Both the capybara and coypu have a stocky body with short limbs. This bulky appearance is extreme in the case of the capybara (right), which uses the natural buoyancy of fatty deposits to offset the skeletal weight when it swims. The long coypu tail often falls victim to frostbite in populations outside South America.

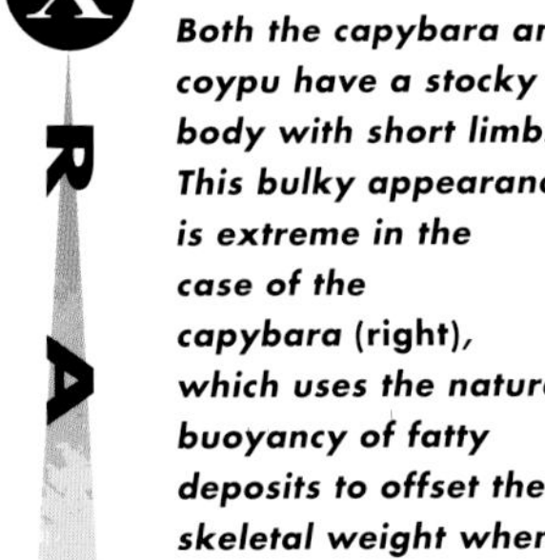

CAPYBARA SKELETON

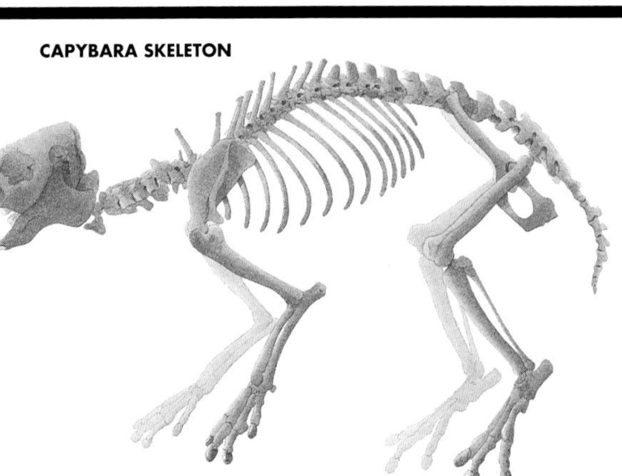

The incisors of the coypu (right) are proportionately larger than those of the capybara (far right), indicating a diet composed of tougher fibers. The capybara's teeth are well suited to constant chewing and grinding. Its incisors have a combined width of 0.75 in (2 cm). All the cheek teeth are rootless and ever-growing.

COYPU TEETH

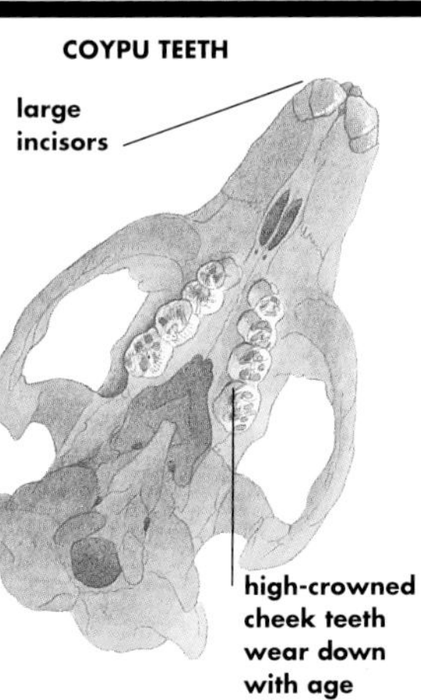

X-ray illustrations Elisabeth Smith

FACT FILE:

CAPYBARA

CLASSIFICATION

GENUS: *HYDROCHAERIS*

SPECIES: *HYDROCHAERIS*

SIZE

HEAD-BODY LENGTH: 41-53 IN (104-135 CM)

TAIL LENGTH: VESTIGIAL (A SMALL, HORNY LUMP)

HEIGHT: 20-24 IN (51-61 CM)

WEIGHT: 77-145 LB (35-66 KG)

WEIGHT AT BIRTH: 3.3 LB (1.5 KG)

FEMALES ARE ABOUT 10-15 PERCENT HEAVIER THAN MALES

COLORATION

REDDISH BROWN TO GRAYISH ON THE BACK AND UPPER PARTS; YELLOWISH BROWN ON THE UNDERPARTS. OCCASIONALLY SOME BLACK ON THE FACE, RUMP, AND FLANKS

FEATURES

FORELEGS SHORTER THAN HIND LEGS; SLIGHTLY WEBBED TOES

LARGE, BLUNT HEAD WITH PROMINENT MORRILLO SCENT GLAND ON TOP OF SNOUT; EYES, NOSTRILS, AND EARS TOWARDS TOP OF HEAD

VESTIGIAL TAIL

TWO PAIRS OF LARGE INCISORS

CAPYBARA

COYPU

HAIR

The capybara's hair (far left) is long and so sparsely distributed that the skin is visible. The coarse hair of a coypu (left) is also long, but it covers a layer of thick, soft underfur (nutria), which keeps the coypu from becoming waterlogged.

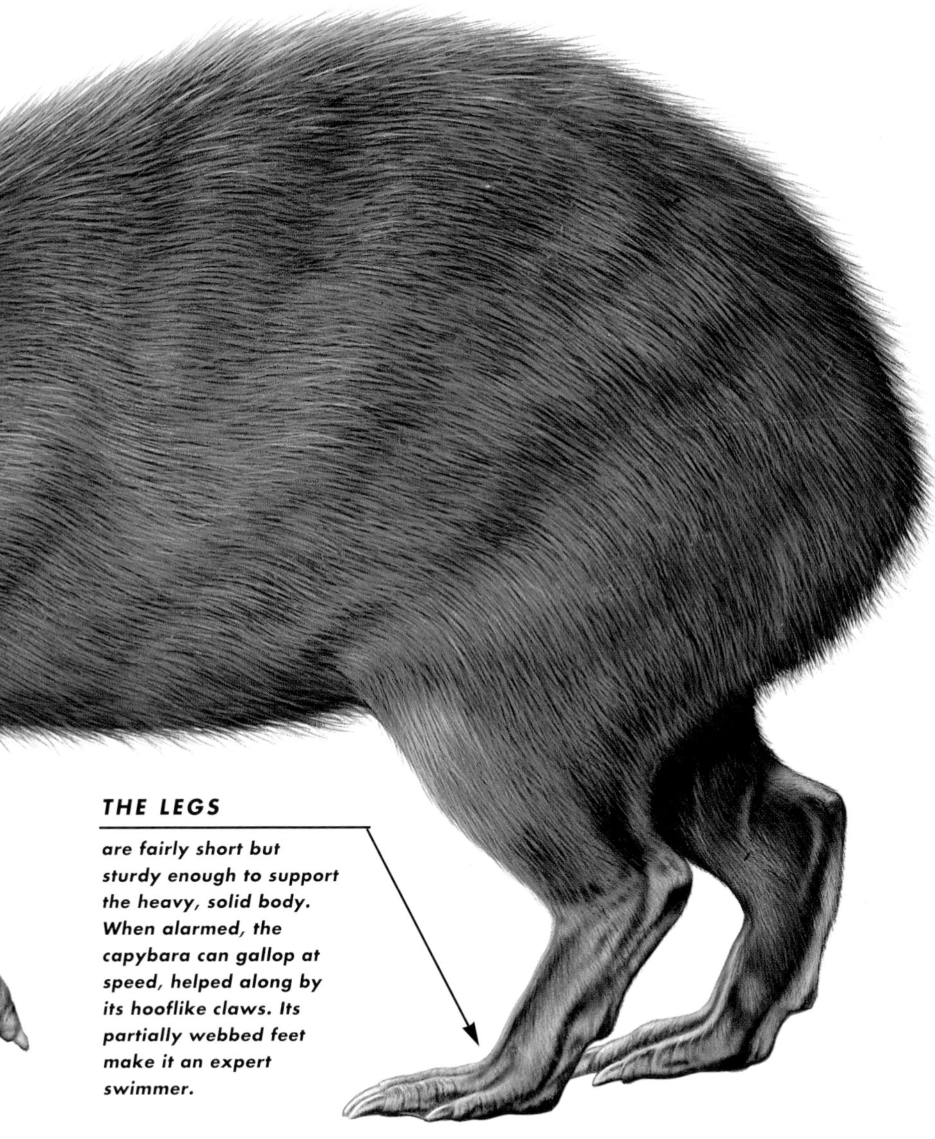

THE LEGS

are fairly short but sturdy enough to support the heavy, solid body. When alarmed, the capybara can gallop at speed, helped along by its hooflike claws. Its partially webbed feet make it an expert swimmer.

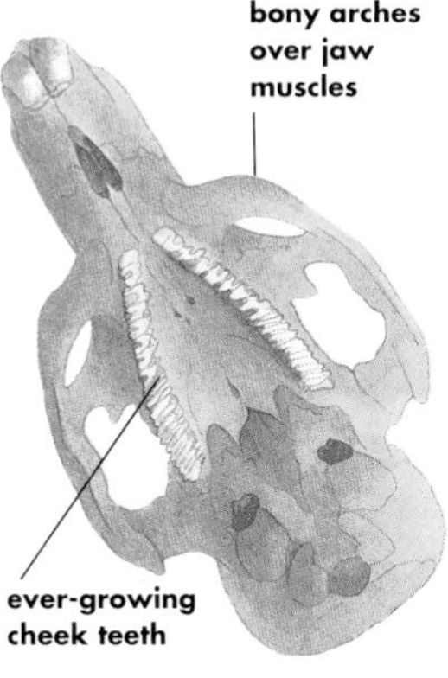

CAPYBARA TEETH

The capybara and coypu both have a large, broad skull with formidable incisors. Typical of the cavylike rodents are the bony arches in front of the eye sockets: These house extra jaw muscles. In addition, each species has a deep muzzle, and the eyes and nose are placed high to enable the animal to see and breathe while almost fully submerged.

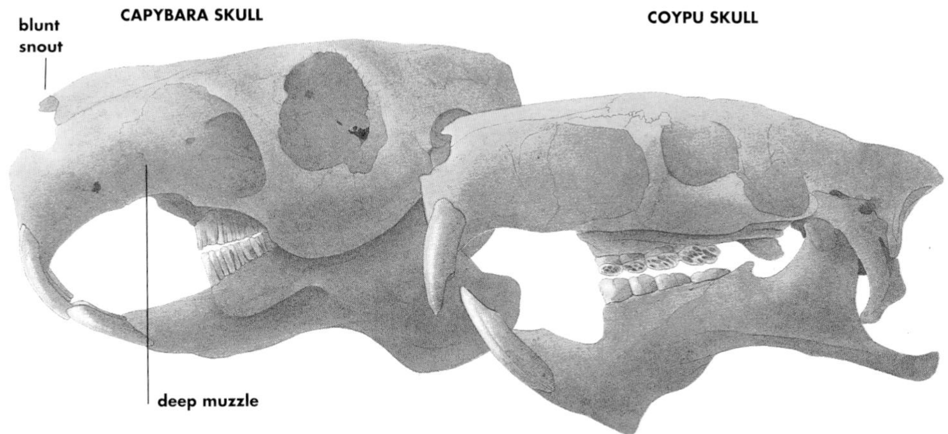

Illustrations Steve Kingston

WETLAND VEGETARIANS

THESE RESOURCEFUL RODENTS HAVE COLONIZED THE WATERWAYS OF CENTRAL AND EASTERN SOUTH AMERICA, LIVING AN AMPHIBIOUS LIFESTYLE MUCH LIKE THAT OF THE NORTH AMERICAN BEAVER

Water is vital to both capybaras and coypus. Capybaras never stray far from water, returning to it to mate, cool off, eat, or escape from predators. Coypus spend even more of their time in the water and sometimes build platforms there, in much the same way as beavers build lodges.

Capybaras range from the humid forests of the north to the grasslands of more temperate South America. There is a perilous balance between reward and risk in their search for food; the food-rich tropics are also home to deadly jaguars and caimans. To reduce surprise attack by predators, capybaras live socially in a group. Humans are the main enemy in the grasslands, clubbing to death any capybara seen to be competing with cattle on grazing land.

A DAY IN THE LIFE

Despite their affinity to water, capybaras spend most of the day on land, where food supplies are more abundant. The group sometimes grazes soon after dawn, moving with a characteristic slow gait. Most of the morning is spent resting in shallow beds in the ground. Close to midday the group enters the water to cool off for several hours.

Once in the water, some individuals might sit upright on their haunches, belly-deep in the water, feeding bits of plants from their forepaws to their mouth. Others might swim around, with little more than eyes, ears, and nostrils peeping from the water. The capybara is a good swimmer, helped by its partially webbed feet. Another factor enables a capybara to swim much more gracefully than other more streamlined animals. Its bulky body contains a high proportion of buoyant fatty tissue, which offsets the weight of the skeleton.

A more frantic version of this noontime dip takes place whenever the group is threatened by a predator. Then the capybaras gallop headlong into the water, with the air alive with the sound of their alarm barks. They then form a defensive "corral"—a close circle with the young in the center and the adults facing outward.

The group leaves the water in late afternoon to graze again until nightfall, then returns to the resting places. The group remains there for the night, sleeping in a series of long naps. Capybaras will alter their routine in the presence of humans, becoming more active by night and remaining in the water or hidden by brush during the day.

TIMID BURROWERS

Coypus, like capybaras, are usually most active at dawn and at dusk. They are timid creatures, and spend most of their time in the rivers and lakes of

Mike Wilkes/Aquila

Richard Coomber/Planet Earth Pictures

Between them, the capybara (above) *and coypu inhabit almost every wet habitat east of the Andes.*

COPING WITH THE COLD

In their native South America, coypus build nests from reeds or other vegetation. However, the introduced feral populations in the colder climates of Europe and North America face real difficulties when lakes, streams, and rivers freeze over. Apart from facing the risk of freezing, coypus are unable to find their way under the ice, as beavers do.

A cold snap can also disrupt some of the coypu's instinctive behavioral patterns. In Germany, coypus have been observed fishing small cubes of ice from the water and carrying them in their teeth to their burrows, where they try to build a nest. Some zoologists suggest that this behavior indicates an instinctive nest-building reaction to any objects of a certain size that coypus see floating on the water.

temperate South America. A shallow lake, with its good supply of plant food, is an ideal environment for coypus. They live in pairs in burrows in the soft soil of the banks. They also build platforms of vegetation in the middle of lakes, using these temporary nests for resting, feeding, or grooming.

Like the capybara, the coypu can submerge for up to five minutes. This skill is used as much in foraging as it is in defense, and the coypu can cut away the roots and underwater stems of aquatic plants before surfacing with a mouthful of food.

Well Groomed

The coypu sits upright to eat, holding plants in its forepaws and gnawing with its incisors. It adopts the same posture for its grooming sessions. Using its stout, sharp foreclaws and the fifth (unwebbed) digit of its hind paws, the coypu runs these "combs" through the fur to remove dirt and parasites. It then rubs the forepaws on two sebaceous glands at the corners of its mouth, transferring the secretion to its fur to keep it lubricated and water-repellent.

A coypu will escape to the safety of the water or its burrow at the first sign of danger. If cornered, however, it arches its back and bares its formidable orange incisors. Although these weapons are mainly used on rival coypus during the breeding season, bared teeth are often an effective bluff against many predators. ■

Coypus rely heavily on water, using the lush vegetation as food or shelter.

HABITATS

The massive Andes Mountain range divides South America into two unequal portions. To the west, a narrow strip of arid land runs down most of the continent's Pacific coastline. Parts of the Atacama Desert in Chile have had no measurable rainfall in over 80 years. The landscape east of the Andes is altogether different. Apart from some of the pampas in the center and extreme south of the continent, most of South America is laced with streams and rivers, marshes, swamps, and lakes.

The capybara lives in the northern half of this territory. This range hardly crosses the Tropic of Capricorn, so the capybara never experiences a wide range of temperatures. Instead, its life might be dictated by seasonal changes in rainfall. Its northern range, in the great basins of the Amazon and Orinoco Rivers, is largely rain forest. There the cycle is from wet to wetter, and the capybara changes its local habitat only because of the presence of predators or humans.

Rainfall is less predictable in other parts of the capybara's range. Many parts of tropical and semitropical South America have pronounced wet and dry seasons. Food supplies dwindle during the dry season, and groups of capybaras are forced to graze a larger local territory or even to share their territory with another group. Land-based but relying on water for food and protection, capybaras live near lakes, ponds, rivers, or in swamps with dense cover.

Hellio & Van Ingren/NHPA

WETLAND DWELLER

Water is even more essential to the coypu. It is clumsier and less well adapted to life on land than the capybara. Its more solitary lifestyle provides

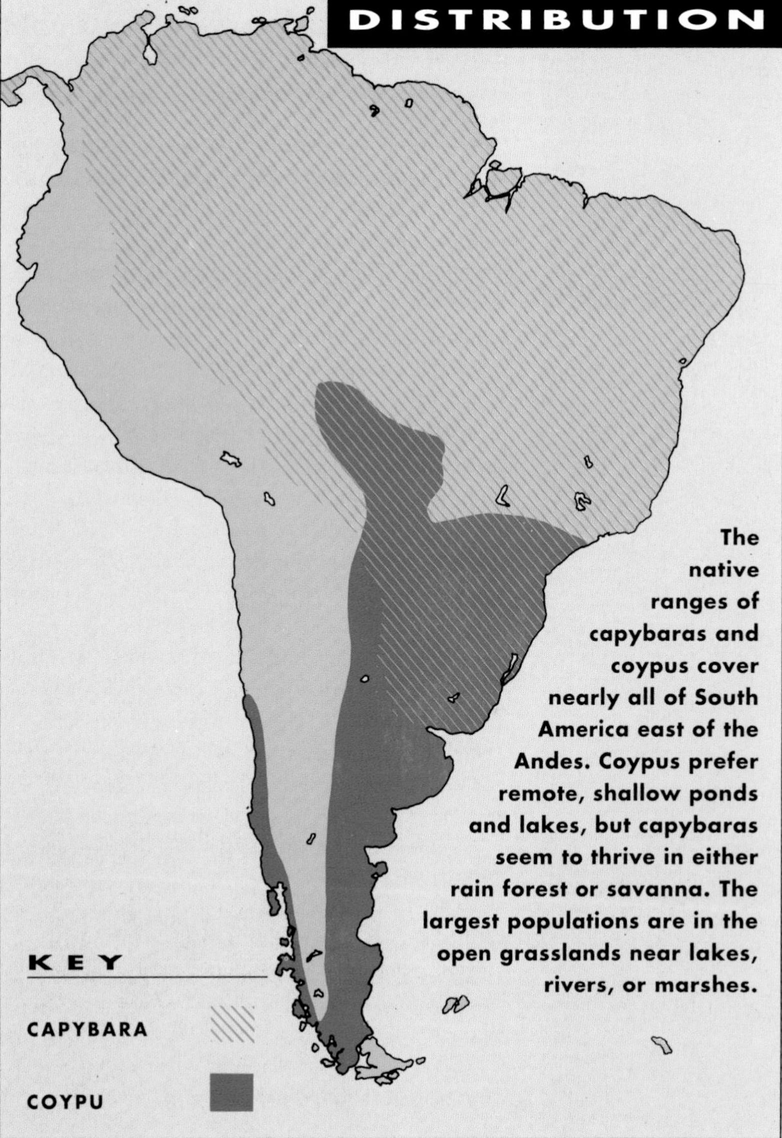

The native ranges of capybaras and coypus cover nearly all of South America east of the Andes. Coypus prefer remote, shallow ponds and lakes, but capybaras seem to thrive in either rain forest or savanna. The largest populations are in the open grasslands near lakes, rivers, or marshes.

L. C. Marigo/Bruce Coleman Ltd.

With its paddlelike webbed feet, the coypu (left) *is a natural swimmer. Those pairs that nest in midwater gain full protection from land predators.*

Capybaras gain much by grazing near the water (below). *At the first hint of an approaching predator, a lookout will give the alarm and the family will dive for cover.*

little or no scope for group protection from predators, so it must always be in or near the environment that provides food and refuge.

Coypus are native to the temperate regions of South America. Their natural habitats, such as shallow lakes and rivers, are less affected by wet and dry seasons than those of the capybara. Coypus must be guaranteed a year-round supply of vegetation for nest-building as well as for feeding. However, they have shown themselves to be quite adaptable within these limits. One population, in the Chonos Archipelago of Chile, flourishes in brackish and even salt water.

Overall, coypus are adaptable creatures whose shy habits and aquatic skills act as good defenses. This very adaptability has led to their success as breeding animals in other parts of the world. With the right combination of water, aquatic plants, and hideaways, coypu populations have flourished on farms in North America, East Africa, and Europe. They have even escaped to become feral in the swamps of Louisiana, on the lowlands of England, and in marshy areas of Scandinavia and Russia. Sometimes the success has brought with it a price; feral coypus can damage the banks of dikes and irrigation ditches, eat through rows of crops, and generally compete with native fur-bearing species.

HUMANS: FRIEND AND FOE

The habitats of both capybaras and coypus are threatened by humans, and not simply by development and pollution. The natural balance of predator and prey has sometimes been upset, only to reemerge in a different form. Historically, larger numbers of coypus than capybaras have been killed, because of their importance in the fur trade.

in SIGHT

NUTRIA

The soft underfur of the coypu, known to the fur trade as nutria, keeps the animal dry and warm in its damp habitat; it is also the reason why coypus have been bred for so long in colonies. The outer fur is long and coarse, nearly concealing the soft, velvety, thick gray underfur.

Processing removes the outer fur and any dense inner hair, leaving only the softest part of the nutria. Captive coypus have been bred to produce the ideal color of nutria. The yellowish white and white lines are the most important, since these furs can be dyed almost any color.

But conservation measures and captive breeding, coupled with the lack of natural predators in their natural habitats, have helped coypu populations stabilize and even increase in South America.

As with coypus, contact with humans has been a mixed blessing for capybaras. On the one hand, they are cruelly clubbed to death when they are perceived to be threatening livestock grazing land. On the other, capybara populations have increased markedly in parts of Colombia and Venezuela, where humans have virtually wiped out the jaguar, the capybara's fiercest natural enemy.

Capybaras in the tropics can distance themselves from these predators without necessarily moving to an area with a prolonged dry season. The solution is to make use of cultivated farmland. Capybaras are common in large plantations of sugarcane, or in fields growing watermelon or rice. These agricultural districts provide rich sources of food, but are as dangerous as livestock pastures if the capybaras are spotted by farmers.

"SOUTH AMERICAN BEAVER"

Coypus in their natural environment are much less threatened by predators and in some respects benefit from the presence of other animals. The aquatic vegetation provides the raw materials for nests built on the water itself; this nest-building earns them the name "South American beaver" in some quarters. However, coypus usually live in burrows along the sloping banks. The tunnels, which are usually short, end in a simple, snug chamber but can be extended if necessary in the more crowded conditions of the breeding season. While their clawed forepaws enable them to burrow well, coypus often take over ready-made burrows that have been abandoned by other wetland animals, such as the giant otter. ■

FOCUS ON

THE ORINOCO

The Orinoco River, together with tributaries such as the Guaviare, Meta, and Apure, drains much of the northern part of the South American continent. This river system creates large areas of tropical wetlands, with rain forest and marshy grasslands stretching from the banks of the Orinoco and its tributaries. Average annual rainfall of more than 88 in (224 cm) maintains the humid, water-dominated nature of the Orinoco habitats. There is a profusion of plant and animal life within the Orinoco Basin. Pungent flowers, such as orchids, attract and even mimic some of the wide range of insects. The food chain is complex and delicately balanced. The jaguar presides at the top of the chain, sometimes turning on a fellow predator such as the caiman. Large herbivores, such as the capybara and the even larger tapir, thrive amid all the aquatic vegetation but are easy prey for the jaguar. This cat usually lies in wait on an overhanging branch but is equally capable of sudden bursts of speed on land or in the water. Not surprisingly, capybaras appear in greatest numbers on those stretches of the Orinoco where humans have hunted the jaguar to local extinction.

Margaret Wilby/Planet Earth Pictures

TEMPERATURE AND RAINFALL

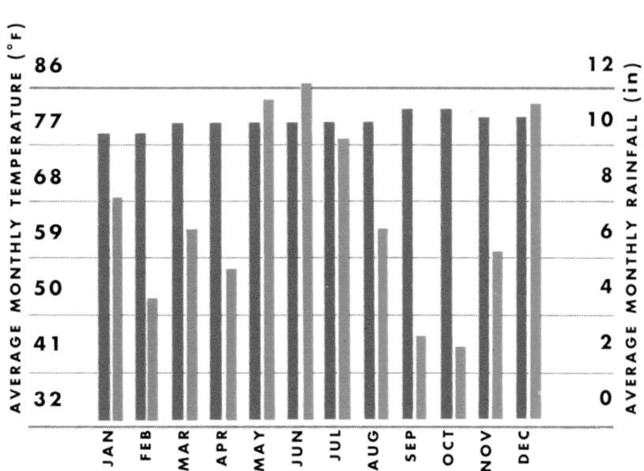

TEMPERATURE

RAINFALL

Warm throughout the year, the Orinoco basin has a typical wet tropical climate. At lower altitudes this climate nurtures rain forests as well as the tropical grasslands favored by capybaras.

NEIGHBORS

The rain forests of South America are home to some of the richest ecosystems in the world. All forms of wildlife can be found, from the sky-scraping tree canopy to the fertile streams below.

JAGUARUNDI

The jaguarundi is a tropical wildcat. Hunted for its coat, it is now endangered in parts of South America.

COMMON WOOLLY MONKEY

These highly agile, fruit-eating monkeys live in the trees, in troops of up to 50 members.

Illustrations Peter Bull

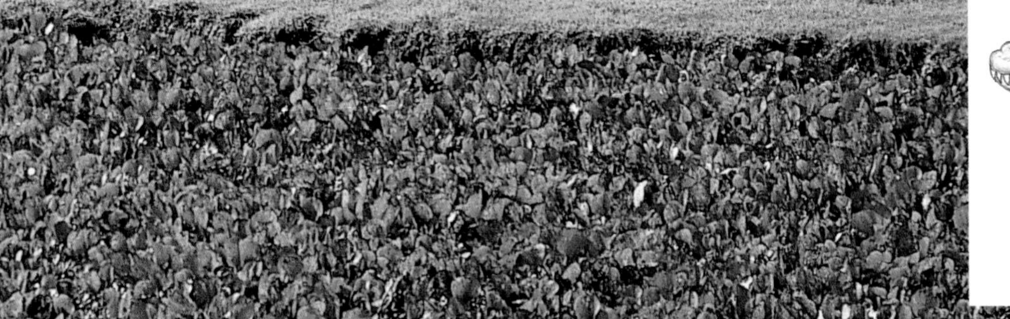

THE ORINOCO

The Orinoco River curves like a letter C from its source along the Venezuela-Brazil border to the Atlantic Ocean near Trinidad. It traces a course along some 1,600 mi (2,574 km) of tropical lowlands, between the Guiana highlands to the east and forms part of the border between Venezuela and Colombia.

ENEMIES

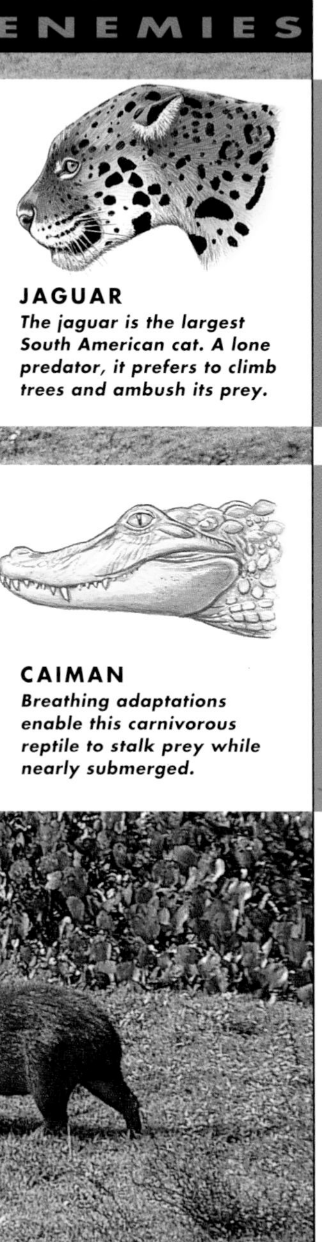

JAGUAR

The jaguar is the largest South American cat. A lone predator, it prefers to climb trees and ambush its prey.

CAIMAN

Breathing adaptations enable this carnivorous reptile to stalk prey while nearly submerged.

GREAT WHITE EGRET

This heron finds its aquatic prey either by standing still in the shallows or by wading slowly.

FER-DE-LANCE

The fer-de-lance is a pit viper that feeds on small mammals in the tropical American lowlands.

GIANT OTTER

The endangered giant otter is the largest otter in the world, reaching 6 ft (1.8 m) in length.

VERMILION FLYCATCHER

These flycatchers perch on tree limbs, waiting to swoop on flying insects. The male is vividly colored.

GREEN IGUANA

The green iguana dwells in trees. It feeds on plants but defends itself with its sharp teeth and claws.

FOOD AND FEEDING

The diet of a capybara reflects its amphibious lifestyle; although it usually eats grasses and chews the bark from trees, it is equally able to nourish itself with water plants.

Early morning and dusk are the main times for grazing, as mornings are spent resting and midday is normally the time for cooling off in the water. Capybaras adopt a more nocturnal feeding pattern in areas where they have been hunted by humans. The pattern of wet and dry seasons also affects how and where capybaras eat. As in other aspects of capybara life, feeding is done as a group.

The group usually sets off together on a grazing expedition. During dry periods they congregate in the few areas where water is still available. Several groups of capybaras might overlap, but they seem to coexist peacefully. Unless disturbed by a predator, the group (or groups) of capybaras will set about grazing the short, dry grasses that remain at the end of the dry season. Observers have recorded how, from a distance, grazing capybara groups resemble a herd of pigs as they move slowly, heads down, across the turf.

Specialized teeth help a capybara deal with this unpromising aspect of its diet. Two large incisors are able to shear the tough grass, while the molars grind it efficiently. There are four molars on each side of a capybara's jaw; the fourth is as large as the other three—yet another grinding advantage. The complex pattern of ridges and channels makes these molars particularly effective.

Capybaras occasionally move on to the pastures grazed by domestic cattle—and the response from farmers is swift and merciless. Groups of youths patrol the fringes of cattle-grazing areas, ready to club to death any capybara that threatens to share the land with the cattle. A similar fate awaits any capybara raiding rice or sugarcane plantations, or found among the ranks of watermelon or corn.

Capybaras rush into water for safety, but they often choose to feed there in the first place. Aquatic grasses, which sprout quickly once the

HOME AND LARDER

An aquatic environment (left) *provides both food and refuge for coypus. They are partial to the succulent herbage growing in and beside streams, lakes, and rivers.*

J. Waters /Planet Earth Pictures

GRAZING THE TURF
In areas where they are free from human persecution, capybaras spend the day grazing the lush waterside turf (above).

Like the big grazing mammals of Africa, capybaras attract birds—such as this cattle tyrant (left)*—that perch on or near the rodents, hoping to snap up any insects exposed in the grasses.*

in SIGHT

HAND TO MOUTH

The capybara has only partially webbed feet; body fat makes the animal buoyant and eliminates the need for full webs. The extra freedom of digital movement enables the capybara to grasp and hold bits of vegetation. The coypu, too, is dexterous. It is often seen holding food in its forepaws and passing pieces up to its mouth.

wet season arrives, are a favorite food. Capybaras will often stand in water up to their stomachs, eating these tender grasses and other water plants. An observer coming across such a feeding group would be treated to the memorable sound of a chorus of contented whimpering.

Broad Diet

Coypus are clumsier on land than capybaras, so they depend even more on the water for their food. This limitation is offset, however, by a wider range of food. Unlike capybaras, coypus do not have an exclusively vegetarian diet; they will also eat mollusks such as mussels and snails.

Several bodily adaptations help coypus find and digest their food, and techniques for food-gathering are practiced virtually from birth. Their deeply webbed feet enable them to swim well, and good lung capacity enables them to submerge for up to five minutes. During these prolonged dives they gather the roots, stalks, and leaves of aquatic plants, which they take back to the bank to eat. There they also gather waterside plants such as sedges and reeds. Like the capybara, they like to eat crops, which often leads them into conflict with humans.

The coypu's sharp claws and distinctive orange incisors quickly cut through all these plants. Such a diet of crude fibers is hard to digest, and bacteria in the coypu's digestive tract break down the cellulose particles. This type of enlarged appendix—and its digestive role—is more normally associated with horses or elephants. ■

Illustrations Peter David Scott/Wildlife Art Agency

SOCIAL STRUCTURE

The basic unit of the capybara social structure is the group, or herd. These usually number about 20 individuals, but are sometimes as large as 50 or 60. A group might be nothing more than an extended "nuclear family" with one adult couple at its core, or there can be more complex structures with several adults of either sex and their offspring.

A fiercely enforced hierarchy underpins the group's structure and is usually led by a dominant male. Dominant males possess prominent and well-developed scent glands on their snouts, and scent marking is a key social and territorial adaptation. Constant threat gestures and aggressive barks and grunts reinforce the dominant male's position. Fighting is rare; he usually chases potential rivals to the outskirts of the group, facing little resistance in the process. The loser in such a confrontation acknowledges defeat with a guttural purr of appeasement like that of a young capybara.

As a result, most capybara groups have a periphery of males whose affiliation is loose. They might try to join other groups, but face similar rebuffs. Sometimes a few of these males band together, in a union that lacks stability but offers many of the protective advantages associated with traditional family-based groups.

Female behavior, by contrast, is marked by cooperation and tolerance. The females practice the nursery or "crèche" system, nursing and caring for each other's offspring. This arrangement

Adrian Warren/Ardea

Banished from the group by the dominant male, junior male capybaras often form their own splinter groups (above).

PAIRED OFF
Unlike capybaras, coypus do not develop complex social structures. Instead, each male/female pair (right) *fends largely for itself.*

MALE RULE
Capybara family groups (left) *are usually led by a dominant male, and contain up to sixty or so individuals.*

in SIGHT

VOCALIZATION

Like most rodents, coypus are rarely vocal; they utter low moans when threatened. Capybaras use a much wider range of calls and noises. When content or while feeding, they often make a soft whimper or low clicking sound; they communicate with weak barks, terse grunts, or shrill whistles. Young capybaras, and losers in conflicts, emit a constant purr.

The important alarm bark is issued by the first capybara in the group to spot a predator. The others respond by standing alert; if the barking continues, they rush into the water to form a protective group.

helps to protect the young, which are at their most vulnerable because they lack the speed and stamina of the adults. Jaguars, feral dogs, and vultures threaten young capybaras on land, while caimans are quick to pick them off in the water. This array of efficient predators accounts for the high first-year mortality rate of capybaras. It also explains why young capybaras remain under the scrutiny of their mother or other adults in the group until the next breeding season. The young capybaras have about six months of "full membership" of the group before reaching sexual maturity.

There is a pronounced seasonal change in the social structure of capybaras. The intolerance of outsiders, typical in the wet season when food is abundant, is softened when the dry season forces more of the animals to share the same feeding space. Several groups might combine into an aggregation of up to 100 capybaras. However, the coming of the rainy season quickly spells the end of these large-scale "marriages of convenience," and the capybaras return to their original groups.

A GATHERING OF PAIRS

Coypus have a much less developed social structure, and the basic unit is the adult pair. The young respond early to the self-sufficient lifestyles of adults. Like capybaras, they are well developed at birth but, without the capybara's safety net of the crèche system, they must soon fend for themselves or be able to accompany their mother.

Coypus sometimes appear to form extended social groups, but on closer inspection these seem more like assemblies of like-minded pairs. These large, informal herds occur either when there is a locally abundant source of food or during the breeding season. In such circumstances, coypus build complex tunnels up to 50 ft (15 m) long, with chambers that contain crude nests. Coypus in such large aggregations usually coexist quite peaceably, provided they have access to personal "hide-aways," although occasional fierce fighting can lead to serious foot and tail injuries. ■

Illustrations Simon Turvey/Wildlife Art Agency

TERRITORY

The notion of territory is important to the social fabric of a capybara group, but, like the social structure itself, the extent of the territory takes its cue from the changing seasons. Dwindling food supplies, and the attendant arrival of other capybaras, can dictate a profound change in how far a capybara group must travel.

The social identity of the group, with its defense system of warning barks and joint protection of the young, means that capybaras need not build elaborate nests. Instead they shelter in thickets or rest in a shallow bed in the ground.

Capybaras cover long distances each day in the search for food, but they return to the same resting place. This base is usually by the water's edge, in order to afford the group a quick escape in case of danger. The daily grazing excursions take place early in the morning or at dusk. The midday swim is usually back at the water by the resting place, although sometimes the group will break off grazing and plunge into the nearest water.

The territory can be as small as 5 acres (2 hectares) or as large as 500 acres (200 hectares), but the average is 25 to 50 acres (10–20 hectares). This territory might become smaller in areas where the dry season reduces the amount of standing water. At such a time also, more than one capybara group will be forced to share the same territory. The local population density of capybaras can rise to about 5 per acre (2 per hectare) at such times, but average densities are about one-fifth of that level when there is less competition for food.

MORRILLO IS A SPANISH WORD MEANING HILLOCK, AND APTLY DESCRIBES THE SCENT GLAND ON A CAPYBARA'S SNOUT

Scent marking plays an important role in establishing a territorial core, as well as giving tangible evidence of the social hierarchy within the group itself. The shiny black morrillo gland, on the top of the snout, becomes more prominent in males during the breeding season. Females have a slightly smaller version of this gland, but the difference in sizes becomes much more pronounced at this time of year. Morrillo size also gives a better idea of the maturity and rank of males, and it becomes apparent which male is dominant.

David Macdonald/Oxford Scientifc Films

The well-developed morrillo gland on this capybara male is evidence of its maturity and high status.

Nick Pike/Wildlife Art Agency

GROUP DUTIES

Capybaras benefit by living in groups (left). *This gives them greater protection against enemies, and they can safeguard vital food supplies from neighboring groups. The adult on the far left is keeping lookout, while a companion marks the territorial border with scent from his morrillo gland.*

Coypus also have well-defined territories, with the burrow or nest acting as the center of a local range. Whether the coypus live as a pair in an individual nest, in a long tunnel, or within a network of coypu passages, they usually confine themselves to a range with a radius of about 600 ft (183 m). Most of the time they are well within this territorial limit, able to retreat quickly to their nest or into the nearest water.

Depending on the availability of food and the presence of predators, a coypu might share its territorial range with anything from 25 to 160 other coypus. Territorial conflict is rare, but these occasional disputes can be bloody. Some coypus bear souvenirs of such battles in the form of scarred or mangled feet and tails.

Coypus are adept swimmers but are more cumbersome on land. As a result, they learn the layout of the land within their circular range; they also make runways through the grass to make escape easier. Although they are often observed by day, they are more comfortable browsing through their territory under cover of darkness. ■

The morrillo excretes a white, sticky secretion that males rub onto the stems of plants. Then they drag their bellies across the marked plants and deposit detachable hairs from glands on either side of the anus. Hairs from the anal glands are coated with hard calcium salts. The exact chemical makeup of these salts is unique to each male, leaving females—and other males—in no doubt about whose marker it is.

DEFENDING THE BURROW

Coypu territories are centered on the burrow or nest, the key point of refuge (right). *The territory is often crisscrossed with pathways.*

LIFE CYCLE

Capybaras and coypus are well developed at birth—able to see, move about, and even begin foraging for food. But there are significant differences in the development of the young, linked to the contrasting social structures of the two species.

Capybaras in tropical areas breed at any time of the year, but reach a peak at the start of the wet season in early May. Those in the more temperate regions of southern Brazil and Argentina breed once a year, at the wettest part of early spring.

Mating takes place in the water, although it is initiated on land. A male approaches a sexually receptive female, who leads him on an elaborate pursuit in and out of the water. This stage may last more than an hour before the female lets the male mount her in the water.

Male and female return to the group during most of the gestation period, which lasts about 150 days. A few hours before birth the female leaves the group and enters ground cover nearby. Litter sizes range from two to eight, with four being the average. The mother returns to the group a few hours after the birth. The newborn young are highly active. This advanced state of development is likely to help them adjust to the mobile lifestyle of the roving group. As a result, the offspring follow their mother to the group after a few days.

Feeding in the Creche

The nursing females of a group jointly suckle the offspring of their group. Lactation usually lasts for about 16 weeks, during which time the young

LIVELY YOUNG

Each litter contains up to 12 young coypus. They are precocial (able to move around freely without help): Their eyes are already open, and they have a thick coat of fur.

GROWING UP

The life of a young capybara

MATING

Capybaras breed during the rainy season, or all year-round in the tropics. They mate in shallow water.

ADULT CARE

Although active, the young are still protected by their mother or another adult for up to six months (below).

GROWING UP

The life of a young coypu

PARENTAL BURDEN

As her young are still highly vulnerable, the mother carries them about on her back (above).

SWIMMING LESSONS

It is only a matter of days before the young join their mother on her foraging trips (below).

Press-Tige Pictures/Oxford Scientific Films

A young coypu (above) *remains with its mother for six to ten weeks, learning how to groom and feed.*

SECLUSION

The mother leaves the main herd to give birth in a thicket. As in the coypu, the young are born with their eyes open (left).

become introduced to the grasses and other foods that make up the adult diet. The young become integrated into the group's pattern of grazing excursions and resting periods. All the while they emit a purring sound, which implies either contentment or a locating signal to their mother—or possibly both.

LARGE AND HUNGRY LITTERS

Coypus normally live in pairs rather than in groups, so the mother has none of the "child care" provisions afforded to her capybara counterpart. There is a September–October (spring) mating peak in the more temperate regions of the coypu's South American range, but mating is nonseasonal in many regions. Females are in heat every 25–30 days, and may produce 2 to 3 litters each year. After mating, the female feeds heavily for the 130-day gestation period. She can give birth to 10–12 offspring, but 3 to 6 are much more common. She is in heat again within a day or two.

The newborn young can follow their mother when they are only a few hours old. Unusually, the mother's nipples are high up on her flanks and nearly on her back; this allows them to suckle while the mother is swimming.

The timing of sexual maturity depends on the birth. Coypus born in the summer attain it in 3 to 4 months, while those born in the autumn take almost twice as long. They find a mate and pair up soon after reaching sexual maturity. ■

FROM BIRTH TO DEATH

	CAPYBARA	COYPU
GESTATION:	148–156 DAYS	128–132 DAYS
LITTER SIZE:	2–8	1–12; USUALLY 5–6
BREEDING:	NONSEASONAL IN TROPICS (PEAK IN APRIL–MAY AT START OF WET SEASON)	NONSEASONAL BUT A SEPTEMBER–OCTOBER (SPRING) PEAK IN COLDER PARTS OF RANGE
WEIGHT AT BIRTH:	3.3 LB (1.5 KG)	8 OZ (225 G)
EYES OPEN:	AT BIRTH	AT BIRTH
WEANING:	16 WEEKS	6–10 WEEKS
FORAGING:	1 WEEK	WHEN WEANED
SEXUAL MATURITY:	18 MONTHS	3–8 MONTHS
LONGEVITY:	8–10 YEARS IN WILD	6 YEARS

Illustrations Robin Budden/Wildlife Art Agency

SAVED BY THEIR SKIN

BOTH THE CAPYBARA AND THE COYPU HAVE BEEN HUNTED FOR THEIR FUR OR MEAT, BUT THEY HAVE ALSO BENEFITED IN SOME UNEXPECTED WAYS FROM HUMAN ACTIVITY—AND FROM HUMAN GREED

In their natural habitats, capybaras and coypus were part of a delicate ecological web for millions of years. Capybaras developed their defensive group structure in response to efficient tropical predators. Coypus had no traditional predatory enemies, but populations grew, declined, or stabilized according to the available aquatic food supply. The native people of South America had no profound effect on the population of either species, despite occasionally hunting capybaras as a source of meat or using the large incisors as ornaments.

The peace was disturbed, however, by the arrival of European settlers in South America 450 years ago. Capybaras were the first to experience these changes. Roman Catholic clergy, noting the aquatic habits of capybaras, grouped them with fish as acceptable food during the Lenten fast. Large-scale cattle ranching, which began early in the colonial period, initiated the systematic slaughter of capybaras that still continues where ranchers view them as pests that deprive livestock of grass.

FASHION VICTIM

The coypu was little disturbed for more than a century after the European conquest, but soon became the target of intensive hunting and trapping. Nutria, its soft underfur, was sent back to Spain as early as the late 17th century, and, within 100 years, had become high fashion in Europe. Coypus were hunted systematically, and numbers began to decline drastically in the face of the demands of the fur trade. By the first decade of the 19th century, numbers were so low in central Argentina that one hatmaker from Buenos Aires realized that he would have to start breeding coypus himself.

The fate of the hatmaker's breeding experiment is now unknown, but it took others nearly a century to reach the same conclusion. The first captive-breeding farms for coypus were established in the early 20th century, initially in South America and later in parts of Europe, North America, and Africa. Coypus took to their new environment with ease, showing themselves to be easily kept and bred, as well as being surprisingly hardy in the face of colder winters. Coypus escaped from many breeding farms, quickly becoming feral in the marshes of Louisiana in the United States, in many parts of eastern England, and in localized areas throughout central and eastern Europe.

These various "foreign" populations took the pressure off their native South American counterparts, which began to recover despite the overall loss of territorial range. Enlightened—or simply pragmatic—measures by the governments of Uruguay and Argentina in the 1950s prohibited the catching of wild coypus.

David Macdonald/Oxford Scientific Films

Capybara pelts, prized for their high-grade leather, are laid out to dry in South America (above).

THEN & NOW

This map shows the parts of the world where coypus have escaped captivity to establish successful feral (gone wild) populations.

FERAL POPULATIONS

The first coypu breeding farms were established in South America in the early 20th century. Demand for nutria soon led to farms in the United States, Canada, England, northern and eastern Europe, southern Russia, Turkey, East Africa, central Asia, and even Japan. Inevitably, some coypus escaped or were introduced in these areas, and feral populations soon developed. Their descendants have formed secure and growing populations.

The vagaries of fashion, having once threatened the coypu with extinction, no longer exert such pressure. At present, nutria is out of fashion and the fur trade is amply supplied with coypus from breeding farms or from feral populations outside South America.

THE CAPYBARA'S FALL AND RISE

The hunting, near-extermination, and subsequent gradual recovery of the capybara have all occurred within South America. It was hunted—sometimes intensively—at a local level, for its meat, hide, and iodine-rich skin. Capybaras were wiped out completely in parts of Peru. But the capybara, unlike the coypu with its high-profile nutria, offered fewer

Adrian Warren/Ardea

Each year in Venezuela, farmers are allowed to cull a percentage of the capybaras on their land.

chances to turn carcasses to cash. Instead, most of the killing was done by those who viewed the capybara as worthless—the cattle ranchers.

In some respects, however, the capybara suffered more in the 18th and 19th centuries because of its perceived worthlessness. The wider public turned a blind eye to, or never learned about, the slaughter of capybaras as ranching became more important. The coypu-protection measures taken by Argentina and Uruguay, by contrast, acknowledged the value of nutria as an export. Cattle ranching was a much more important industry, and few people were prepared to challenge the ranchers' claims that capybaras were intrusive pests.

More recent studies have proven that capybaras do not really compete with livestock. They graze almost exclusively on short vegetation near water, leaving the longer grasses to the cattle and horses. Even where long grasses are not available, capybaras can eat plants that livestock cannot digest.

ALONGSIDE MAN

ENLIGHTENED CULLING

Humans have begun to treat the capybara more mercifully during the 20th century, thanks to a policy that could be described as enlightened culling. The success of capybara breeding farms has grown alongside the marketing of a range of capybara products. The chief product is capybara meat, once the colonial Lenten fare, and, before that, the choice of native South Americans. Capybara hide is tanned to make a high-grade leather. The skin, which is rich in iodine, is processed for use in the pharmaceutical industry.

The need to conserve stocks of coypus goes back nearly 200 years, largely because of their money-making nutria. Coypu farms, in South America and beyond, produce vast numbers of these furs. Even now, with nutria comparatively out of fashion, several million coypu furs are exported from South America each year.

Maurice Tibbles/Survival Anglia

Recognition of this peaceful coexistence led the government of Colombia to ban the hunting of capybara in 1980. More important, it has led to an increasing number of capybara breeding farms. Ranchers realize that they can gain new income with little outlay and with no real threat to their livestock. Ironically, many of the capybara breeders are the same cattle ranchers who once did their best to exterminate the rodents.

Venezuela has taken the lead in promoting and licensing these breeding ranches. Capybaras roam in their natural environment, although some ranches are irrigated to offset the worst droughts of the dry season. Ranches are usually licensed to take 30–35 percent of the population at an annual cull, usually in February when the capybaras congregate around water holes. These unmanaged capybara populations yield about 7 lb of meat per animal per acre (8 kg per hectare), each year.

One aspect of humankind's presence has benefited capybaras in their natural habitats. Hunting has driven jaguars to near-extinction in most of Colombia and Venezuela. Without their fiercest natural enemy, and protected by new hunting restrictions, capybara populations are increasing in some of these tropical wetlands. Sadly, however, the jaguar now faces a far less secure future.

There are many similarities in the survival stories of capybaras and coypus. In each case their worst enemy—humankind—has had a change of heart and has come to recognize the importance of protecting these South American rodent giants. ■

No longer seen as a threat to livestock, capybaras are enjoying a warmer relationship with humans.

INTO THE FUTURE

The reversal of the drastic decline in capybara and coypu populations during the 20th century might prompt cynics to argue that these species are simply the lucky beneficiaries of human greed. After all, goes this argument, where would they be if it had been shown that capybaras really did squeeze out domestic livestock, or if nutria had not been seen as a source of revenue worth preserving?

These sentiments have some validity: National and international conservation agreements can legislate a well-meaning sentiment, but enforcement is almost impossible in countries with developing areas and basic human needs. The depressing evidence is there, in the form of rhino horn, ivory, and products made from the Siberian tiger.

Likewise, capybaras and coypus continued to be killed even after this slaughter was made illegal. The Venezuelan ban on hunting capybara was largely unheeded until 1968, when a study shed light on the interrelationship of the capybara with other species in its grasslands habitat. This study also introduced the basic features of the breeding programs, which have since succeeded in Venezuela and in other South American countries.

The success of bred and feral coypu populations outside South America in the first half of the 20th century shook the governments of Argentina and Uruguay into recognizing the importance of maintaining coypu stocks. Breeding farms began to be seen as guardians of a vital natural resource.

There is now a great incentive to harvest capybaras and coypus. Even with the strict controls on culling, this managed system offers the chance of a steadier and greater income than by hunting these animals in the wild. As a result, capybaras and coypus are now well represented in most of their original South American habitats. Controls on hunting must remain, to maintain current levels, but the overall picture remains healthy for both species. ■

PREDICTION

CAPTIVE-BRED "DECOYS"

Captive breeding will continue to take the pressure off wild populations. Coypu farming will become less attractive if world opinion continues to frown on the fur trade; breeding populations will decline, but by the same token reestablished wild populations will be less threatened.

FERAL POPULATIONS

It is estimated that feral coypus living outside South America now greatly outnumber those in the original coypu habitats. Coypus have shown that they can survive winters far colder than any in their original South American range.

These burgeoning transplanted feral populations now account for much of the world trade in nutria. Louisiana alone has a coypu population of more than 20 million; most of these are descendants of just 20 coypus that were brought there in 1938. This rapid population growth is not always welcome, however; coypus are known to ruin crops and damage waterways with their burrows. Farmers in England, for example, have viewed coypu control as a necessity for more than 40 years; indeed, as a result of culling campaigns in the area, coypus may well be extinct there.

SAVING THE WETLANDS

Capybara ranching has had an unexpected side effect—it helps preserve some native South American habitats. Breeders recognize that open water is essential for the survival of capybaras. Having realized that capybaras in this environment do not threaten the food supply of domestic livestock, ranchers are now prepared to preserve tracts of swampy and marshy land bordering the grasslands. This stops a drive for draining grasslands that goes back centuries. Capybaras benefit, along with many other species of plant and animal life.

Illustration Evi Antoniou

BISON

RELATIONS

Bison belong to the cattle family, Bovidae. Other members of the family include:

DOMESTIC CATTLE

BUFFALO

ANTELOPES

GRAZING ANTELOPES

GAZELLES

DUIKERS

GOATS & SHEEP

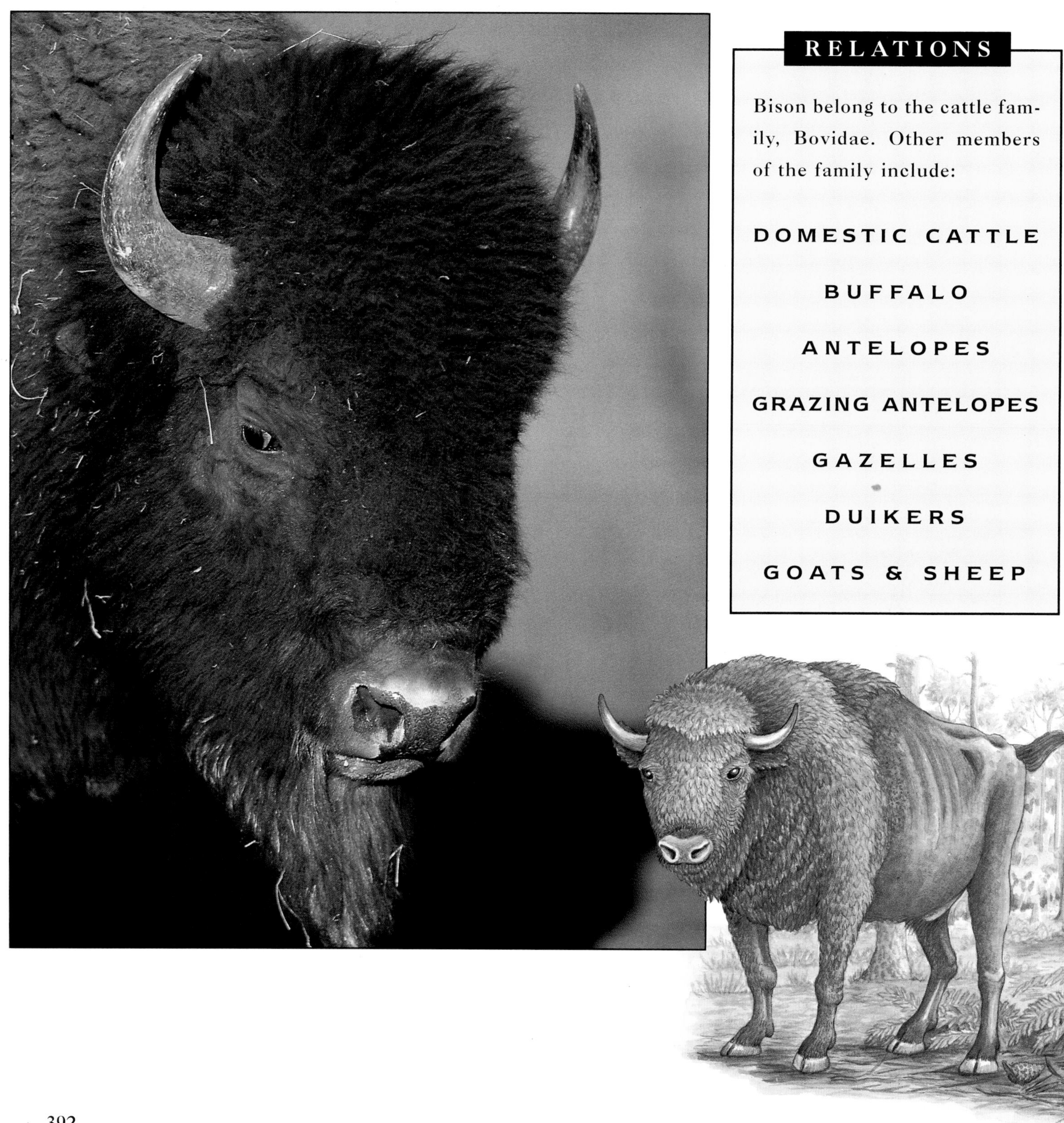

Kenneth W. Frink/Ardea

Bison are artiodactyls, or grazing mammals with an even number of toes. Like true cattle and buffalo they are part of the Bovini tribe of wild cattle.

ORDER

Artiodactyla (even-toed ungulates)

FAMILY

Bovidae

SUBFAMILY

Bovinae

TRIBE

Bovini (wild cattle)

GENUS

Bison

SPECIES

bison (American bison)

SUBSPECIES

bison bison (plains bison)

bison athabascae (wood bison)

SPECIES

bonasus (European bison)

HORNED AND HARD-HEADED

PAWING PROUDLY ON THE DUSTY PLAINS, A PAIR OF BULL BISON CRASHING TOGETHER IN COMBAT DURING THE MATING SEASON IS ONE OF THE GREATEST DRAMAS NATURE HAS TO OFFER

The American bison is one of the timeless images of the American West. Nearly 6.6 ft (2 m) high at the shoulder, and weighing up to a ton (2,200 lb), a bull exudes brute strength. A massive, low-hung head and thick mantle of fur over the forequarters add to this powerful and bulky appearance.

A creature of the plains, the bison finds nourishment in the grasses and herbs that grow in a habitat that often stretches, treeless, to the horizon. Outside the mating season, bison spend their time grazing the open grasslands, eating mainly at dawn and dusk and chewing the cud through the day.

A related species lives in the forests of Eastern Europe. The European bison, or wisent, is even larger than the American bison, with longer legs and larger hindquarters, but it looks less bulky, and, unlike the grazing bison of the American plains, the European bison is primarily a browser, preferring the buds and shoots of its wooded environment.

Plains bison (below) *are chiefly grazers; they once roamed the American prairies by the thousands.*

Stephen Krasmann/NHPA

Bison are members of the Bovidae (BOV-id-eye) family, which includes mainly horned, grazing mammals. The family originated in the tropics of the Old World about ten million years ago, but its members have shown a remarkable ability to adapt to changes in geography or climate. Some settled in arid or marshy habitats by spreading east to west or southward. But with the arrival of the Pleistocene ice ages, which began two million years ago, a few of these mammals ventured into colder northern parts.

One was the yak, which at one time extended its Asian territory as far north as Siberia. Another was the bison, which also seems to have originated in southern Asia. From there they extended their range into the temperate regions of Eurasia. A map of their greatest historical range would shade in a swath from Ireland to the Korean peninsula. Even at the height of the Pleistocene ice ages, bison inhabited

Although leaner than its American cousin, the European bison is still a force to be reckoned with.

William S. Paton/Bruce Coleman Ltd.

THE BERING EXPRESS

The Bering Strait, only 36 mi (58 km) wide, separates Siberia from Alaska at a latitude just south of the Arctic Circle. But during the Pleistocene ice ages, when increased glaciation reduced sea levels, the strait became a land bridge linking Asia and North America.

The bridge offered many species the opportunity to spread beyond Eurasia. The bridge functioned as a filter, for only cold-hardy species could use it; Alaska and Siberia are bywords for subfreezing temperatures, and the Pleistocene climate was even colder. This harshness imposed severe "immigration restrictions" on animals trying to take this northern route to the New World. However, species ranging in size from bison and musk oxen to tiny rodents made the crossing and settled, sometimes at the expense of native species. One of these newcomers—human—was destined to have the most profound impact.

most parts of Europe not directly covered by glaciers. The cave art of Vallon-Pont-d'Arc in southern France throws new light on bison and other European animals that survived against the odds in that frozen climate. The caves, once used by a tribe of humans, were only rediscovered in 1994 after being sealed off in a sudden landslide eighteen thousand years ago. Lively naturalistic paintings line the cave walls, depicting not only bison but woolly rhinos, lions, bears, horses, wild oxen, reindeer, mammoths, and leopards. The bison species on the cave walls was the steppe wisent, *Bison priscus*; it did not survive the post-glacial period, but it displayed many of the features that helped bison adapt to cold—in particular, a thick coat of fur.

Bison Superhighway

Bison entered Alaska from Siberia about a million years ago, when a land bridge existed across the Bering Strait. Like other animals—and humans—they used this entry point to spread deep into North America. An ice-free basin east of the Rockies provided an "express route" to the south. Other bovids that took the same route live on in North America as bighorn sheep, mountain goats, and musk oxen.

One of the earliest bison species, the giant bison, *Bison latifrons*, pushed through into what is now the southeastern United States about ten thousand years ago. Its horn cones extended to 6.5 ft (2 m), compared with about 26 in (66 cm) for the present-day American bison. It died out, but was followed by two new races of bison—one of which, *Bison occidentalis*, proved to be the ancestor of the modern American bison.

The end of the Pleistocene was a period of great turmoil in North America. The climate was becoming more seasonal and the grasslands were spreading. Many of the huge species died out: North America lost three genera of elephants and six of edentates, as well as equids. These animals may have died out because, unlike bison, they were not ruminants and therefore could not digest the grasses—but other scientists cite the arrival of hordes of human hunters as the cause of the extinctions.

Scientists also disagree on the exact origins of the modern American bison. Fossil evidence suggests that American bison in their current form are relatively new, having become a smaller species about 5,000 years ago. American bison comprise two subspecies: The more familiar American subspecies is the plains bison, *Bison bison bison*, with its bulky build and grazing habits. The wood bison, *Bison bison athabascae*, is native to a more northern region, with the dividing line roughly following the U.S.–Canadian border.

The wood bison is less stocky and has longer legs than the plains bison—in fact it looks very like the European bison. It seems that bison resembling the European species stayed nearer the Bering land bridge, while those venturing further south evolved into the new subspecies—the plains bison. ■

THE ORIGINAL BISON?

The image of the American bison, familiar to anyone who has seen a Western film, is really that of the plains bison, just one of two subspecies. The other, the wood bison, resembles the European bison in its darker, less stocky appearance and its browsing habits. Like the European bison, the wood bison is actually larger than the plains bison.

This superior size fits a pattern seen in other cattle, such as the yak, and in goat antelopes, such as the musk ox. Greater size is important in dealing with the colder climates in these continental extremes. The similarities of wood bison to European bison could also suggest that the interaction of bison in North America and in Eurasia continued until recently. The plains bison's current body type is probably a recent adaptation to the milder climate of the southern grasslands.

THE BISON'S FAMILY TREE

There is some debate about the classification of American and European bison as different species. Some scientists argue that they should be considered two races of the same species on the basis of their interbreeding in captivity. Others go further and maintain that both should be classified under the much larger Bos *(true cattle) genus of the Bovini tribe.*

EUROPEAN BISON

Bison bonasus

(BIE-son bo-NAS-us)

The European bison, sometimes called the wisent, is the heaviest terrestrial mammal in Europe. It has a less stocky appearance than the American bison, with its longer legs and more upright head. The European bison prefers more wooded habitats, which suit its browsing (rather than grazing) feeding pattern.

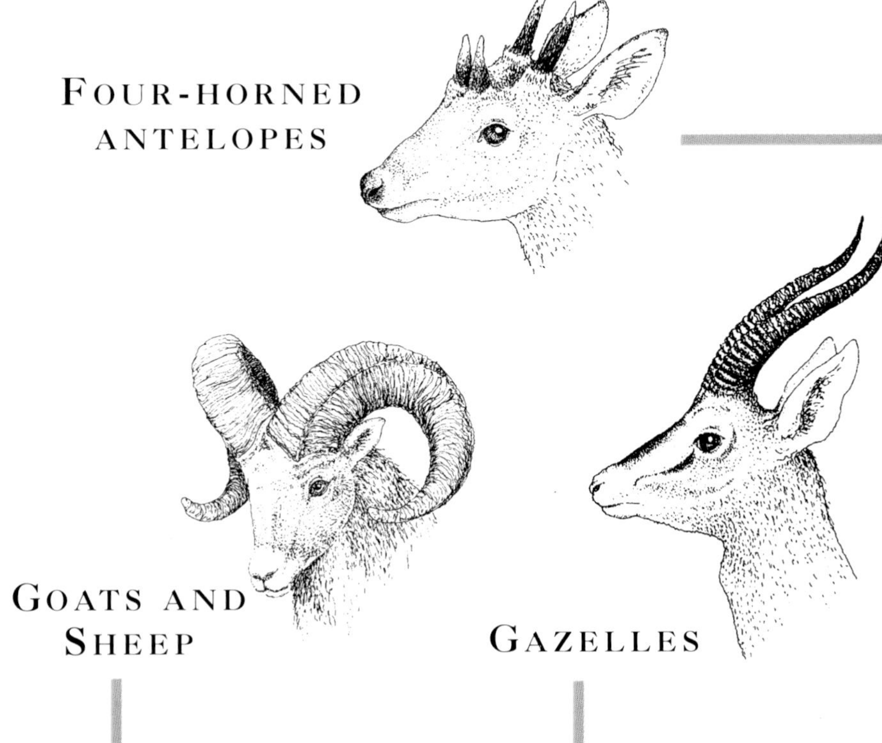

AMERICAN BISON

Bison bison
(*BIE-son BIE-son*)

The American bison is easily recognized by its massive forequarters, covered in heavy fur, and the comparatively dainty rump. Until its near extinction in the 19th century it grazed the plains of the American West in herds numbering 50,000 or more. Most American bison now live in parks and refuges. American bison are often—but incorrectly—referred to as buffalo.

BUFFALO AND OTHER CATTLE

SPIRAL-HORNED ANTELOPES

WILD CATTLE (BOVINI TRIBE)

SUBFAMILY BOVINAE

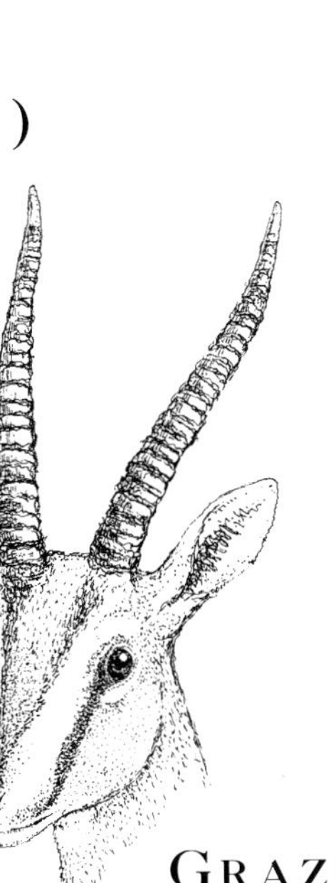

GRAZING ANTELOPES

DUIKERS

FAMILY BOVIDAE

B/W illustrations Ruth Grewcock. Bison Steve Kingston

ANATOMY THE AMERICAN BISON

Bulls of both species can attain shoulder heights of up to 6.6 ft (2 m). The massive forequarters and heavy mane of the American bison (above left) belie the fact that the European bison (above right) is actually larger.

THE HUMP

that characterizes the American bison is a buildup of muscle and tissue over long bony outgrowths from the dorsal part of the spine.

PROTECTIVE FLEECE

A thick mantle of fur covers the bull's head and most of his forequarters. Apart from serving as winter insulation, the thick mane protects the bull's head from damaging horn thrusts in breeding battles with other males.

THE HINDQUARTERS

are smallest in the plains bison, which has a relatively smaller pelvis than both the wood bison and the European bison.

THE TAIL

of the American bison is shorter than that of the European bison. Its short length limits its usefulness in fending off insects: Bison prefer to roll in dust or mud to rid themselves of insects.

THE HOOVES

are cloven; they are broad to support the bison's bulk and to make it easier to walk on snow. The print resembles a comma and its reflection, but is much wider than it is long.

X

AMERICAN BISON SKELETON

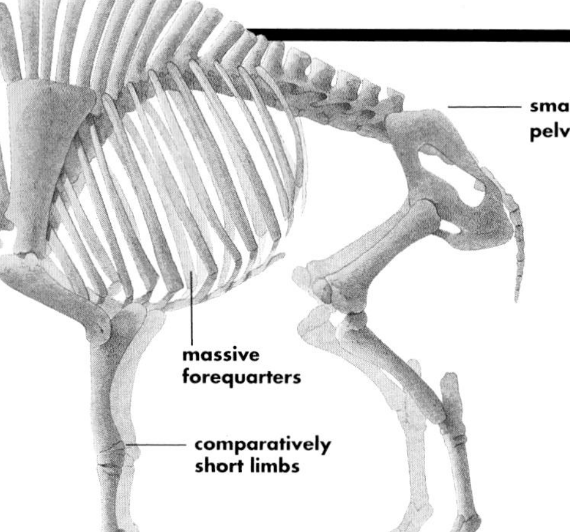

The American bison has far more massive forequarters, shorter legs, and a stockier appearance than the European bison. In effect, this species is more low slung and front heavy, qualities that are emphasized by the lower positioning of its head and its smaller pelvis.

AMERICAN BISON SKULL

The broad row of lower inciso and massive molars a ideally suited shearing ar chewing gras

molars

X-ray illustrations Elisabeth Smith

AMERICAN BISON

EUROPEAN BISON

As a plains grazer, the American bison has evolved for a more herd-based lifestyle than its European counterpart.

HORNS

Both sexes have short, sharp horns that turn upward. They are effective in defense and are used, or at least brandished, by bulls in rivalry battles.

THE FACE

changes in shape as the bison grows, and is a good indicator of the animal's age. In bulls the jowls gradually fill out, while females retain a relatively slim muzzle even in maturity.

THE HAIR

on the body behind the mane is short and pale, although it often appears dark as the bison enjoys rolling in dust.

FACT FILE:

THE AMERICAN BISON

CLASSIFICATION

GENUS: *BISON*

SPECIES: *BISON*

SIZE

HEAD–BODY LENGTH: 7–11.5 FT (2.1–3.5 M)

TAIL LENGTH: 20–24 IN (50–60 CM)

HORN LENGTH/BULL: 26 IN (66 CM)

SHOULDER HEIGHT: 5–6.5 FT (150–200 CM)

WEIGHT/MALE: UP TO 2,200 LB (1,000 KG)

WEIGHT/FEMALE: 1,320 LB (600 KG)

WEIGHT AT BIRTH: 66 LB (30 KG)

COLORATION

THICK FUR ON HEAD, NECK, SHOULDERS, AND FORELEGS IS BROWNISH BLACK

SHORTER FUR ON REMAINDER OF BODY IS PALE IN COLOR

CALVES ARE REDDISH BROWN

FEATURES

"FRONT-HEAVY" APPEARANCE WITH LOW, BROAD SKULL, STOCKY FOREQUARTERS, AND COMPARATIVELY SMALL RUMP

THICK MANTLE OF HEAVY FUR ON THE HEAD AND FOREQUARTERS

HUMPED SHOULDERS

SHORT, SHARP HORNS

MALES CONSIDERABLY LARGER THAN FEMALES

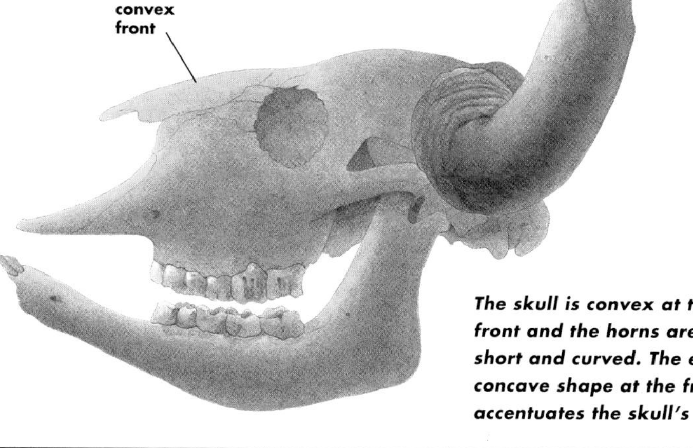

The skull is convex at the front and the horns are short and curved. The extra concave shape at the front accentuates the skull's bulk.

HORN STRUCTURE

Bison horns have a permanent bony core encased in a hardened sheath. These differ from antlers, which grow and are shed seasonally. There are distinct burrs on the bull's horns before they meet the skull; these are absent on the cow.

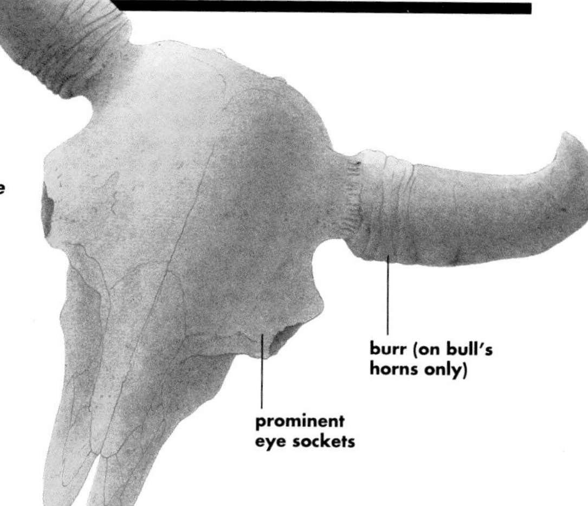

Main illustration Rachel Lockwood/Wildlife Art Agency

PRAIRIE RANGERS

PLAINS BISON HAVE EVOLVED TO MAKE THE MOST OF NORTH AMERICA'S ROLLING, GRASSY PRAIRIES. EVEN TODAY, THESE GIANT GRAZERS LIVE IN HARMONY WITH THEIR EXPANSIVE ENVIRONMENT

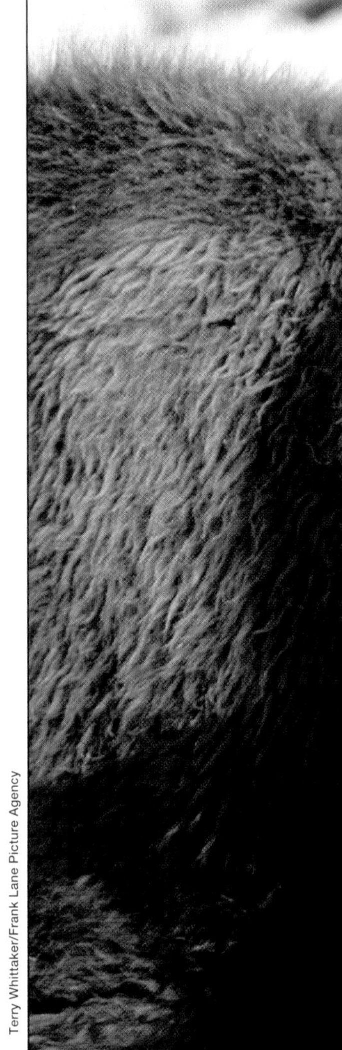

Terry Whittaker/Frank Lane Picture Agency

Midday visitors to the Yellowstone National Park begin to form a circle, a park ranger advising them to keep a safe distance from a steaming hole at the center. Old Faithful, one of the world's most famous geysers, is about to make a dramatic appearance. The people stir nervously—the idea of nature letting off steam begins to seem a bit threatening. Suddenly the hot summer air is filled with a loud and terrifying roar. The ranger reassures his audience, telling them that it is breeding time for the herds of wild bison living in the park. Moreover, there is no danger from these raging bulls, as they are about 3 miles (5 kilometers) away.

SURVIVING AGAINST THE ODDS

Much of the popular awareness of bison is the result of westerns, with their stirring images of teeming herds massed under the "big sky" of the American prairies. The four-footed extras in these shots are captives, destined to be rounded up and returned to safe wildlife reserves once the camera crew has conjured up a view of a bygone era. Bison now live in clearly demarcated areas, a far cry from the vast tracts of open prairie that provided their natural home. But a century or so of living in such relatively confined areas has not changed much of the bison's behavior, and its role in the local ecology has also been maintained.

The bison is a herbivore, occupying a place at the lowest level of the Great Plains food pyramid. Like other herbivores, such as prairie dogs, jackrabbits, and many bird species, it must be on guard against predators such as wolves and coyotes. Such hunters pose no threat to adult bison, but will prey on young calves in early summer.

We rightly consider the bison to be a victim, having been driven nearly to extinction in the 19th century, but in many respects it is a survivor. It is the largest creature in its natural habitat, but some 10,000 years ago it would have shared this space with other huge mammals, collectively known as "megafauna." None of these other animals—including various types of elephant and horse as well as mammoths and giant sloths—managed the transition into a post-ice age environment that saw huge grasslands cover the interior of North America.

The growth of these prairies also saw a corresponding decline in the variety of plants available, but the bison was able to survive and multiply in these conditions. Bison also showed they were remarkably able to provide themselves with another essential: water. The Great Plains of North America constitute a region that has few lakes; moreover, the rivers and streams often dry up in the

Jeff Foott/Survival Anglia

Dust baths condition the coat, removing parasites and loosening dead skin (above).

AMAZING FACTS

HIDDEN RESERVES

Bison have an appearance that suggests cumbersome movement and sluggish behavior. This image is strengthened by observing them sitting for hours chewing the cud rather vacantly. But looks can be deceiving. European bison can jump over streams 10 ft (3 m) wide and fences 6.6 ft (2 m) high from a standing position. A bison herd, sensing danger, can reach speeds of up to 30 mph (48 km/h).

summer months and freeze in the winter. Such places are vital, and bison will often use the luxury of a good watering hole or riverbed to give themselves a mud bath—the ultimate relief from insect pests.

Bison trails still exist in parts of the United States that have not seen a bison in over a century. These trails, appearing as deep grooves on the prairie floor, lead to and from water supplies. Countless generations of bison would follow these trails, even using them in the winter, with a herd stretched out in single file to follow the tracks of the leaders in the deep snow. These are the behaviors of the plains bison, the most abundant bison now living. They are also the only bison still roaming wild in large herds, albeit within a national park. Few films have been made with roles for wood bison or European bison, yet they have adapted to environments as distinct as those of the plains bison.

Forest browsers

The wood bison lives farther north than the plains bison, preferring the coniferous forests of the Canadian interior and eastern Alaska. Both the wood bison and European bison get their food primarily by browsing. The European bison samples a wide range of vegetation as it moves through the swampy mixed-growth forests of Eastern Europe.

Both types of bison survive in a chilly habitat that is damper than that of the plains bison, yet like the plains bison, these animals have shown a strong historical talent for adapting to a changing world. The European bison avoided sharing the fate of the aurochs, a giant ancestor of modern cattle, which became extinct in 1627. But no matter how adaptable or officially protected, all bison still present a big target for trigger-happy hunters. Even today, poaching of bison, with its implied disregard for the survival of the species, remains a concern. ■

These young bulls are not fighting in earnest, but merely sparring to hone their combative skills.

HABITATS

The plains bison is a creature of the prairies, and proved itself capable of multiplying successfully within that environment even in the presence of humans. Yet most evidence suggests that the modern bison evolved in surroundings more like those in which the wood bison and the European bison now live: mixed forests with swamps and marshes.

The climatic changes that culminated in the series of ice ages called for special adaptations in animals. Greater bulk, providing nutritional fat reserves and increased insulating qualities, enabled certain bovids to thrive in the cold forest environment that developed. Representatives of the genus *Bison* were one such successful group, as were musk oxen, yaks, and aurochs.

Fossil evidence suggests that the bison fanned out from their origins in southern Asia near the end of the Pliocene era, about two million years ago. They swept into the forests of temperate Eurasia, establishing themselves across a wide band, from the Atlantic seaboard eastward to the Volga and the

Stirring scenes such as these were once common across the entire prairie belt of North America.

DISTRIBUTION

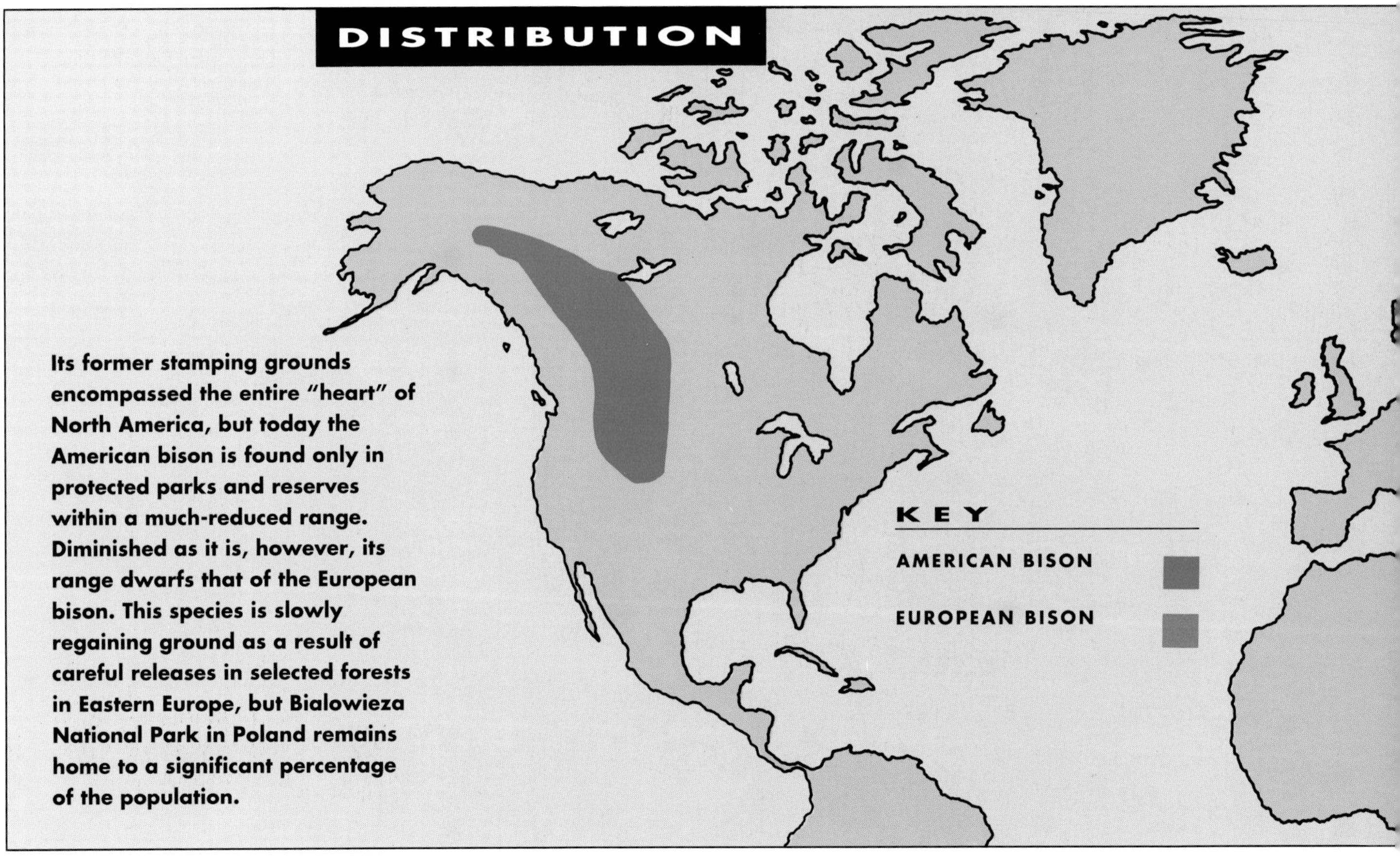

Its former stamping grounds encompassed the entire "heart" of North America, but today the American bison is found only in protected parks and reserves within a much-reduced range. Diminished as it is, however, its range dwarfs that of the European bison. This species is slowly regaining ground as a result of careful releases in selected forests in Eastern Europe, but Bialowieza National Park in Poland remains home to a significant percentage of the population.

KEY

AMERICAN BISON

EUROPEAN BISON

Franz Kamenzind/Planet Earth Pictures

Caucasus. The modern European bison developed in these surroundings, and, like today's American bison, it had two subspecies. The lowland, forest version still exists, but there seems to have been a separate mountain subspecies that lived on the forested slopes of the Caucasus and other ranges.

European bison had also thrived in the forests of northern Russia, with isolated pockets in the woods near the Urals and beyond. Some had been reported surviving into the 20th century in northeastern Siberia. These northern herds perhaps hark back to the time when bison crossed over the Bering Strait into North America during the Pleistocene ice ages. The terrain that they encountered would have been similar to the familiar Eurasian forest: The Canadian wood bison's similarity to the European bison indicates how little adaptation was needed to thrive in the new environment.

THE PRAIRIE BELT

The north-central region of North America retained its forest character in the period following the retreat of the glaciers, but further south there were great changes. Forests of spruce and other trees yielded to the march of grasslands across much of the Great Basin—the heart of the continent. Before white settlers arrived, the prairies formed a vast ocean of grass that extended to the low, distant horizons. This ocean extended from the deciduous forests of what are now Pennsylvania and Ohio to the Rockies in the west, and from the Mackenzie River in Canada south to the Gulf of Mexico. The vast valley of California was once a sea of grass; drier grasslands extended through Arizona and southwestern Texas and into Mexico.

Within this huge region there is a great range of rainfall. Much of the western area is semiarid, as it is cut off from Pacific moisture by the Rockies, while in the much wetter east, humid air flows north from the Gulf of Mexico. Consequently, two types of prairie have developed. Shortgrass predominates in the west, on the high plains under the shadow of the Rockies, where blue grama and buffalo grass grow. Away to the east, from eastern Oklahoma to Ohio, the tall-grass prairie lies—before it was cleared for farmland. Here, bluestem, prairie cord grass, and Indian grass grew tall enough to hide a man upon a horse. An intermediate zone, between the tall and short grasses, is known as the mixed-grass prairie. This still survives in patches, where little bluestem, June grass, and western wheat grass grow. Bison country centered on the fertile swath of grassland from the Mississippi to the Rockies.

The prairies—such as they remain today—owe much of their fertility to the fact that, westward from the Mississippi, they slope up to altitudes of around 2,950 ft (900 m) at the point where they meet the Rockies. Rainfall washed sediments down from the mountains, providing a rich bed for the grasses. Sadly, this means that the prairies are now heavily farmed, and the nutrients are much depleted.

Yellowstone has long been a refuge for living symbols of the American wilderness.

David Schultz/Tony Stone Worldwide

The bison, an effective ruminant, was able to populate this terrain and extend its range despite the arrival of the first humans. Its dental and digestive adaptations enabled it to thrive on all species of grass, and its bulk and fur provided a bulwark against the cold winters. None of the mammals that once populated that region of North America—horses, mastodons, camels, llamas, elephants, and rhinos—survived into the post-Pleistocene period. Some died out as a result of climatic change; others were easy targets for early human hunters; still others could not survive on the narrower vegetable "menu" served up by the prairies. Pronghorn antelopes are the only other bovid to have survived on the prairies.

THE MARCH SOUTH

Bison moved steadily south and east from their origins in the northwest corner of the continent, first colonizing the shortgrass prairies but already established in the much richer tall-grass prairies well before the Europeans arrived in the 16th century. Making up for their poor eyesight with a well-developed herd instinct, bison were able to defend themselves, particularly their vulnerable calves, against prairie predators such as the wolf, coyote, and bear.

The natural size of a bison herd—then as now—was not much more than about 60, methodically grazing a range of about 11 square miles (28 square kilometers) in summer and 38 square miles (98 square kilometers) in winter. Numbers would be hugely swollen during seasonal migrations. Bison would undertake twice-yearly treks in huge aggregations numbering a million or more, searching for fresh grass or for milder weather conditions. Even today wood bison in northern Alberta can be observed migrating some 150 miles (241 kilometers) each November and May, between the forested hills and the Peace River Valley. ■

FOCUS ON

BIALOWIEZA FOREST

Bialowieza Forest in northeast Poland encompasses the last tract of primeval lowland forest in Europe. The forest covers more than 463 sq mi (1,200 sq km), straddling the border with Belarus about 124 mi (200 km) east of Warsaw. Some 13,300 acres (5,386 hectares) on the Polish side have national park status and are recognized as a United Nations Biosphere Reserve and a World Heritage site.

Pine, oak, and ash woodlands give way in places to peat bogs, marshes, and meadows. The forest is also the home of the largest herds of European bison. European conservationists joined forces in 1919 after the last wild bison in the forest was killed by poachers. They set up a breeding program with three captive Bialowieza bison—two cows and a bull—in 1929.

The bison population grew steadily and in 1952 the first animals were released into the wild. Then as now, they were kept under close observation, with every new bison given a name and listed in a pedigree book. The international rescue program is now acknowledged as a success story, and nearly 400 bison now browse in the equally preserved forest.

Darak Karp/NHPA

TEMPERATURE AND RAINFALL

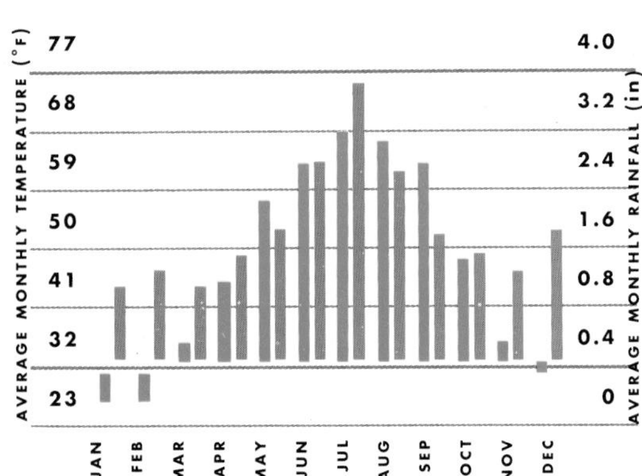

TEMPERATURE

RAINFALL

Away from the bitter chill of the North Sea and Arctic, the land near Warsaw enjoys a climate bordering on the continental. Summers are wet and warm and the winters, though cold, are not so harsh as they would be further east.

NEIGHBORS

Bialowieza is rich in oak, lime, hornbeam, and ash trees, and is a refuge for beavers. Woodpeckers and eagles find prey in and around the forest, parts of which have never been managed.

GRAY WOLF

Gray wolves are powerful, intelligent pack hunters that bring down prey as large as deer and horses.

LYNX

The lynx is a lone hunter, stalking its prey on the ground by night or lying in wait in low vegetation.

Illustrations Joanne Cowne

RUSSIA
LITHUANIA
POLAND
WARSAW
BELARUS

BIALOWIEZA

The National Park lies on the Poland–Belarus border. It occurs in Brest and Grodno provinces in Belarus and in Bialystok, Suwalki, and Lomza provinces in Poland. A former royal hunting ground, the forest is protected on both sides of the border.

BIALOWIEZA NATIONAL PARK

WOODPECKER

The greater spotted woodpecker drums loudly upon tree trunks to find insect larvae.

OTTER

The elusive otter lives along riverbanks and in wetlands. Its webbed feet and strong tail help it to swim well.

MOOSE

The moose is the largest of all deer species. It feeds alone on woody stems and aquatic plants.

EUROPEAN BEAVER

Unlike its American cousin, the European beaver usually burrows into a riverbank rather than building a lodge.

EAGLE OWL

With its tufted crown, the eagle owl is the largest European owl, killing prey as large as hares.

FOOD AND FEEDING

The American bison no longer have the luxury of migrating great distances in search of food, so they must demonstrate more resourcefulness in feeding themselves in the confines of Yellowstone National Park and other refuges. Even there, bison exhibit some seasonal preferences, migrating to the higher ground for the summer and back to lower valleys during the winter.

In summer the plains bison eat herbs and prairie grasses. These are the shorter grass species of the drier, western prairies rather than the taller species of the prairies further east. Bison will browse if the need arises, but they prefer grazing. In fact, their foraging activities stimulate the growth and spread of grasses in much the same way that elephants "husband" the African savanna.

A bull bison will often amble over to a tree on the edge of a wood, rubbing his head and neck against it and even grabbing the trunk between his horns. Pushing his bulk into the job he will shake the tree until it rocks and then snaps. The timber soon dries and becomes tinder, and can spread flames quickly to nearby woods. Burnt woodland is usually replaced by grasses, so in effect the bison has widened his feeding range.

LAZY DAYS

Bison need a lot of food to fuel their vast bulk—and this food demands plenty of digestion time. So they spend the day quietly regurgitating and rechewing (below).

THE DAILY GRIND

Bison usually feed in the morning or at dusk, with the herd slowly covering up to two miles (three kilometers) a day in search of grass. When grazing, a bison uses its tongue to gather grass in a bunch, which is gripped between the lower incisors and upper palate and ripped up. Bison have no special means of conserving moisture, so they rely on supplies of fresh water.

Plains bison take care not to exhaust their food resources. They practice an effective form of "crop rotation," allowing each area of grass to grow back before returning to graze it (left).

FOREST FEAST

European bison (below) *are spoiled for choice in their rich homelands. Tender shoots and tree buds are popular, but they will also eat grass.*

in SIGHT

PERFECT CATTLE?

The plains bison represents an evolutionary success in utilizing and digesting the short grasses and herbs typical of the dry western prairies of the American Great Basin. A herd of domestic cattle requires far more grazing space than its bison counterpart—a fact that has not escaped the notice of cattle ranchers.

An obvious solution would be to produce a bison/cattle cross, which would have these space-efficient eating qualities while retaining the hardiness against disease that characterizes domestic cattle. Efforts so far have proved commercially unsuccessful. The two species can breed, but some of the hybrid offspring are infertile. There is also concern that the presence of a number of bison/cattle hybrids will create unwanted opportunity for cattle genes to creep into the relatively small bison population.

They spend the day in comparative inactivity while they digest. Like other ruminants, bison have multiple stomach chambers, enabling them to digest food with a high cellulose content. They chew and swallow the food, then regurgitate and chew it again. The contents of the rumen—the first stomach division—begin to ferment at 104°F (40°C) with the aid of cellulose-loving bacteria that live in the bison's digestive system.

In colder weather plains bison eat mainly moss, lichens, and dried grasses. They uncover a thin layer of grass by pawing at the snow or by "sweeping" it away with their furry heads. They will eat snow if supplies of fresh water are unavailable or frozen.

BROWSING BISON

The wood bison eats mainly leaves, shoots, and the barks of shrubs and trees. European bison feed on branches, shoots, bark, moss, and lichen. Like the wood bison, they will also graze, but European bison fully exploit the richness of a mixed forest like Bialowieza. Over the course of the year they sample the food from a variety of forest habitats, favoring special seasonal "treats" such as acorns in the autumn and evergreen shoots in the spring. ■

Illustration Stephen Message/Wildlife Art Agency

SOCIAL STRUCTURE

Bison social structure is based on the herd. It is essential as a form of protection against predators, a means of passage through snow-covered ground, and as the basis for bison breeding patterns. Like other wild cattle, bison have poor eyesight, so gathering in numbers is a good defensive ploy.

We can only imagine the vast bison herds that once roamed Europe and much of Asia—even their natural habitat has been reduced to protected pockets of woodland. American bison, on the other hand, have the numbers and space to assemble in slightly larger herds, which give zoologists a few insights into the qualities of the bison herd.

Top cows

Bison society is led by the females, and some small groups are made up of adult females, young bulls no older than three years of age, young cows, and calves. Adult bulls remain at the edge of such groups. This, in effect, is the "core" bison social unit, and by necessity it is the largest type of grouping that European bison establish. Age counts towards status in these groups, so it is the oldest females that direct the herd's movements. Discipline is more easily achieved in these compact groups; the notorious stampedes have traditionally occurred in larger herds, in which the "line of command" is confused.

Within a stable bison society, the senior females dictate where the herd travels and when.

Bulls, by virtue of their extra size and strength, provide defense and—at least during the intense mating season—view each other as potential rivals. Females, more watchful of their young and also more vulnerable, achieve their aims through consensus. Although a group or even a small herd might be directed by a small number of "elders," each female plays a part in directing actions. Guide animals in these maternal groups are always on the lookout for stragglers, such as calves or tired adult cows. This "female solidarity" also extends to offspring, as suckling calves can approach any lactating cow.

Franz J. Camenzind/Planet Earth Pictures

COLLISION

If neither bull backs down, a bloody conflict breaks out (right), *and they slam together with bone-cracking force amid the flying dust.*

SHOWING OFF

At the start of a conflict between bulls (left), *each stands proudly to show off his profile and bellows with all the force of his lungs.*

BOWING OUT

When tempers rise the inferior bull (below right) *often lowers his head in a submissive gesture of defeat.*

in SIGHT

NATURAL SELECTION

Natural selection implies that some traits or variations are emphasized over others because of specific survival advantages associated with those traits. Traits that enhance survival obviously tend to prolong opportunity for reproduction, and the net result is more animals with the genes for these useful traits.

Size is a complex trait that is the result of several factors, including food supply, predators, climate, and social structure. A smaller body is easier to feed but harder to keep warm and also more susceptible to predators. Where males and females are dimorphic (different sizes) as in the bison, it is suggested that the costlier but larger body size of the male provides an advantage in male competition for mating. The female's smaller body size is probably the ideal balance for feeding (even when nursing a calf), maintenance of body temperature, and competence against predators.

Illustrations Kim Thompson

Apart from those bulls living individually on the edges of these matriarchal groups, there are small "bachelor herds" of bulls. Adult bulls and cows mingle only during seasonal migrations and during the summer breeding season, and at other times they remain apart, unless there is a threat from predators, such as wolves. Faced with such enemies the herd forms a "corral." Surrounding the calves and facing outward are the cows, and forming an outer circle are the adult bulls, stamping, snorting, and providing a none-too-subtle warning to would-be attackers.

BULLISH BEHAVIOR

A bull's bulk and power are related to a breeding pattern in which a single male mates with as many females as possible. Physical dominance—implied or achieved in battle—leads to a bull's breeding success and a chance to pass on his genetic inheritance. There are many rituals to establish dominance. At a basic level, a bull might simply move toward another animal until it moves away. Faced with a subordinate adult male, the bull will simply sway his head to display his horns, or make a short charge. Many conflicts end at this stage, with the other animal retreating.

Much more memorable are the fierce exchanges between evenly matched bulls. These dramas are played out with the tension and ritual of a Spanish bullfight—except that both combatants are bulls. The battle begins with the bulls contracting their stomach muscles to exchange deafening roars. Then they scratch the ground with their hoofs before edging toward each other with backs arched and tails swaying. Each lifts a forefoot slowly, and the exchange erupts into an all-out battle, with bulls charging each other with lowered horns, aiming to pierce the other's rib cage or flank. The battle is often over within half a minute, with the loser nursing deep wounds or fractures. Death is fortunately rare, although some fights are prolonged and noisy. ■

REPRODUCTION

Bison follow time-honored behavior patterns when it comes to mating. Some 90 percent of breeding takes place over a two-week period in mid- to late summer; this is so the young will be born at the height of the following spring, when grass and other vegetation will be most lush.

Breeding patterns among American bison are linked to a system of social dominance, reflected in the great difference in stature between bulls and cows. Size—and the power that it confers—is a key factor in male breeding success, as a dominant bull can displace a subordinate from a cow in heat. In this way the one-third of the bulls that are dominant mate with about two-thirds of the cows each year.

Cows might be bystanders during these great battles, but the theme of male dominance also suits their priorities. All cows are destined to be "single mothers," as bulls play no part in the nurturing of the young. Male competition is often used indirectly by cows as a mate-choosing strategy. A cow in estrus will often run through the entire herd. This attracts the attention of all the bulls and triggers a wave of competition among them. The male that can successfully keep all other males away usually wins the attention of the cow.

WELCOME RECRUIT

Gestation lasts about nine months, and the female leaves the herd before giving birth. Within several hours of its birth, a calf has enough confidence and coordination to run around its mother and they both rejoin the herd. They are welcomed back, and most of the bison pay social calls to satisfy their curiosity about the new arrival. The bison calf sometimes capitalizes on the goodwill of the herd to find a teat on the nearest familiar female.

As young calves gain a bit more independence, they join up in small groups and chase each other around, staging mock battles. Young females soon begin to distance themselves from the fray, and most males must leave these groups after about a year. By then they are weaned and mothers are probably ready to give birth again. Newly weaned females remain with mothers and their other offspring while young males join male herds, where they find themselves at the bottom of the social "ladder."

Females are at their most fertile between the ages of three and fifteen, during which time they give birth to two calves every three years. A female with a young calf will not mate until several months after the normal breeding season, which means that she will not be ready to mate until the following breeding season.

FROM BIRTH TO DEATH

BISON

GESTATION: AMERICAN BISON AVERAGES 285 DAYS; EUROPEAN BISON 260–270 DAYS
LITTER SIZE: 1, RARELY 2
BREEDING: JULY–SEPTEMBER
WEIGHT AT BIRTH: 33–66 LB (15–30 KG)
JOINS HERD: 3 HOURS
WEANING: 7-12 MONTHS
SEXUAL MATURITY: 2–4 YEARS
LONGEVITY: 20–30 YEARS

John Davis/Wildlife Art Agency

BIRTH
Usually a single calf is born, away from the herd (below). *It can stand upright, albeit very shakily, after only 15 minutes.*

MOTHER'S MILK
Although the newborn calf mimics the adults by nibbling at grass, it mainly suckles (below).

in SIGHT

TENDING BULLS

Although bison bulls play no part in raising their own offspring, they make every effort to insure that their own genes are passed on. A bull stays with a cow for about an hour after mating, repulsing any other bulls and thereby making sure that it is his sperm that fertilizes her. He will block her path if she tries to move away, and might even mount her again.

This sense of genetic exclusivity, known as tending, is similar to that of canids but the comparison ends there: Canids such as wolves pair for life and both parents share the responsibilities of nurturing the young.

Mary Clay/Planet Earth Pictures

WELCOME!

The other bison nuzzle the recent addition to the herd, fawning over it delightedly (below).

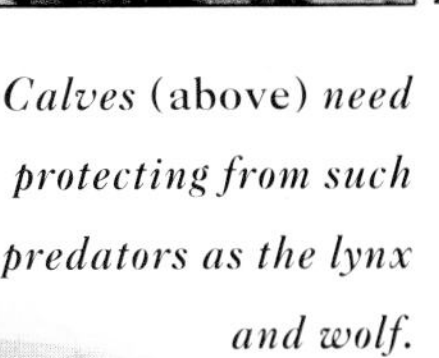

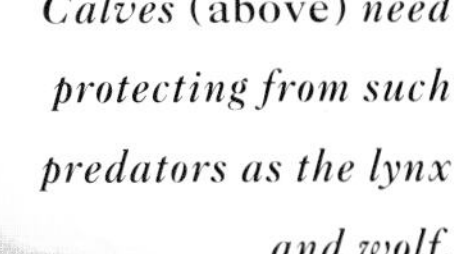

Calves (above) *need protecting from such predators as the lynx and wolf.*

BACK FROM THE BRINK

HAVING SLAUGHTERED THE BISON TO WITHIN A WHISKER'S BREADTH OF EXTINCTION, HUMANKIND THEN MADE LAST-DITCH ATTEMPTS TO SAVE THIS MAGNIFICENT BEAST—AIDED BY ITS OWN NATURAL RESILIENCE

The easiest way to illustrate the decline of the bison would be to plot them on a graph, with numbers running up the vertical axis and time running from left to right along the horizontal. Taking the end of the Pleistocene ice ages (about 10,000 years ago) as the start, the subsequent case histories of European and American bison would look startlingly different. Only at the end of the 19th century would their positions look similar—and equally alarming.

It is impossible to say precisely how many European bison there were at their peak, although it is safe to assume that they once numbered in the millions. Plotted across the millenia, however, their "population line" would slope steadily downward. The reason for this decline was the corresponding increase in the human population of Eurasia. Agricultural clearances probably played the biggest part in this decline, as bison lost huge swaths of their preferred forest habitat. The development of crossbows and then gunpowder put further pressure on the European bison, and numbers began to decline even more sharply in the 15th century.

Pressure on the European bison became acute. By the beginning of the 19th century herds survived in only two regions—the Bialowieza Forest between Poland and Belarus, and on the northern slopes of the Caucasus. Hunting restrictions imposed by European noblemen and Russian czars offered

The plains bison (below) *stood in the way of the pioneering U.S. government of the 19th century.*

Ken Cole/Natural Science Photos

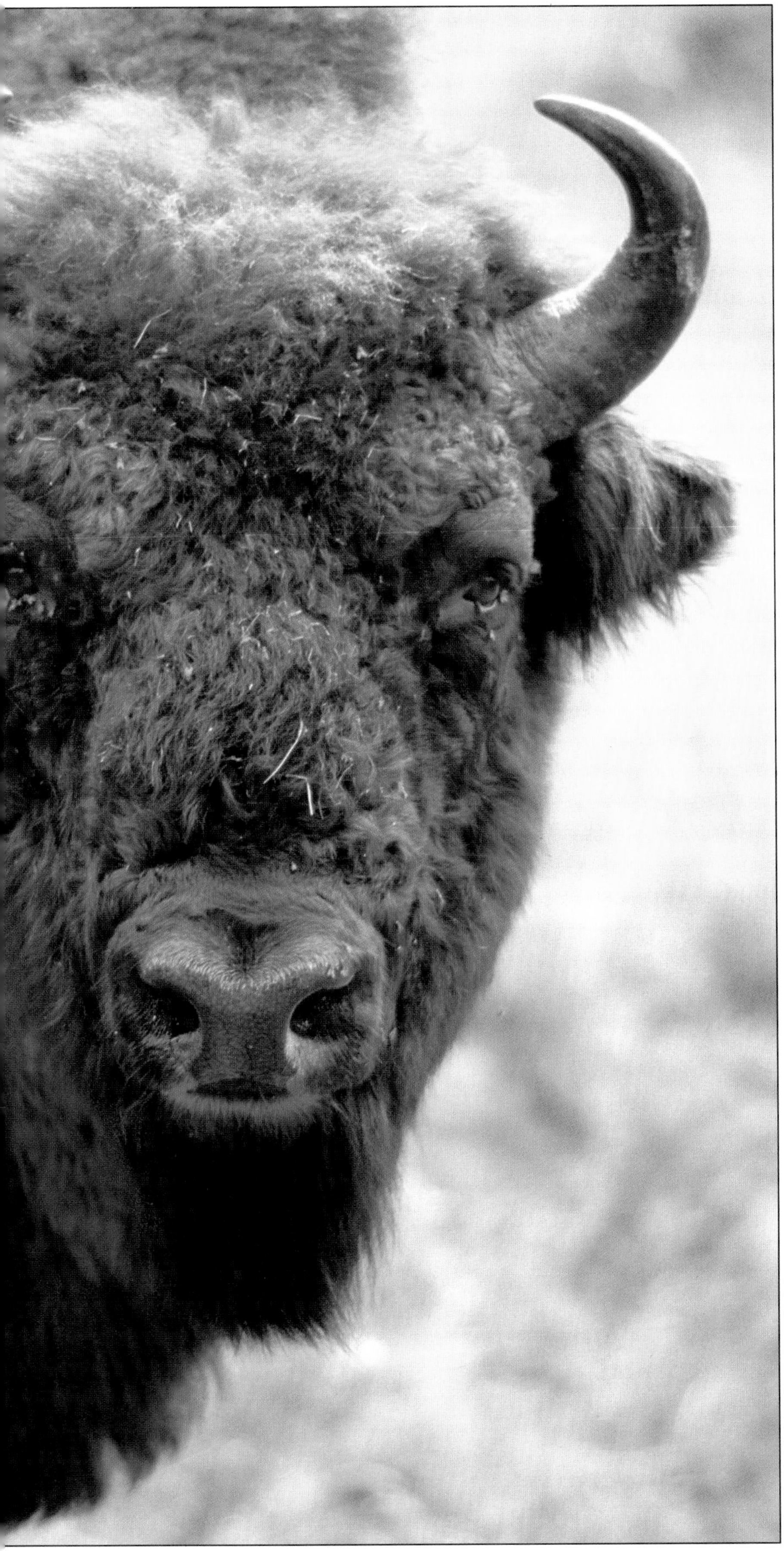

C. Dani & Ingrid Jeske/Natural Science Photos

THEN & NOW

This map shows the former and current distribution of the European bison.

FORMER DISTRIBUTION — CURRENT DISTRIBUTION

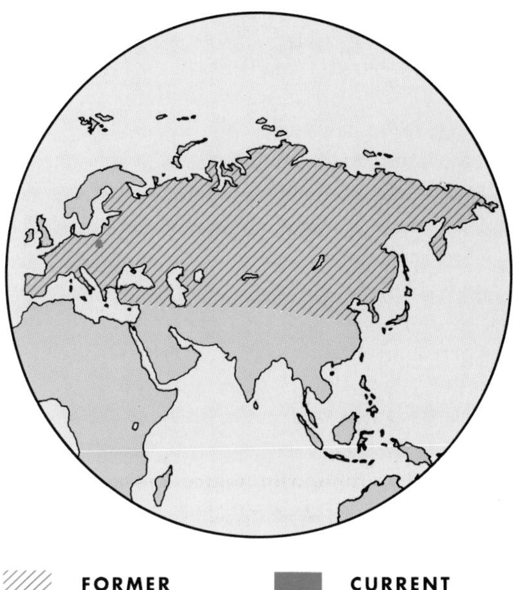

Fossils show that, some 2,000 years ago, the European bison roamed the Eurasian forests from Spain east to the Sea of Okhotsk. Deprived of its natural habitat by the advance of agriculture, it survived into this century only in Bialowieza and the Caucasus. The First World War put an end to the former population, while the Caucasus herds died out in the 1920s. Luckily, release programs involving zoo animals have succeeded in a few forests in Poland, Romania, and the former USSR.

some protection, but even these herds were endangered. A census carried out in 1930 indicated that there were only 30 surviving European bison—all in captivity. It was only through the dedication of the international team of conservationists, with a breeding program based in Bialowieza, that the species was saved from extinction. Scientists now estimate the European bison population to be nearly 3,000, with about 400 roaming wild in Bialowieza.

Plotting the population of the American bison would present a drastically different picture. Instead of a steady downward slope over the millenia we would see an upward slope—sometimes dramatically so—reaching heights of 60 million or more.

Today, "wild" herds of European bison actually descend from released captive stock.

That upward slope would continue across more than 95 percent of the horizontal axis, and then plunge almost vertically downward to nearly zero.

The Native Americans

The relationship between the American bison and humans accounts for this different picture. Like its European relative, the American bison has shared its range with humans since the end of the ice ages. But through most of that period its human neighbors were the Native Americans, and in particular the nations known collectively as the Plains Indians.

Archaeological findings in Colorado, dating back some 8,000 years, reveal evidence of hunting techniques almost identical to those used by the Plains Indians of the 19th century. The hunters used two types of "bison drive"—the pound and the jump. Both techniques relied on the skillful use of scouts, often disguised under wolf or coyote skins.

For the bison pound, scouts would guide 50–60 bison from a larger herd into a natural canyon, up to 4.3 miles (7 km) long. At the end of this "funnel" the bison would be driven into a wooden stockade; a ditch dug at its entrance prevented bison from retreating. The main body of hunters

> Before the advent of firearms, Native Americans tackled only the smaller bison herds

would surround the pound, slaughtering the bison with spears. The Plains Indians used similar decoy techniques in the jump, driving bison off a cliff to their death. White pioneers who later found the mass bison graveyards at the feet of these cliffs found heaps of bleached, cleanly picked bones stacked several yards high, the accumulation of hunting through several millenia.

Both of these techniques would provide a band of humans with several months' worth of food. But although effective, these traps could only work during the twice-yearly migration of bison. At other times bison would be more scattered—and better able to defend themselves. This subsistence level of human predation therefore had little or no effect on the overall bison population, which continued to grow as bison extended their range.

The white settlers

The arrival of white European settlers in the 15th and 16th centuries affected the bison in two stages. The first was with the spread of a European import—the horse. Plains Indians soon learned how to capture and breed horses and their riding skills rapidly gained renown. With this new mobility, they

Richard Packwood/Oxford Scientific Films

ENDANGERED SPECIES

GENOCIDE

"It is in the nature of the Buffalo...to recede before the approach of civilization, and the injury complained of is but one of those inconveniences to which every people are subjected by the changing and constantly progressive spirit of the age." These were the words of U.S. Commissioner of Indian Affairs William Medill in 1846, after the Sioux complained that white immigrants were killing or driving off the game on which they depended.

The Sioux were not the only Native Americans whose way of life revolved around the bison. Similar pleas came from other tribes—the Blackfoot, Cheyenne, Arapaho, Comanche, and Apache. These people had carried on the hunter-gatherer way of life that had prevailed on the Great Plains since the end of the last ice ages. But this "primitive" way of life was an irritant to a country bursting to "go west."

Americans of this period believed in "Manifest Destiny," a doctrine stating that it was the destiny of the United States to take over the whole of North America. The U.S. government gave its full support to a policy of eliminating the bison. The railroad companies, laying tracks across the continent, slaughtered bison to feed their workmen and when the rail lines were complete they even allowed passengers to shoot bison from railway cars.

The range of the bison became more and more constricted, either with outright killing or when vast crop fields replaced

Conservation Measures

- By 1889 there were only 835 bison left in the whole of North America. Fortunately, Yellowstone National Park had been established in 1872. The federal government had set aside its 2.2 million acres (900,000 hectares) as a way of preserving the natural beauty of the Yellowstone River Valley. In doing so, it also gave a new lease on life to the remaining herds of plains bison, but it would take the efforts of future conservationists to help bison populations begin to grow again.

grassy prairies. The last bison had disappeared from east of the Mississippi River early in the 19th century; by the 1860s they were gone from the southwest.

The greatest slaughter was reserved for the prairie heartland; some 200,000 were killed in Kansas alone in 1872–1873, and from 1870–1875 around 2.5 million bison were killed each year. Echoing the opinions of Commissioner Medill, President Roosevelt summed it up with a shortsightedness characteristic of the period: "The many have been benefited by (the extermination of the bison); and I suppose the comparatively few of us who would have preferred the continuance of the old order of things, merely for the sake of our own selfish enjoyment, have no right to complain...."

BISON IN DANGER

ALL BISON ARE DECLINING TO A GREATER OR LESSER DEGREE AND ARE GIVEN PROTECTION ACROSS MOST OF THEIR RANGE.

EUROPEAN BISON	VULNERABLE

VULNERABLE MEANS THAT THE ANIMAL MAY MOVE INTO THE ENDANGERED CATEGORY IF THREATS REMAIN UNDIMINISHED. *ENDANGERED* MEANS THAT THE ANIMAL IS IN DANGER OF EXTINCTION AND ITS SURVIVAL IS UNLIKELY UNLESS STEPS ARE TAKEN TO SAVE IT.

Adrian Warren/Ardea

WHERE THE BUFFALO ROAMED: THE PRAIRIES TODAY HAVE BEEN PARCELED UP FOR FARMLAND.

were able to hunt bison in greater numbers. Greater contacts with white traders also led to the spread of firearms, especially rifles, which increased their hunting ability even further. Even so, the Plains Indians would not commit wholesale slaughter of the bison, which had a spiritual as well as a nutritional role for their society.

The second stage of white contact was more direct and led to the precipitous decline in the bison population. The great plains at the heart of North America—along with the bison and Plains Indians that lived on them—stood in the way of the westward expansion of the United States. In the early 19th century the bison were systematically slaughtered to make way for railways and farms, or simply because these large animals made easy targets for people caught up in the frenzy of trophy hunting. The decimation of Plains Indians culture was an obscene, but hopelessly predictable by-product of this mandated carnage. By the end of the last century plains bison numbered fewer than a thousand. Many of these lived in Yellowstone National Park, established in 1872 and still the home of the only remaining wild herd of these bison.

BISON SOCIETY

Specific measures to protect the bison only came with the new century. In 1905, the Bronx Zoo's director, W. T. Hornaday, established the American Bison Society. The Society had a high profile from its inception, counting among its supporters President Theodore Roosevelt—although, ironically, he was an ardent big-game hunter. Building on successful breeding programs in zoos and conservation sites, the Society released bison into protected areas. This led to reintroduced populations in Montana, Oklahoma, Nebraska, and North and South Dakota.

Similar measures bore fruit in Canada, where the woodland subspecies had also been threatened with extinction. Breeding programs in Alberta and

- The breeding program in Bialowieza National Park, set up in 1929, is proving to be a great success in preserving the European bison.

- For its part, the American wood bison's future relies in part upon the herd that roams Wood Bison National Park. This park, established in 1922, covers nearly 17,370 sq miles (45,000 sq km) of plains and forest, where moose and bears also roam free.

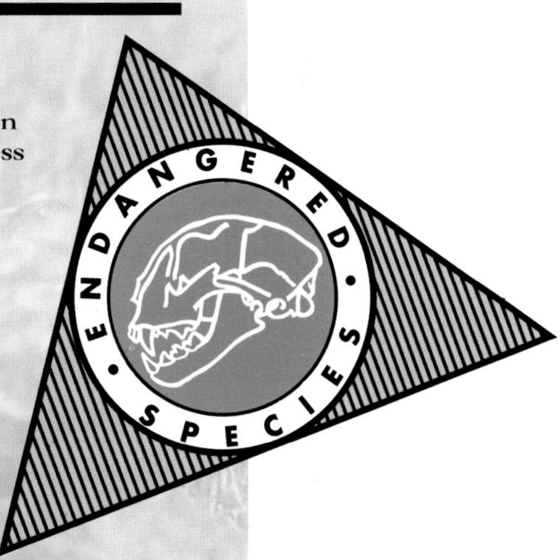

Alberta and Northwest Territories helped numbers increase, despite a misguided attempt to interbreed wood and plains bison, which introduced tuberculosis. In 1957, however, conservationists discovered a residual population of about 200 wood bison, rather fittingly, in Wood Bison National Park. This group has been subjected to careful management to keep them separate from the mixed plains bison population, and the herd now numbers 2,500. They live in 6 separate wild and captive groups.

The story of the decline of the American bison and its recovery is among one of the most remarkable in conservation history. The thoughtless and systematic extermination of the species was interrupted at the last hour by an emerging conservation consciousness. The American bison is unlikely to recover its numbers in the tens of millions but is now safe from extinction. Apart from animals in bison reserves, there are tens of thousands of bison on private ranches.

ALONGSIDE MAN

THE HEART OF A CULTURE

French fur traders traveling west from the Mississippi and Missouri rivers in the 18th century found that they could survive long, cold winters on a diet that consisted mainly of pemmican. This foodstuff, which Plains Indians traded in return for weapons, horses, and cooking utensils, consisted of dried bison meat enriched with fat and dried fruit. Pemmican was a staple food of these Native Americans. It lasted well and—with the addition of fat and fruit—insured that their diet did not run the risk of protein poisoning. And like so much of Plains Indian life, it centered on the careful exploitation of bison.

Hunting with primitive bows and arrows, the native hunters needed all their skill and cunning to kill a bison, and no part of a slaughtered animal was wasted. Skins and furs were used for clothing or for shelter; the skin and tongue of rare white bison were worshiped as fetishes, and as offerings to the Sun God. Bones could be fashioned into cooking utensils or children's toys. Even the sun-bleached bison skulls served a practical purpose. Scouts would arrange these near the entrance of bison drives in the belief that the bison would be attracted by the sight of their "white brothers."

A MIRACLE BIRTH

Despite a history of problems, the current social concern about animal welfare and conservation has benefited the bison, and an unusual occurrence in 1994 seems to have offered an uplifting postscript to the tragic relations between bison, Plains Indian, and white American.

Jeff Foott/Survival Anglia

The bison was a vital element of the Native American way of life (above), *until U.S.-government policy did away with both hunter and hunted.*

On August 20, 1994, David Heider was astonished to see that one of the cows in his small herd of bison had given birth to a white calf. This news was considered noteworthy in his small farming community of Janesville, Wisconsin, but Heider was not prepared for the reaction of the Native American population to this new arrival. Within days of the birth, Native Americans began arriving to see the calf, and to leave offerings. Some had traveled for days from the American East Coast or from Canada, and local police had to control the traffic bringing more than 1,200 visitors a day.

There was a simple and profound reason for this commotion. According to the beliefs of the Plains Indians, the calf was the embodiment of the White Buffalo Calf Woman, the spirit who created the bison. Her return would herald an era of peace and prosperity. According to Chris Macarthur, a Lakota visitor from Saskatchewan, the calf was "the most sacred gift of the gods." By way of a comparison, Macarthur speculated on the excitement that would surround Christ's return to Earth. He left an eagle feather, since the eagle flies nearest the Creator.

Heider agreed to name the calf "Miracle" and to respect the beliefs of all who came to see her. In doing so, he even turned down an offer of $250,000 for the bison—some twenty times the normal trading price for a bison calf—from someone aiming to cash in on this tourist attraction. Most of his neighbors opted to respect his decision and put up with the extra traffic and upheaval.

Time alone will tell whether Miracle's white fur darkens as she grows older, but the events surrounding her birth and first months suggest that she has already acted as a bridge between two cultures. Perhaps the new spirit of reconciliation will grow and mature with her. ■

INTO THE FUTURE

Few conservationists in 1900 would have bet on the survival of the bison at the end of the century—yet it seems as though their worst fears have not been realized. Natural refuges, enlightened breeding programs, and a better understanding of genetics have pulled both bison species back from the brink of extinction. The outlook is probably best for the plains bison, which now numbers over 100,000, although many of these bison derive from captive stock.

The only herd to have remained completely wild lives in Yellowstone National Park, where natural patterns of herd behavior can be observed. The separation of the sexes and the dramatic battles between bulls continue as they would have 150 or, equally, 8,000 years ago. Even the seasonal migrations, which once produced herds of a million or more, have their diminutive parallel within Yellowstone. The bison shift their grazing ground with the season, moving into the fresh upland grass in the spring and back to the lower—and milder—valleys for the winter season. The Yellowstone bison even face some of their old predatory enemies—wolves, coyotes, and bears.

Some "purists" argue, however, that this unspoiled refuge is still a sort of cage. Bison wandering beyond the park are often shot by ranchers who fear that the bison will bring disease among their cattle. They would seem to argue for a sort of protected status for the bison, akin to the position held by cows among the Hindu population of India. Such a move seems extremely unlikely, and ranchers point out that the bison population is increasing despite these killings.

European bison have a less certain future. Most live in small, scattered communities and are vulnerable to local disasters such as forest fires, droughts, floods, or the effects of pollution. These isolated populations also face the risk of inbreeding. ■

PREDICTION

CONCERN FOR SMALL POPULATIONS

Plains bison seem assured of a healthy passage through the next century. There is more concern for the smaller and more scattered populations of wood bison and European bison. Their survival will depend on continued breeding intervention by humans as well as the setting up—in the case of European bison—of more refuges.

EUROPEAN THREATS

There are still grave concerns about the future of the European bison as a species. In the early 20th century, soon after the last wild bison was killed in Bialowieza, a small population of European bison also died out in the Caucasus. This group of bison might have represented an upland subspecies of European bison. A new herd has been released in this region, but these bison are American-European hybrids. Other hybrid herds exist in Eastern Europe that may "swamp" the native species. Still, the greatest threat is the expansion of human population which continues to put pressure on habitat for all wildlife. European bison populations will continue to exist only as long as people are willing to set aside suitable forest habitat and offer long-term protection.

WOOD BISON

The position of American wood bison is closer to that of the European bison than it is to the plains bison. Small, scattered populations also characterize this subspecies, causing similar concerns about inbreeding and genetic drift. There is an additional worry about interbreeding with the plains bison, introducing disease and rendering the wood subspecies impure. These concerns are addressed in the special management programs set up by Canadian conservationists. The program seems to be succeeding, and there are now some 3,000 "pure" wood bison living in Canada and perhaps some scattered populations in remote parts of Alaska.

Illustration Carol Roberts

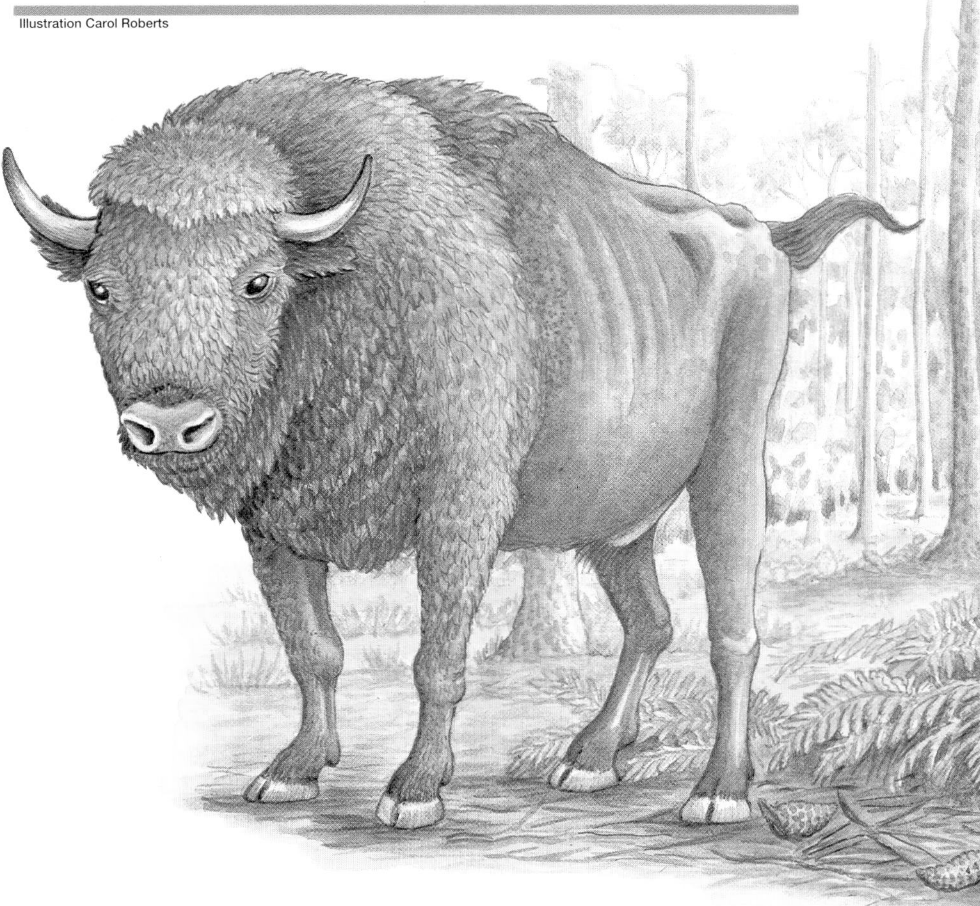

WILD CATTLE

RELATIONS

Wild cattle belong to the order Artiodactyla and the cattle family, Bovidae. Other bovids include:

DUIKERS

GRAZING ANTELOPES

GAZELLES

DWARF ANTELOPES

BISON

Lex Hes/Natural Science Photos

Wild cattle are bovids—members of the family Bovidae, which also includes duikers, grazing antelopes, and the pronghorn.

ORDER

Artiodactyla (even-toed ungulates)

FAMILY

Bovidae

SUBFAMILY

Bovinae

GENUS

Bubalus (Asian buffalo)

four species

GENUS

Bos (true cattle or oxen)

four species, plus all breeds of domestic cattle

GENUS

Synceros (African buffalo)

one species

WILD COUSINS OF THE COW

CONTENTED COWS GRAZING IN HOME PASTURES ARE A COMMON SIGHT AROUND THE WORLD—BUT THESE ANIMALS HAVE A NUMBER OF WILD RELATIVES, NOT ALL SO MILD-NATURED AND EVEN-TEMPERED

The 11 wild cattle species include the African buffalo and the American bison—which is also known, wrongly, as a buffalo. Other species range from India to Southeast Asia. Cattle belong to a group known as the even-toed ungulates, or Artiodactyla, which includes animals ranging from pigs to giraffe. Cattle are distinguished by their horns, which consist of a core of bony horn encased in true horn and, unlike the antlers of deer, are not shed annually.

The earliest origins of these animals go back some 50 million years, but it was not until about 20 million years ago that recognizable bovids appeared. According to fossil finds, they originated in France, the Sahara, and Mongolia. Ten million years later, vast numbers of bovids appeared, until, 2 million years ago, more than 100 different genera roamed the earth. Modern cattle evolved during this time; one species was a giant African bovid, an ancestor of today's African buffalo. In its wild state, the

The gaur (below) *is closely related to domestic cattle and lives in small herds.*

E. A. James/NHPA

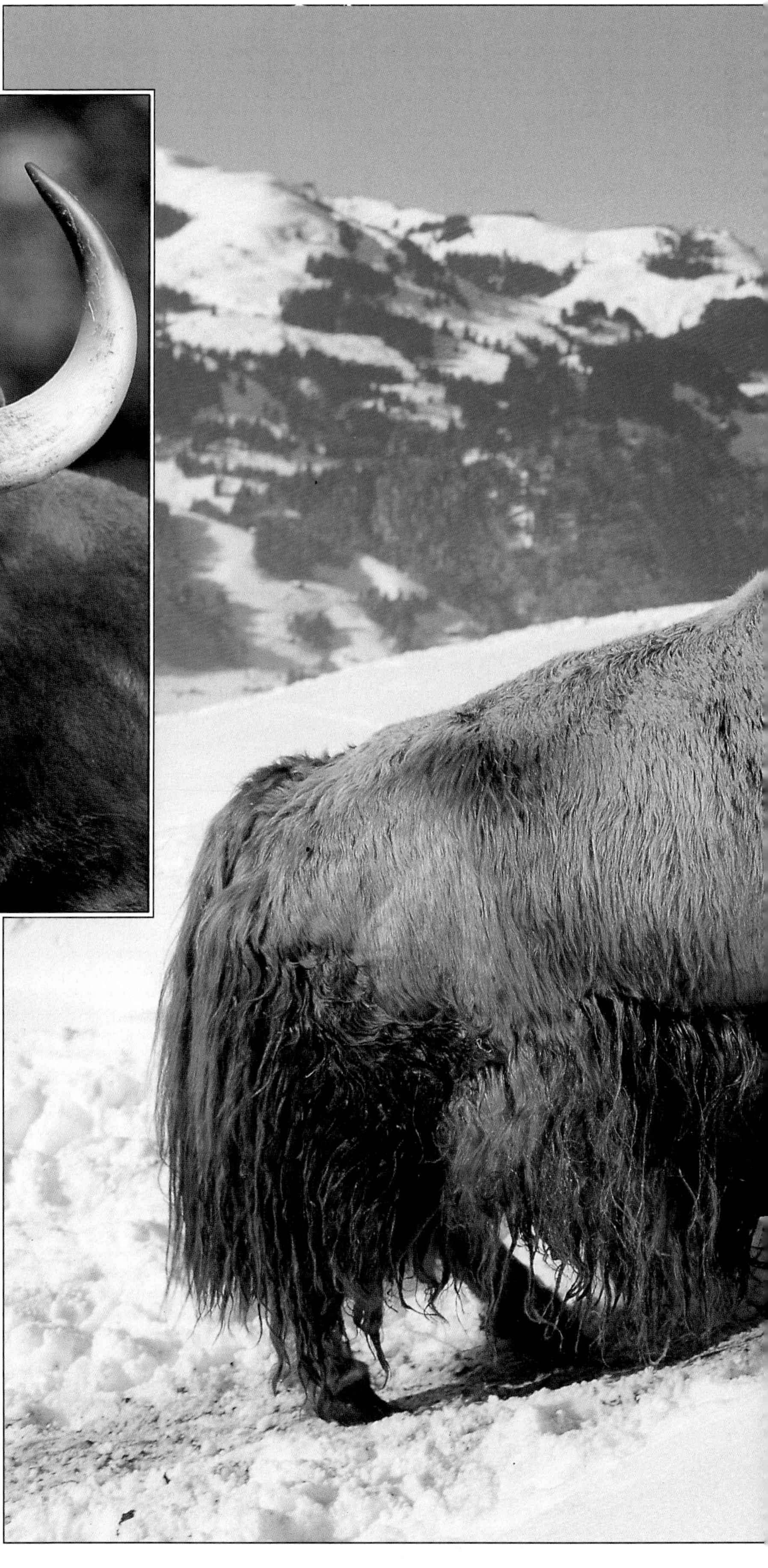

African buffalo is probably the most numerous of all wild cattle species. With its reputation for being one of the most dangerous of Africa's big-game animals, it has never been domesticated.

WATER BUFFALO

Close to the African buffalo in body size, and sporting a vast spread of horns, is the Asian or wild water buffalo. The best known of the four species in the genus *Bubalus* (bew-BAH-luss), it is also probably the most widely domesticated. In fact, it has served humans for so long and so widely that there are various domestic breeds of this animal. Usually these are much smaller, reaching about 1,210 lb (550 kg) in weight as against a top weight of more than double this in the wild species. They vary in color from black or brown and white, to pure white. Feral herds of water buffalo wander in many areas—in Asia, Europe, and South America, but perhaps most noticeably in northern Australia, where there are some 250,000 feral water buffalo, descendants of animals imported in the 19th century.

Hans Reinhard/Bruce Coleman Ltd.

in SIGHT

THE NEW VU QUANG

We might think that, by now, all species of mammal are well known to humans. Not so, it seems. The kouprey was discovered as late as 1936, but there has been a discovery even more recently than this. In 1992 an entirely new species of wild cattle was found in Vietnam; it has been given the name of the vu quang ox, *Pseudoryx nghetinhensis* (syoo-DOR-iks gay-tin-EN-sis).

Small by wild cattle standards—it measures only 31–35 in (80–90 cm) at the shoulder—the vu quang earned its genus name from a resemblance to the Arabian oryx. However, DNA tests show that it is most closely related to members of the subfamily Bovinae. It has a shorter tail and smaller feet than are usual in wild cattle, and it also has a black-and-white patterned head, although its overall color is black. It was discovered in the evergreen montane forests to the north of Vietnam.

The other three species in the *Bubalus* genus are the mountain and lowland anoa and the tamarau—one of the world's rarest mammals. Looking almost more like antelope, the anoas could be described as miniature water buffalo—they are the smallest, many consider the most primitive, and also apparently the oldest of all wild cattle species in the world today. Coat color varies from brown to near black, often with patches of white. The slender, pointed horns reach a maximum length of 14 in (37 cm) in the lowland anoa, but are usually much shorter; in the mountain anoa, they grow to 5.7 in (14.6 cm).

The rare tamarau is a little bigger than the anoas but still considerably smaller than the wild water buffalo. Its woolly coat is a dark brown to gray black, and its short, thick horns grow to a length of around 20 in (0.5 meter).

OXEN

The remaining genus of wild cattle, *Bos*, takes in the animals most frequently known as oxen. They include the most northerly living species, which is also one of the largest of all, the yak, together with three other species—the banteng, gaur, and kouprey. Also included are all breeds of domestic cattle, which are descended from a now-extinct species belonging to this genus, known as the aurochs (OR-ox).

Subzero conditions present no trouble to the yak, the most cold-tolerant of any wild cattle species.

The yak has also been domesticated over many centuries. The dense, long dark brown coat of the wild yak and the immense horns, which curve outward and forward to a length of 38 in (96 cm), contribute to the overall impression of huge bulk.

The gaur, sometimes known as the Indian bison, has a pronounced shoulder hump and is another huge bovine. However, it has a smoother coat than the yak, which makes it look smaller, and may vary in color from a rich chestnut brown to almost black, usually with white "stockings." Other key characteristics are two dewlaps—a small one below the chin and a larger fold that hangs between the forelegs. Its stout, up-curving horns may grow to 28 in (71 cm).

The banteng is perhaps the most handsome of wild oxen. A little smaller, yet more graceful than the gaur, it looks like some of the various breeds of domestic cattle. The big horns are almost crescent shaped, and the coat is usually a rich reddish brown—darker in males—with various white markings.

The kouprey is another species in which males have a dewlap between the forelegs; in old animals this may reach almost to the ground. Its coat is paler than those of the gaur and banteng, and the long tail has a bushy tip. The female has delicate, lyre-shaped horns, unlike the male's huge, curving pair. As the animals get older, the horns tend to get frayed at the tip, apparently from long service in digging and investigating tree stumps. ■

ANCESTORS

THE AUROCHS

The vast aurochs, said to have resembled the gaur in size, gave rise to many of today's domestic cattle breeds. In prehistoric times it was found in open forests and their margins, as well as steppes, over most of Europe east to the Urals and Caucasus, as well as parts of Asia and northern Africa. The males were a rich dark brown with long curved and spreading horns. Females were smaller, and paler in color.

Domesticated some 6,000–8,000 years ago, it was so widely hunted that its range was already restricted 2,000 years ago, and by about the 11th century, aurochs were scarce everywhere. Their last strongholds were the forests of east Prussia, Lithuania, and Poland. In the mid-16th century there was only a small herd near Warsaw; less than a century later only one remained. It died in 1627, and with it the species became extinct.

Color illustrations Steve Kingston

THE WILD CATTLE'S FAMILY TREE

The species within the family Bovidae are so diverse that they are further divided into subfamilies. Within the wild cattle subfamily, Bovinae, there are three tribes: the Bovini, which contains the wild cattle discussed here and also the bison; the tribe Boselaphini, which contains the four-horned antelopes; and the tribe Strepciserotini of spiral-horned antelopes.

ASIAN BUFFALO

Bubalus

(boo-BAH-lus)

The four species of Asian buffalo are the Asian water buffalo, the lowland anoa, the mountain anoa, and the tamarau. Ranging from Nepal and India to Malaysia and the islands of Mindoro and Sulawesi, the smallest and rarest of all wild cattle belong to this genus. The best known of all, the water buffalo, is one of the most widely domesticated of wild cattle and appears in many areas outside of its natural range in various forms.

FOUR-HORNED ANTELOPES

GOATS AND SHEEP

GAZELLES

BISON

TRUE CATTLE OR OXEN

Bos
(boss)

The four true species of oxen are the yak, the gaur, the banteng, and the kouprey. Of these, the yak is the hardiest and has been the most widely domesticated. All four species are massive. This group also includes the domestic cattle breeds.

AFRICAN BUFFALO

Syncerus caffer
(sin-CARE-us CAF-er)

The most dangerous and feared of all wild cattle, this is the only African species. There are basically two forms—the Cape buffalo and the forest buffalo. The Cape buffalo may weigh twice as much as its forest relative. It is also usually black, whereas the forest form is more often red. The horns of the forest buffalo are also shorter.

WILD CATTLE TRIBE BOVINI

SPIRAL-HORNED ANTELOPES

DUIKERS

SUBFAMILY BOVINAE

GRAZING ANTELOPES

BOVIDAE

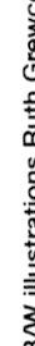

ANATOMY: THE AFRICAN BUFFALO

The African buffalo is the largest and most feared of the wild cattle. The mountain anoa (above right) is the smallest, measuring up to 5 ft (1.5 m) long and weighing up to 660 lb (300 kg).

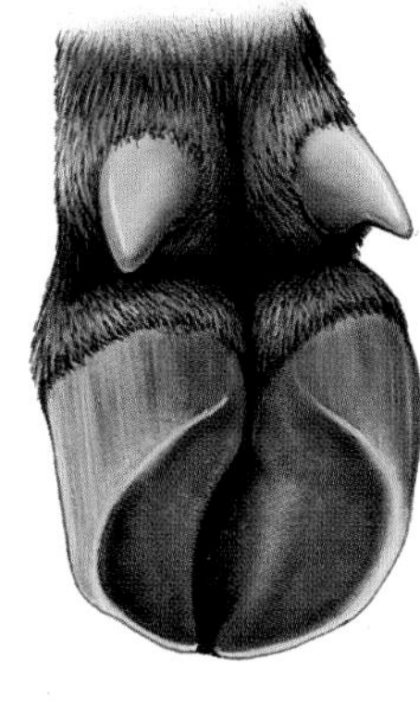

AFRICAN BUFFALO HOOVES

The cloven hooves are exceptionally broad, with a wide spread for easy wading in swampy conditions. As in all artiodactyls, they have evolved to retain an even number of toes.

THE HEAD

is massive, with a prominent forehead. The broad muzzle is naked and permanently moist, and the nostrils are broad and flared. The eyes are comparatively small.

THE EARS

grow at right angles to the head, but hang droopily behind and below the horns. They are set far back and made to look even bigger by the fringe of soft hairs.

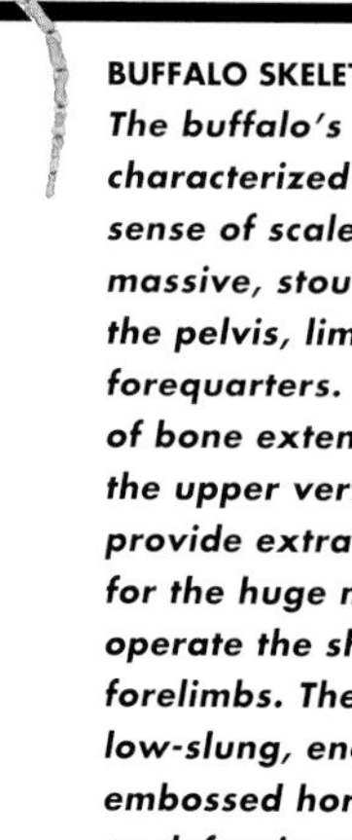

X-RAY

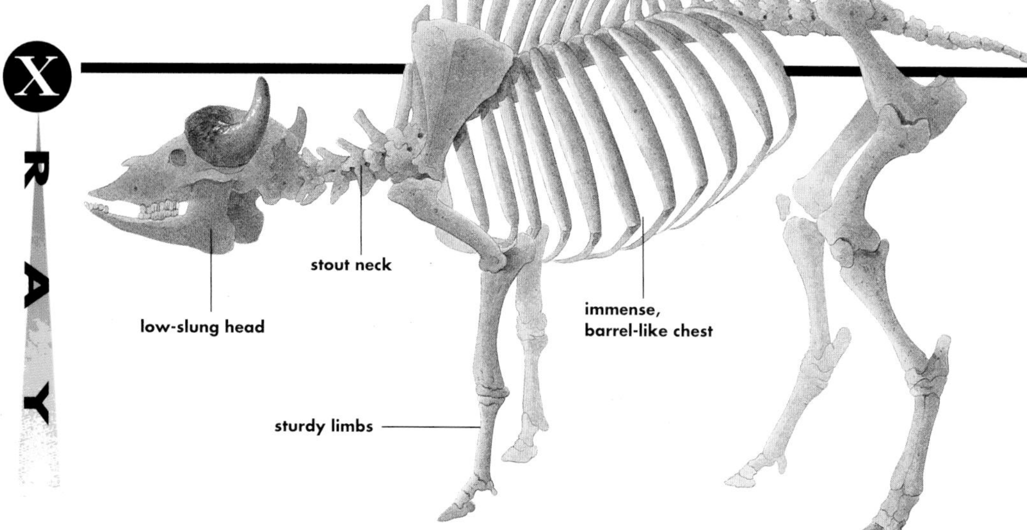

BUFFALO SKELETON

The buffalo's body plan is characterized by its sheer sense of scale—there are massive, stout bones in the pelvis, limbs, and forequarters. Long fingers of bone extending from the upper vertebrae provide extra anchorage for the huge muscles that operate the shoulders and forelimbs. The skull is low-slung, enabling the embossed horns to serve as defensive weaponry.

X-ray illustrations Elisabeth Smith

Horn shape and size vary widely among the wild cattle. Those of the yak grow to a length of 37 in (95 cm). The water buffalo's elegant, backswept horns are the longest of any bovid, and measure 48 in (122 cm) along the outside edge—the record length is 76 in (194 cm). By comparison, the tamarau's stout horns measure a mere 20 in (51 cm).

THE BODY

is typically "cattle shaped," with a thick neck and strong shoulders. The humps of other cattle, such as the gaur and zebu, are formed from two massive muscles surrounded by fatty tissue.

THE TAIL

is slender, ending in a tuft of hairs. Of all the wild cattle, the kouprey's tail probably has the bushiest tip.

THE COAT

is dark brown to black in the male. The female's coat is paler in color. As animals mature, the coats become more sparse, particularly so in old bulls, when the dark brown hide often shows through. White patterns of grizzled hair may appear on the head.

FACT FILE:

THE AFRICAN BUFFALO

CLASSIFICATION

GENUS: *SYNCERUS*

SPECIES: *CAFFER*

SIZE

HEAD–BODY LENGTH: 6.8–11 FT (2.1–3.4 M)

HEIGHT TO SHOULDER: 3.3–5.5 FT (1–1.7 M)

AVERAGE LENGTH OF HORNS FROM ROOT TO TIP: 3.3 FT (1 M)

TAIL LENGTH: 28 IN (71 CM)

WEIGHT: 660–1,984 LB (300–900 KG)

MALE IS 30–50 PERCENT LARGER THAN FEMALE

WEIGHT AT BIRTH: 88 LB (40 KG)

COLORATION

ADULT BULLS ARE DARK BROWN TO BLACK. HAIR GRADUALLY THINS OUT AS ANIMALS MATURE, UNTIL LARGE PATCHES OF DARK HIDE ARE EXPOSED. THIS MAY BE ACCOMPANIED BY PATCHY MARKINGS ON THE FACE. COWS ARE PALER IN COLOR, AND CALVES ARE A REDDISH BROWN

FEATURES

MASSIVE, TYPICAL BOVINE APPEARANCE

LONG, SHALLOW CURVING HORNS, MEETING IN A HELMET, OR "BOSS," ON THE CROWN IN MALES

HORNS TAPER TO A POINTED TIP

LONG, DROOPING EARS FRINGED WITH HAIRS

PERMANENTLY MOIST MUZZLE

LONG TAIL ENDING IN A BUSHY TIP

BUFFALO SKULL
The horn helmet, or "boss," adds to the great size of the cranium. In spite of their size, the horns are surprisingly light and may help the animal to float in water.

large cranium

tapering muzzle

HORNS
The male's horns (below) are massive and spreading, and their central base forms a "boss" on the skull. Viewed from the front, they form a shallow W shape. The female's horns are similar but smaller, and there is no central boss.

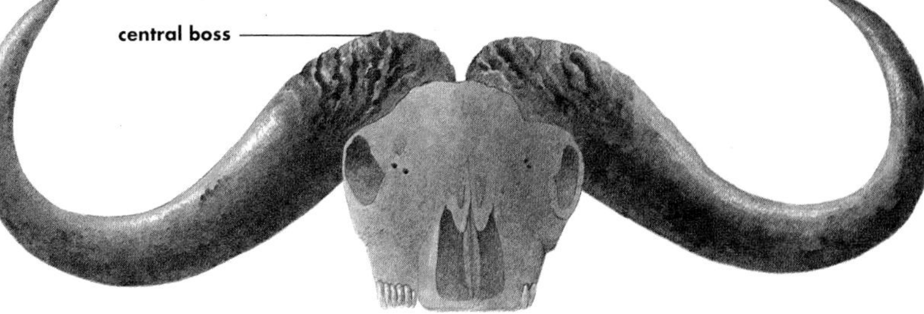

Main illustration Kim Thompson. Heads Ruth Grewcock

Wild Under the Skin

Left to themselves, wild cattle display the placid bovine contentment that we see in domestic cows. But when they are disturbed or threatened, the story can be very different

The lifestyle of wild cattle has evolved to suit their feeding and watering needs and their defense against predators. In some cases, their sheer size may deter enemies, but the weak and young will always offer an easy target to a determined carnivore, so all wild cattle have special protection measures.

The most obvious of these are the horns; the fact that both sexes posses them shows that they are not simply connected with male display. But these may be ineffective against, for example, lions attacking from behind, so most wild cattle rely on herding behavior; by forming large groups, they gain safety in numbers. A whole herd may be alerted to the presence of a predator by just one member, and the weaker members will instantly gain protection by being shepherded to the safe core of the group. Not all wild cattle are herders, however. Anoas spend much of their lives alone, or perhaps in a pair; they are protected in their forest domain, where they weave cautiously through the dense thickets.

Another safety measure comes through nocturnal activity. When studied in western Zambia, African buffalo—which are as well equipped as any wild cattle to defend themselves—were found to do more than half of their grazing by night. The water buffalo is very sensitive to heat, so besides wallowing in water, most of its activity takes place at night. Certainly all cattle spend the greater part of daylight hours resting in the shade, chewing the cud.

Pests and Parasites

Besides feeding, watering, resting, and protecting themselves from predators, another factor determines certain aspects of wild-cattle behavior. This is their need to avoid the many insects and other parasites that plague them, as well as to avoid the intense heat that dominates the habitats of some. The naturalist David Attenborough described large animals, buffalo in particular, as "walking menageries," referring to the many parasites inside and on their bodies. These include ticks, which bore into a buffalo's hide; leeches in its mouth that it has picked up from water holes; tapeworms in its gut; roundworms deep in its muscles; and flukes feeding on its liver. There is nothing a buffalo can do about the internal parasites, but it has ways of dealing with the biting insects and ticks. To some extent, it is aided by birds: Cattle egrets and oxpeckers sit on its hide and pick off many of the parasites.

The other method employed by African buffalo is to wallow in a muddy water hole. Some animals—mainly the big bulls—will lie in the mud for hours on end, with just their heads exposed. When they emerge, their whole bodies are caked in mud; this

Mary Plage/Bruce Coleman Ltd.

Jean-Paul Ferrero/Ardea

Wallowing gives the water buffalo an insect-proof coat of mud and refuge from the heat (above).

ENGLISH CATTLE

Wild cattle have never been native to England and yet there exists today, in the grounds of Ros Castle in Northumberland, a herd of feral cattle. Known as Chillingham cattle, they resemble the aurochs and are certainly descended from it, although their exact origin is unknown. Unlike some species or breeds of cattle, they usually move away from the herd to give birth, which they do standing up. They then lick the calf to stimulate it to defecate. The licking also helps to give it an immunity against flies. Within the herd, there is a dominant bull at any one time, usually holding sway for two or three years. He alone may mate with the cows—until he is deposed by a younger and fitter rival.

While over the centuries many stately homes and castles of England have had herds of feral cattle, known generally as English park cattle, the Chillingham herd is the most ancient, dating from around 1220. Interestingly, through the centuries, these cattle have decreased slightly in size.

will soon dry and harden in the sunshine. The mud pack forms a barrier against the insects; sooner or later, the buffalo will rub against a tree, dislodging the barrier and its cargo of parasites.

The water buffalo is also helped by birds in removing external parasites. It, too, is a great wallower, even more so than many African buffalo. When it takes a dip in the mud, only the nostrils remain exposed. If the water is shallow it lies on its belly and, shoveling with its horns, splashes mud over itself. Once again, the wallowing serves a dual purpose: escape from, and ultimately a mud barrier against, insects, and a way to avoid the heat.

SUPER SENSES

The most highly developed of all senses in wild cattle is that of smell. This is what is employed in the first instance to find food, detect enemies, and initiate social communication. An African buffalo can detect the scent of a predator more than 1,500 ft (457 m) away. If it senses that the best form of defense is attack, it will charge with its head raised and its nostrils flaring, using the sense of sight as well as smell to pinpoint its target. ■

Their sheer bulk gives most wild cattle, such as the yak, a measure of superiority over their predators.

HABITATS

As we associate domestic cattle with open pastures, it may come as a surprise to discover that wild cattle have successfully colonized a wide variety of habitats, from open woodland to dense forest, scrub-covered steppe to open savanna, swamp and other wetlands to high mountains. The ancestor of so many of today's domestic cattle, the aurochs, kept mainly to open scrubland, river valleys, and the fringes of the forest.

The yak probably lives at a higher altitude than any other mammal. An inhabitant of the high plains of Tibet and its neighboring areas, it is at home not just in the alpine tundra but also among the ice and desert regions of the high mountains, way beyond any area inhabited by humans. It will venture to altitudes of at least 20,000 ft (6,096 m) when foraging.

Hot and cold cattle

As a group, wild cattle can dwell equally successfully in some of the hottest and coldest areas on earth. We have seen how they deal with extreme heat—by being active at night, resting in the shade, and cooling down in muddy wallows. At the other end of the scale, the yak and the bison rely on two special adaptations to cope with extreme cold. One of these is the extreme thickness and length of their coats; the other the "central-heating" effect of the action of microscopic organisms in their gut as they go to work on fermenting the ingested food.

Across its wide range—at one time it occurred in most of Africa south of the Sahara—the African buffalo occupies varying habitats. Each environment, however, must provide plenty of water, grass, and dense cover. The Cape buffalo is best adapted to the open savanna, whereas the forest buffalo, as its name suggests, is more at home in the swampy woodlands of West Africa.

The natural habitat of the Asian water buffalo originally spanned from India and Nepal across to Vietnam, Malaysia, and the Philippines. Within this wide area it was strictly an inhabitant of wetlands—marshy grasslands, swamps, and leafy river valleys. Its broad, long hoofs and remnant dewclaws enable it to pad across soft wet ground with ease. Both species of anoa are natives only of the Indonesian island of Sulawesi, while the tamarau inhabits the Philippine island of Mindoro. All are basically forest dwellers, but they also need water. As their names suggest, the mountain anoa is found in the highlands, the lowland anoa in the foothills. The tamarau, once found over most of Mindoro, has now withdrawn to areas of mountain forest up to

FOCUS ON

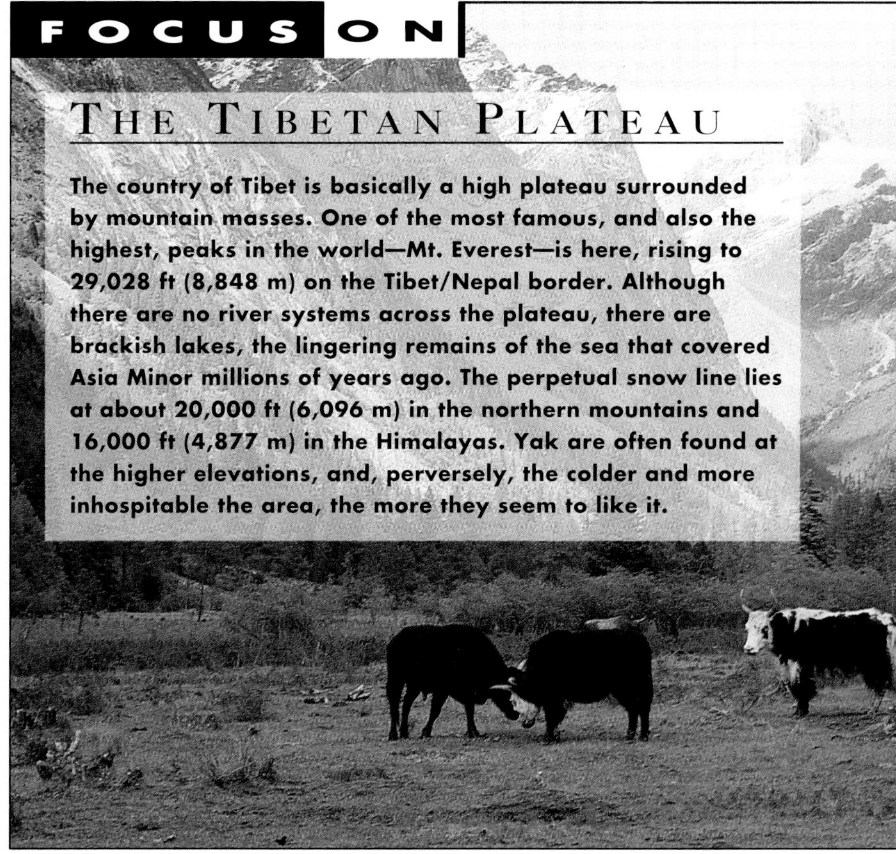

The Tibetan Plateau

The country of Tibet is basically a high plateau surrounded by mountain masses. One of the most famous, and also the highest, peaks in the world—Mt. Everest—is here, rising to 29,028 ft (8,848 m) on the Tibet/Nepal border. Although there are no river systems across the plateau, there are brackish lakes, the lingering remains of the sea that covered Asia Minor millions of years ago. The perpetual snow line lies at about 20,000 ft (6,096 m) in the northern mountains and 16,000 ft (4,877 m) in the Himalayas. Yak are often found at the higher elevations, and, perversely, the colder and more inhospitable the area, the more they seem to like it.

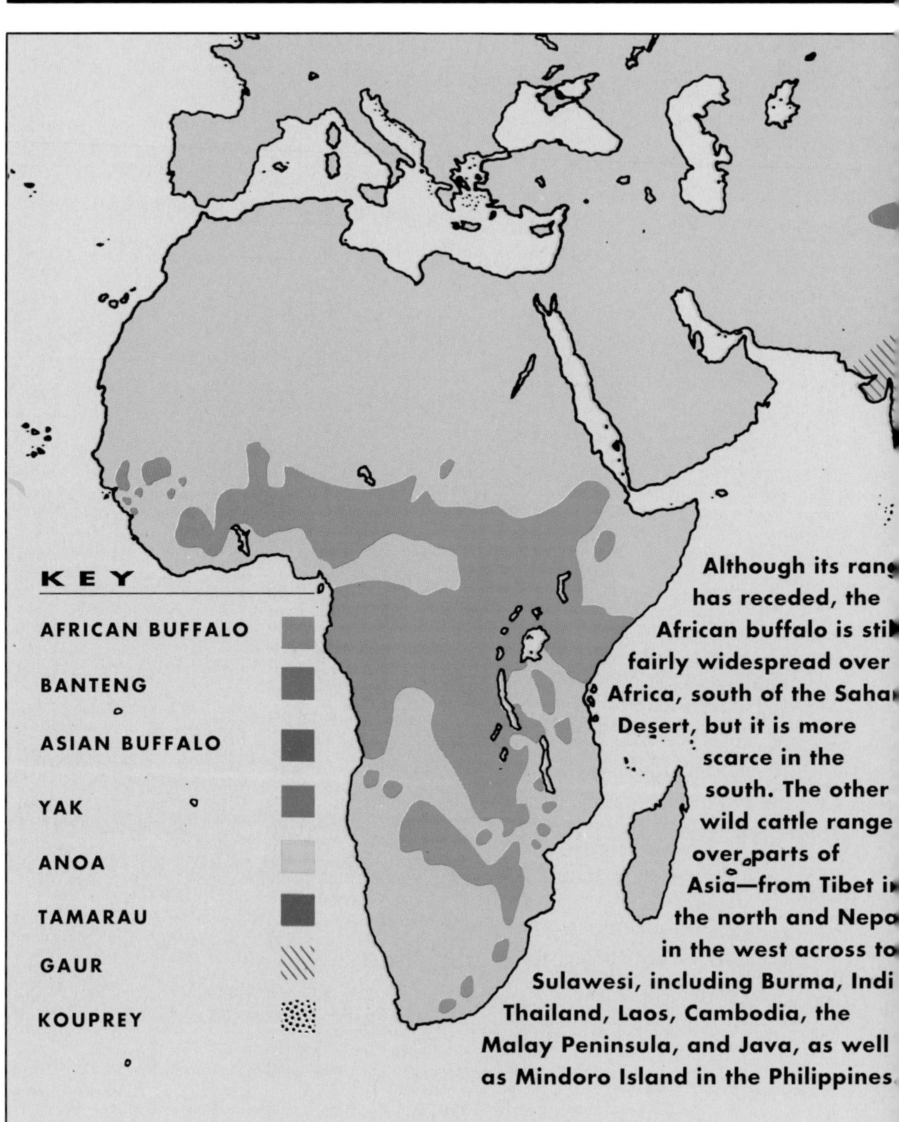

Although its rang[e] has receded, the African buffalo is sti[ll] fairly widespread over Africa, south of the Saha[ra] Desert, but it is more scarce in the south. The other wild cattle range over parts of Asia—from Tibet i[n] the north and Nepa[l] in the west across to Sulawesi, including Burma, Indi[a,] Thailand, Laos, Cambodia, the Malay Peninsula, and Java, as well as Mindoro Island in the Philippines.

Charles McDougal/Ardea

altitudes of 5,900 ft (1,800 m). It prefers dense vegetation, but will wander into more open land to feed.

Like that of nearly all wild cattle, the range of the banteng has been reduced and fragmented over the decades. Once it was found throughout Burma and Thailand, across Malaysia and other parts of Southeast Asia to the islands of Java and Borneo. It favors wooded hills and mountains to heights of 6,500 ft (2,000 m). Unlike many of its relatives, it can tolerate aridity, so it moves into the hills during the monsoon period; in the dry season, it wanders back into the valleys to feed on the new grass.

SOUTH AMERICA AND AUSTRALIA ARE THE ONLY PARTS OF THE WORLD THAT CONTAIN NO TRULY WILD CATTLE

The banteng's close relative, the gaur, is now found only in scattered groups in Nepal, India, Burma, western Malaysia, and scattered parts of Southeast Asia. It, too, is principally a forest dweller, although it often grazes and rests in open, grassy glades and roams the upland tropical forests to elevations of 5,900 ft (1,800 m). Although the gaur bathes in water holes, it does not depend on these for relief from the heat. Instead, it loses body heat through its hump and large dewlaps; its coat, too, is very short.

The kouprey's alternative name of Cambodian forest ox gives the clue to its home area; it is a native of northern Cambodia as well as neighboring parts of Thailand, Laos, and southern Vietnam. It is found in similar types of habitat to the gaur—hilly country with open woodlands. Prone to wandering during the course of the day, it finds plenty of grazing in the clearings, while the woodland provides sanctuary from the sun and predators. ■

DISTRIBUTION

The gaur finds refuge in the remaining forest blocks of India and Southeast Asia. In the tropical parts of its range, its dewlaps and thin coat help it to radiate excess heat.

Anup & Manaj Shah/Planet Earth Pictures

FOOD AND FEEDING

Wild cattle feed mainly on grasses, and also need ready access to water. Being so large, most species need to eat a lot of fodder, but their ruminant digestive system enables them to extract the maximum nutrition from a low-protein diet.

Cattle sniff out their food, and gather it mainly by wrapping their highly mobile tongue around a bunch of grasses. This wad is then gripped between the incisors and upper palate and ripped off. Lacking the mobile lips of, say, horses, wild cattle cannot easily crop shorter grasses, but they can make short work of stems at least 6 in (15 cm) long.

The food passes to the first chamber of a four-compartment stomach. This is known as the rumen, where the chewed food is softened by microbes. It is then brought back up by strong muscles in the gullet and is mashed again in the mouth—this is known as "chewing the cud." Swallowed again, the food passes through the other three stomach compartments, where more microscopic organisms ensure that the cellulose in the plants is completely broken down for digestion and all nutrition extracted.

Cold comforts

The yak can survive happily and comfortably in temperatures as low as -40°F (-40°C) and will even bathe in icy rivers and lakes. The yak's thick, hairy coat and its taste for high-elevation plant forms contribute to its cold-hardiness. The yak has one of the poorest diets of all wild cattle—mosses and lichens, which it strips from rocks with its rough tongue. The lower plains offer more in the way of mossy grasses and herbs, but the yak visits these only in the depths of winter. The yak feeds mainly in the early morning and evening, spending the rest of its day enduring violent snowstorms while calmly chewing the cud.

WATER BUFFALO *find good grazing in riverside clearings* (right). *Feeding in a herd enables them to keep a wary eye out for predators.*

COOLING OFF *Watering holes also make ideal wallows. Water buffalo will happily spend hours immersed* (right), *safe from the sun's burning heat and protected against biting insects.*

A banteng placidly crops the grass in Ujong Kulon National Park, Indonesia (above). *Like the gaur, the banteng will feed by night to avoid humans.*

in SIGHT

WATER OF LIFE

Wild cattle cannot easily conserve moisture, and the often hot conditions of their habitat make liquid intake a daily necessity. An African buffalo visits a watering hole at least once in a 24-hour period, usually in daylight. At such a time it is most at risk from predators, and it is not unusual for a young or weak buffalo to be seized and dragged beneath the water by a crocodile. It is said that in order to avert this danger, some buffalo will wait while the more aggressive animals go ahead to paw the surface and scare off the crocodiles. An adult buffalo needs about 7.5 gallons (34 liters) of water daily; it can drink this amount in about six minutes.

Illustration Darren Harvey/Wildlife Art Agency

For all its bulk, the African buffalo is a fairly modest feeder. Chiefly a grazer, it also takes foliage from trees and bushes. Because it feeds on grasses that are too tall and coarse for many ruminants, the African buffalo plays an important role in opening up grasslands for the other plains beasts.

As with many wild cattle and other ruminants, a 24-hour period is broken up into sessions of grazing, followed by resting while chewing the cud, followed by resting or sleeping. The African buffalo tends to feed slightly longer by daylight in the dry season and a little longer by night in the wet season.

Feeding time for the massive gaur depends very much on who else is in the neighborhood. Where humans have scarcely penetrated its habitat, it will feed by day; in other areas, where it is subject to constant disturbance, it is entirely nocturnal. Equipped with a remarkably long tongue, the gaur feeds on both dry and succulent grasses, and on young shoots and fruits. In the bamboo jungles where it is occasionally found, it often cannot reach the foliage on the tall plants and relies instead on vegetation crushed to the ground by elephants.

Bearing in mind its watery habitat, we should not be surprised that the water buffalo feeds mainly on the lush grass and herbage that grow beside, or even in, the marshes, rivers, and lakes. Its close relative, the anoa, also feeds on the water plants it comes across in woodland swamps, as well as herbs and grasses that grow on slightly drier terrain. Reported to have a particularly broad diet, the anoa includes ferns, saplings, palm, ginger, and fallen fruit on its menu. It will also occasionally browse on the leaves of various bushes and trees. ■

DEFENSES

Wild cattle will always attract the attention of carnivores as a source of protein. In Africa, only the lion poses any real threat to the mighty African buffalo; generally, hyenas and leopards leave it alone. In other areas, tigers and leopards spell trouble, particularly for the smaller cattle species. Muscles and horns go some way toward deterrence, and these are backed up in most species of wild cattle by the natural herding instinct.

Safety in numbers

Most, although not all, wild cattle live in herds. In the case of the African buffalo, old bulls are often solitary, although they will generally be found not far from a herd. While a lone animal would normally present a more tempting and easy target to a predator than a number grouped together, the old bull does get protection from its sheer size, as well as its particularly impressive horns.

Within a grazing herd, there are always some animals instinctively on the lookout for danger. These are the older, more experienced animals—maybe a bull, or a female with young. Having seen or smelled a predator, the "lookout" animal alerts the others in a number of ways; it may simply stand stock-still, head raised, nostrils flared, and every muscle tensed, while gaurs tend to toss their heads up and down and open their mouths. A warning alarm call is usually given; females respond instantly by giving a special call to summon their young to their side.

MIXED FORTUNES

Cape buffalo repel a single lioness, while hyenas creep in to pick off an old bull that has lost the strength to retaliate.

Defensive action usually involves flight; the herd takes off as one, keeping the weak and young on the inside, where they are best protected. If a single adult buffalo is chased by a lion, it cannot usually outrun it, having a top speed of only 30–35 mph (48–56 km/h) over a short distance. If cornered, however, a buffalo may turn and face its aggressor.

Raging bulls

All wild cattle have a variety of dominance or threat displays, and these are most apparent among bulls. An African buffalo may stand side-on to the enemy with his head held high, pulling in his chin to show off the muscles of his neck to best effect. His height and bulk will be at their most impressive in this

Stan Osolinski/Oxford Scientific Films

Bloodied but unbowed, a Cape buffalo bull bears the scars of many fierce battles.

Illustrations Robin Budden/Wildlife Art Agency

in SIGHT

FOREST LONERS

Forest-dwelling cattle species, in particular the anoas and tamarau, do not usually form herds, since their tangled environment is less suitable for community living. Since they lack safety in numbers, their first form of defense is to hide in the undergrowth.

If detected, they generally flee, crashing through the vegetation in ungainly leaps. When cornered, however, they react in a manner typical of their kind. With a ferocity that must prove daunting to many an attacker, they charge with head lowered, ready to spear their assailant with their sharp, pointed horns.

Gaurs may often encounter an elephant in the course of their daily activity. While this animal is usually an equally peaceful creature, tempers may flare over feeding grounds. Gaurs have been seen approaching elephants in an obviously aggressive manner, with heads lowered and moving from side to side. If the aggression becomes more intense, the gaur will increase its speed and throw its head in the air, tossing its impressive horns from side to side. This is generally enough of a display to persuade the elephant to beat a retreat! ■

position, and may be sufficiently daunting to repel the attacker. If need be, it resorts to head-tossing, jabbing its horns into the ground or a nearby bush, or stamping at the ground with a heavy cloven hoof.

Many witnesses have seen an African buffalo turn the tables on its lion aggressor and charge toward it. Faced with a fast-moving ton of flesh tipped with horns, a lion will take the sensible option and run for its life—but if the buffalo catches it, it can gore and toss the big cat into the air with a single blow from its deadly weaponry. Such attacks may involve more than one buffalo, for this species shows a high level of concern for the other herd members. Blind or injured animals are often given such full protection by other group members that they can stay with the herd and are no more at risk than their healthy compatriots.

A herd at rest, chewing the cud, would seem to be more vulnerable to attack. Therefore, in order to minimize the danger, the cattle usually retire to a sheltered and shady spot where they are less visible to marauding predators. Their keen sense of smell will warn them well in advance if danger, in any form, is approaching.

CAUGHT BY THE CAT

Cattle can never afford to relax their vigilance—as discovered by this adult gaur singled out and ambushed by a tiger (below).

SOCIAL STRUCTURE

The wild cattle that congregate in herds may be found in groups of fewer than 20 animals to more than 1,500. The higher number is most associated with the African buffalo, although herds of this size are inevitably becoming increasingly rare.

Wild cattle are not territorial, but all occupy a home range. This varies greatly in size from species to species, and even within a species, depending upon the type of terrain combined with the availability and quality of the grazing. Home ranges often overlap, which accounts for the huge herds, in which individual groups graze side by side. Open terrain clearly allows the space for the largest herds.

Buffalo herds

A typical African buffalo herd contains units of females with their young of up to about three years old but, despite the modular nature of such a herd, it still remains remarkably stable. Within it, the older calves tend to associate in subgroups. Females stay within the group, increasingly distancing themselves from their mothers from the age of three or four.

At about three years old, the young males break away and begin to form bachelor herds. Such groups are generally associated with the female/sibling herds, ready to assert dominance at breeding time. As bulls get older, they often become solitary—not for any antisocial reasons but rather because their ever-increasing size means they neither need the protection of a group nor have the inclination to move far around a home range in the more restless fashion of cows and calves. They will stay within a small area that provides all their needs—sufficient grazing, sufficient shade for resting, and usually a

in SIGHT

MALE AGGRESSION

Buffalo are irritable creatures, and bulls often fight over a challenge for supremacy. One bull approaches another in measured strides and may toss its head and bellow. A subordinate responds to such an advance by dropping its head and jutting its chin out, and even placing its nose under the aggressor's belly in appeasement. It then wheels around and gallops away. But if the challenged animal stands its ground, both bulls toss and sway their heads and paw the ground. They then circle around each other, 65 ft (20 m) or so apart. Usually these encounters end with one bull losing interest and moving away, but if the challenge continues, it becomes very violent. With deep growls, the two animals charge at each other, head stretched out. Just before they clash, they drop their heads to take the impact on their horn bosses; the weaker animal will then take flight.

CLASH OF TITANS

The big, bony boss on the male banteng's skull leaves us in no doubt as to its purpose when tempers flare over breeding rights (below).

John Davis/Wildlife Art Agency

muddy pool where they can wallow. They remain on perfectly friendly terms with any passing herds, although woe betide any young bull that attempts to bathe in a big bull's mud wallow!

The activities of a herd appear perfectly coordinated. They graze together, each one feeding individually, but always move on as a group. After feeding, they move to a shady spot to rest and chew the cud, often lying down close-packed against each others' flanks. Although few wild cattle undertake huge migrations, they may frequently move over some distance. Yak, for example, move up to higher, colder areas in the summer; gaurs move to higher feeding grounds in the dry season; and African buffalo with large home ranges may move as a group quite some way at the beginning and end of the rainy season.

When a herd of African buffalo set out on such a journey, they move into a definite formation, particularly when passing through wooded country. A number of individuals, not necessarily dominant males, take up position at the front and side of the herd, acting as pathfinders. They are followed by the herd members in clusters, with the young and any weak or sick members on the inside or toward the back. Young males will often be ranged around the outside of these groups. If a herd is under attack from a lion, for example, and has taken the defensive path of flight, they will often be led by an experienced female, the bulls staying at the back, ready to turn around and face their attacker if necessary.

Riverside herds

Water buffalo associate in similar herds in the wild, although they tend to be smaller than those of the more abundant African buffalo. Larger groups often form at nighttime when herds congregate at the same spot to rest. In the morning, they disperse into smaller groups, moving to their traditional grazing grounds. The distances between resting and grazing areas mark the extent of the home range of any particular group. It will always include a stretch of water, and members of the herd may be found together in a river or lake, cooling themselves by splashing in the muddy water.

Young bulls are often found within the group—again, old bulls tend to be solitary—but the dominant member of a herd is always a female. As the bulls get older, they tend to group together in the typical bachelor herds but associate with the female-dominated herds only in the breeding season. Even then they do not control or dominate the females, who will chase them off after mating. ■

Huge herds of African buffalo join forces at a watering hole to drink and graze (below).

Nigel Dennis/NHPA

LIFE CYCLE

Wild cattle give birth to coincide with the most favorable natural conditions. Depending on the species and the location, this may be during the rainy season or the months with the most favorable temperatures. The bulls join the females as the latter become sexually receptive, but there is often fierce competition between bulls for females; usually there is a dominant bull who fights any others that try to lay claim to a female, and he certainly has the first selection of cows.

Gestation periods vary between species. The anoa may give birth after only 275 days, while the African buffalo gestates for roughly 340 days. Calves may be born within the herd—in the African buffalo —or the female may give birth on her own and rejoin the herd later; this is the case with the gaur.

CALVING

The calf is highly developed at birth and is up on its feet soon after birth. In some species, however, such as the African buffalo, it is some hours before the newborn can follow the female and it remains fairly uncoordinated for many weeks. This can be a problem when a herd takes flight from a predator; the mother usually drops out of the herd to hustle her calf along, but she may be forced to abandon it.

The mother licks the calf vigorously after birth, and thereafter may strengthen the bond by licking it on its head and neck. The first drink the calf takes from its mother is full of substances that help to give it immunity from disease.

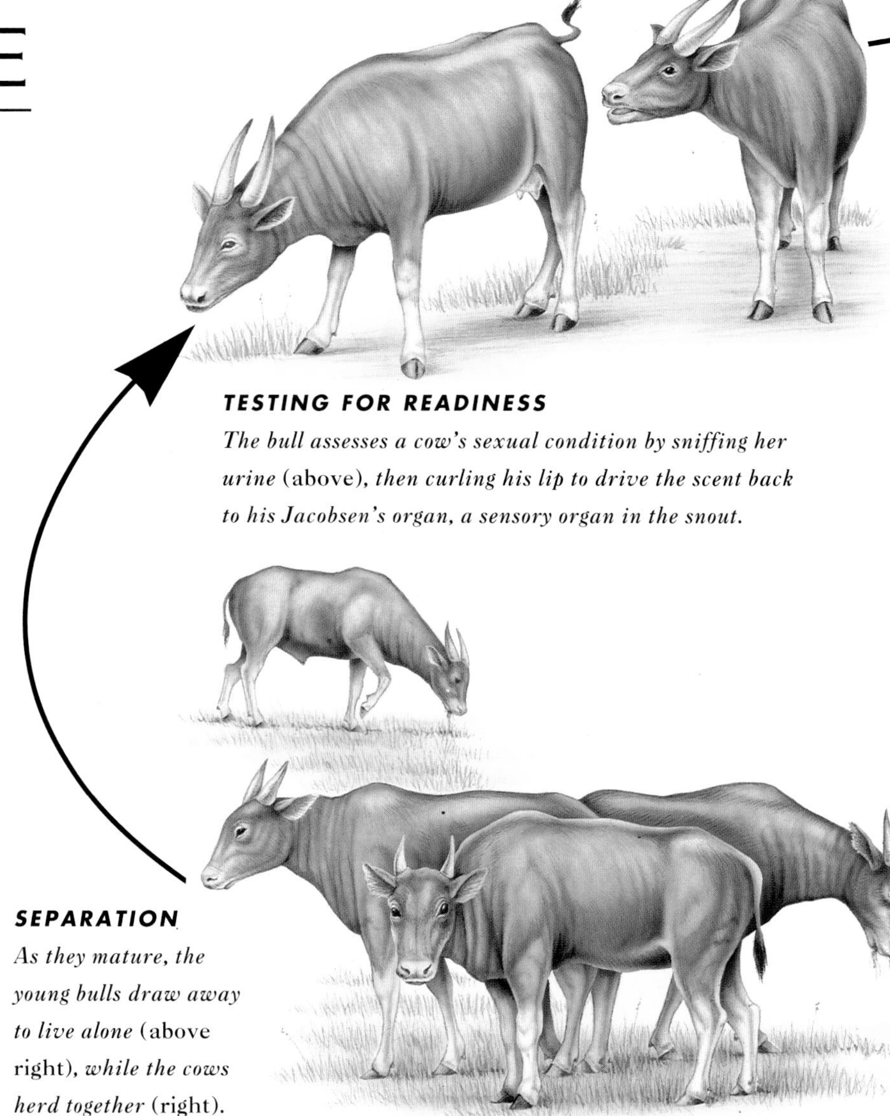

TESTING FOR READINESS

The bull assesses a cow's sexual condition by sniffing her urine (above)*, then curling his lip to drive the scent back to his Jacobsen's organ, a sensory organ in the snout.*

SEPARATION

As they mature, the young bulls draw away to live alone (above right)*, while the cows herd together* (right).

Martin Harvey/NHPA

in SIGHT

SACRED CATTLE

Any visitor to India will have seen the huge cattle that walk the streets of towns and villages, untroubled by people or traffic. And woe betide anyone who harms them, for these animals are sacred to Hindus. According to the Hindu mythology, the milk of a cow once saved the life of one of the gods, Krishna, who was being persecuted at the time. Seen as an incarnation of Vishnu, the universal God, Krishna is the most revered Hindu deity, and the cow has become the life-giving "mother" of all Hindus. The meat must not be eaten, and should anyone harm a cow, the act is considered a mortal sin, more serious than the murder of a fellow human being.

GROWING UP

The life of a young anoa

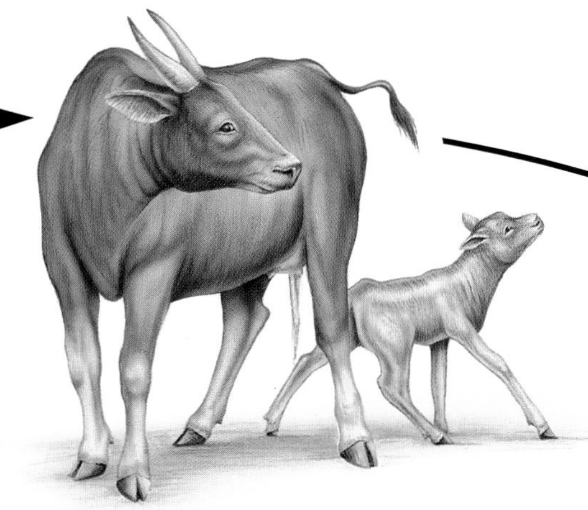

EARLY TO RISE

Almost as soon as it is born, the calf staggers to its feet on wobbly legs (above). *The mother licks it clean, then nudges it gently toward her udders.*

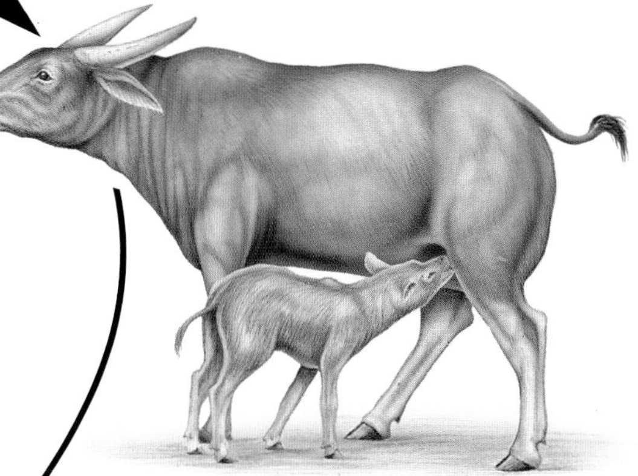

HEALTH DRINK

The calf's first drink is rich in vitamins and protective bacteria. During the course of the day, the calf suckles from each teat in turn (right).

MOTHER LOVE •

The cow's close bond with her calf remains strong, at least until she gives birth again, and the two graze side by side (left).

Nursing takes place at irregular intervals during the day and may continue for anywhere from three to ten minutes. In most instances the calf is weaned after six to nine months, although it may go on suckling up to within two or three months of the next calf's birth. During this time, a cow keeps in contact with her young with various calls. In spite of the bond between mother and calf, however, when a new calf is born, the female takes no further interest in her older offspring. Nevertheless, they generally stay nearby for another year or so. As they grow, the calves spend more time in each others' company; they indulge in play sessions, practicing dominance displays, fighting, and other social gestures.

In general, females can breed two or more years before males. For example, African buffalo cows first calve at about five years—although they are able to do so a year or two earlier—while males may not mate for another three to four years. In most other species, sexual maturity comes earlier. ■

Joanne van Gruisen/Ardea

From the start, the mother forms a strong bond with her calf, nursing and watching over it.

FROM BIRTH TO DEATH

AFRICAN BUFFALO	WATER BUFFALO
GESTATION: ABOUT 340 DAYS	**GESTATION:** 300–340 DAYS
NUMBER OF YOUNG: 1, RARELY 2	**NUMBER OF YOUNG:** 1, RARELY 2
WEIGHT AT BIRTH: 77–110 LB (35–50 KG)	**WEIGHT AT BIRTH:** 77–88 LB (35–40 KG)
WEANED: UP TO 9 MONTHS	**WEANED:** 6–9 MONTHS
SEXUAL MATURITY: 3.5–5 YEARS	**SEXUAL MATURITY:** 2 YEARS
LONGEVITY: 18 YEARS IN THE WILD	**LONGEVITY:** 25 YEARS IN THE WILD

Illustrations Richard Tibbits

Once They Were Wild

Some of the most recent finds of large mammals have been new species of wild cattle. Sadly, these latecomers may be set for extinction within decades of their discovery

At one time, the African buffalo was one of the most numerous and widespread of even-toed ungulates and could be seen in almost every corner of the African continent south of the Sahara. The range of the water buffalo stretched westward from Nepal and India, encompassing the whole of southern and Southeast Asia. And of the yak, an explorer wrote at the end of the 19th century, "On one green hill there were I believe more yak visible than hill." Today the numbers of all species of wild cattle are a pale shadow of their former glory, and in some instances they are heading toward extinction.

As far as we know, some species of wild cattle have always been comparatively rare. The island species—the anoas and tamarau—having been denied the huge range of some of their relatives, are bound to be more restricted in numbers. When their habitats began facing pressure from spreading civilizations that required ever more farmland or simply harvested the trees in their forest homes, survival for island species became even less tenable. These animals live more solitary lives than most other wild cattle species; once their habitat becomes sparse and fragmented, their chances of meeting breeding partners become more tenuous. Indeed, the tamarau is now among the most endangered of all wild cattle.

The anoas

Both species of anoa have been excessively hunted. Since they generally avoid areas inhabited by humans, the reason for hunting is probably not that they are seen to compete with domestic cattle for grazing. Nor have they been widely hunted for meat, but more likely for sport: for their hardwearing, handsome hides and impressive horns.

Both species of anoa are confined in the wild to remote and ever-diminishing areas, and in the case of the lowland anoa, there appears to be no effective captive management program. A few mountain anoas have been bred in captivity, but their best hope still remains with gaining protection from the governments and people in their homelands, so that they can regain numbers in the wild.

Trouble for true cattle

Three species of true cattle or oxen—the banteng, gaur, and kouprey—are also likely to have been naturally rare even before humans invaded their homelands. This has a lot to do with their distribution and the nature of their environment. All these cattle are primarily forest dwellers, but within the forest they seek open spaces where the grass grows

Alain Compost/Bruce Coleman Ltd.

Hunted for sport in Sulawesi, the anoa is also highly vulnerable to parasitic infestation (above).

THEN & NOW

This map shows the former and current distribution of the Asian water buffalo.

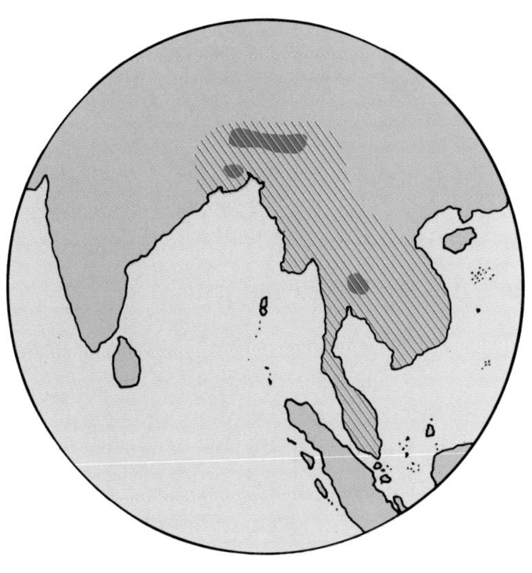

FORMER DISTRIBUTION

CURRENT DISTRIBUTION

The decline in the Asian water buffalo's range has been almost as dramatic as that of the American bison. The species once occupied suitable lush forests from eastern Nepal and northern India east to the Malay Peninsula. It has suffered from much the same problems as other wild cattle species: hunting, habitat loss, competition with domestic stock, and disease. Its main stronghold today lies in northern India.

more abundantly. In many areas, the forest was once so dense that such places were scarcer, so numbers of these animals were naturally limited. Later, settlers began to open up the forest, creating exactly the kind of environment favored by these animals. Unfortunately, the settlers had earmarked the new pastures for their own domestic cattle and not for the wild beasts, which they regarded as competition for precious food sources. Already subjected to all the accompanying threats of habitat loss—fragmented populations, reduced chances of breeding, fast-diminishing grazing—at least two of these three species were also hunted by local farmers.

The kouprey was discovered fairly recently; it was not known until 1936, when it was first seen as a hunting trophy in the house of a Monsieur Sauvel,

Mary Clay/Planet Earth Pictures

Sadly, the magnificent horns of the increasingly rare yak are greatly coveted as hunting trophies.

a French vet, from whom it takes its species name. Ever since that date, the species has faced problems of a different nature. Its limited range in Cambodia, Laos, Thailand, and Vietnam has been the scene of conflict. During the Vietnam War, its native forests were carpet-bombed with explosives and defoliants (leaf-stripping chemicals), which killed animals as indiscriminately as they did people. From an estimated 1,000 animals in 1940, this number had halved in ten years and had fallen to only 100 by the beginning of the 1970s. There have been only occasional sightings since then, and the kouprey's current status remains unknown. Some people believe it may already be extinct in the wild.

Trophies from the wild

The remaining species classed with these three—the yak—may now be facing possible extinction, after a heyday of superabundance. This is even more tragic in that the yak is one of the few wild animals whose habitat remains largely untampered with by humans. The nature of its terrain—bleak, icy, and inhospitable—means that it offers little in the way of resources to civilization. Instead, the yak's demise in the wild has been largely the result of overhunting by trophy hunters, even though it has had official protection for some years.

THERE ARE FEW HOPES OF MONITORING ANY EFFORTS TO CONSERVE THE YAK IN ITS HOSTILE NATIVE ENVIRONMENT

The wild water buffalo has declined greatly in numbers over the decades of the 20th century. In its time, the range of the water buffalo was as wide as any species of wild cattle; wherever there was suitable watery habitat between eastern Nepal and southern Malaysia, the water buffalo was part of the scene. Some authorities claim it may have even lived in the wild in parts of Europe.

Now it is extinct over huge areas, largely displaced by domestic cattle, as well as through loss of habitat and, in some areas, hunting. Today, there are thought to be only a few truly wild herds—that is, animals descended from native stock, as opposed to the feral descendants of domesticated buffalo. Of about 1,000 apparently wild buffalo in India at the end of the 1980s, it was thought only about one-tenth of these were free from the genetic influence of domestic animals.

Domestic conflict

Dire though the effects of habitat destruction have been on wild cattle, the main threat over the centuries to most species has come through the

ENDANGERED SPECIES

THE TAMARAU

The tamarau, or Mindoro buffalo, is one of the rarest mammals in the world today. Shy and yet aggressive, it has retreated into the densest forests in its mountainous home on the small Philippine island of Mindoro, but with deforestation ever on the increase in Southeast Asia, it is far from safe there.

The tamarau was formerly listed merely as a subspecies of the Asian water buffalo. It certainly looks like a cross between an anoa and a mainland water buffalo: The coat markings ally it with the anoas, while its skull is similar to that of the buffalo. It is now known that, like the anoas on Sulawesi, it developed as a separate island form and so its independence has now been fully recognized. During the ice ages, Mindoro was still connected to the main landmass, whereas Sulawesi split away some time earlier—around four or five million years ago. The tamarau is therefore a "younger" species than the anoas, having become separated from the main lineage at a later date.

The tamarau was once also found on the nearby island of Luzon; how it became extinct there is not clear. In more recent history, when the tamarau was still relatively common, it could be seen grazing in more open country—but this brought it into conflict with the farmers who wanted the land for their domestic grazing stock. Natives of the island have also hunted the tamarau, using spears and pit traps.

Conservation Measures

- The plight of the tamarau has long been recognized, so much so that a preserve in Mindoro—the Mt. Iglit Game Preserve—was created earlier in this century with the aim of protecting this species. There are also preserves on Mts. Calavite and Sablayan.
- A captive breeding program has helped to increase tamarau numbers, but the species is still endangered.

Anup & Manaj Shah/Planet Earth Pictures

Normally, a modest level of hunting does not affect an animal's status, but when a species is as threatened as the tamarau, it can spell disaster. In addition, many animals died as a result of rinderpest in the 1930s, as well as other diseases imported onto the island by domestic cattle.

There have been but a few, brief sightings of tamarau in the wild, now that it has retreated from open pastureland. Two observers in 1961 spent many days on Mindoro, in particular the Mt. Iglit Game Preserve; they managed to spot only one individual. In spite of the protection given to the tamarau by creating preserves, illegal poaching has continued, as has the loss of habitat. By 1970 the number of tamarau on the island of Mindoro had fallen from an estimated 10,000 at the beginning of the century to fewer than 150.

WILD CATTLE IN DANGER

THE CHART BELOW SHOWS HOW THE INTERNATIONAL UNION FOR THE CONSERVATION OF NATURE (IUCN) CLASSIFIES THE STATUS SOF WILD CATTLE IN ITS 1994 *RED DATA BOOK*:

GAUR	VULNERABLE
BANTENG	VULNERABLE
WILD YAK	ENDANGERED
KOUPREY	ENDANGERED
WILD WATER BUFFALO	ENDANGERED
LOWLAND ANOA	ENDANGERED
MOUNTAIN ANOA	ENDANGERED
TAMARAU	ENDANGERED

VULNERABLE INDICATES THAT THE ANIMAL IS LIKELY TO MOVE INTO THE ENDANGERED CATEGORY IF THINGS CONTINUE AS THEY ARE. *ENDANGERED* MEANS THAT THE ANIMAL IS IN DANGER OF EXTINCTION AND ITS SURVIVAL IS UNLIKELY UNLESS STEPS ARE TAKEN TO REMOVE THE THREATS FACING IT.

Tom McHugh/Photo Researchers/Oxford Scientific Films

ONCE SAFE FROM HUMANS ON ITS ISLAND REFUGE, THE TAMARAU IS RUNNING OUT OF SAFE HAVENS.

● Following the recent discovery of the vu quang, in Vietnam, by a joint team from the Vietnam Ministry of Forestry and the World Wide Fund for Nature, efforts are under way to protect the newly found species. The Vietnamese government has already increased the size of the Vu Quang Nature Preserve in the provinces of Ha tinh and Nghe an.

introduction of domestic cattle. Domestication has brought with it various effects—competition for grazing, the generation of new breeds more suitable and more likely to serve human needs, and the introduction of diseases that attack wild species as readily as domestic breeds.

By and large, it is true that land fit for wild cattle will also support domestic stock. In the case of open grassland, this is obviously so; all that is needed is fencing to prevent the domestic stock from wandering away into the wilderness. The wooded areas that were home to some species of wild cattle were less suitable for domestic animals but could soon be made more amenable by clearing them and letting the grass come through in greater abundance. Natually, as soon as farmers have commandeered land for livestock, they are keen to keep away any other grazing animals. Fences not only keep domestic animals in; they also keep wild species out. When this fails, as it often does, farmers and ranchers the world over have no compunction in shooting the wild animals that they view merely as pests.

The value of cattle to humans became apparent many thousands of years ago. Sheep and goats, perhaps because of their more manageable size, were domesticated before cattle, but we know that cattle, in the form of the now-extinct aurochs, came under human influence around 8,000–6,000 years ago. Water buffalo were first domesticated in the Indus Valley 1,000 years later, soon spreading east and west to the Middle East and China. Cattle clearly have great value to humans—they provide milk, meat, and hides for clothing and various artifacts; in

ALONGSIDE MAN

BUFFALO BULL FIGHTS

Wild cattle have had a special place alongside humans for centuries, helping them in their daily toil and providing them with sustenance, clothing, and often revenue. In some areas, the cattle were seen as having special significance beyond this. On the island of Sulawesi, native home of the anoas, Toradja people sacrificed water buffalo at a funeral feast. The greater the wealth and the higher the rank of the deceased, the greater the number of beasts were killed. After the feast honoring the departed, it was traditional to present the head of the buffalo to the grieving relatives; the horns were later fixed to the outside of the house.

At some of their celebrations, the Toradja staged fierce fights between two buffalo bulls. At the start of these, the bulls appeared to perform a kind of ritual, arching their necks and raising their noses to the sky, sniffing the air to make sure they were detecting the scent of another male. Fixing one another with their eyes, they began to jab their horns savagely into the ground, increasingly working themselves into a rage. Then they approached one another, slowly and cautiously beginning to fence with their long horns. Ultimately, they backed off before charging headlong at one another, hunching their shoulders and lowering their heads so that the impact was taken at the base of the horns. The weaker one was knocked off its feet.

addition, they have been used to pull agricultural implements and as beasts of burden.

In achieving domestication of a wild species, the normal course of events is to breed selectively the most desirable and useful animals over numerous captive generations. The water buffalo, the yak, the banteng, and the gaur are wild cattle that all now have a domesticated version, of which there are far more in existence than the wild species. An interesting variation on the wild form is seen in the domestic version of the banteng. Known as the Bali cattle, this animal achieves sexual maturity phenomenally quickly: Both sexes are capable of breeding from the age of about 21 months. This has obvious benefits for cattle farmers.

The only species of wild cattle absent from the rarity lists of conservation organizations is the African buffalo. Nor has it been domesticated, largely because of its ferocious reputation. However, its numbers have declined dramatically from the countless figures they once reached for two reasons: hunting and disease.

SHOTGUNS AND RINDERPEST

Hunting has long been undertaken by big-game hunters anxious to pit their skills against these most "fearsome" of game animals. However, the greater threat has certainly come from farmers and ranchers who saw these beasts as unacceptable competition for their domestic cattle once they started importing them onto the grasslands. Although the African buffalo was never persecuted to the same degree as the American bison, its numbers nevertheless fell with the colonization of much of its range.

Disease imported through domestic stock has been a problem for many wild cattle, for inevitably they are prone to the same infections and illnesses. But what really brought African buffalo to their knees and wiped them out in the thousands was rinderpest, a cattle disease that swept across Africa in the 1890s. This viral infection affects sheep as well as cattle and causes a raging thirst, high fever, diarrhea, and lesions of the skin and mucous membranes. It is nearly always fatal. Imported to the continent by domestic cattle, it hit the African buffalo harder than any other animal, and it was estimated that for each one that survived, 10,000 died. Millions of domestic cattle were also killed. It says a lot for the resilience of this animal that, once the epidemic had passed through, the survivors recolonized much of their former range so rapidly and successfully that today, in certain places, they need to be culled in order to preserve the environment. This is mainly in the various preserves where they are given protection.

Okapia/Oxford Scientific Films

The domesticated form of the banteng is used widely as a beast of burden in the rice paddies of Indonesia.

The domestication of the African buffalo has recently been reconsidered, since it is thought that their nature is basically peaceful and friendly—aggression being aroused only by threat. This would aid local economies, as buffalo are more efficient grazers than domestic cattle, their meat is superior, and, in spite of falling victim to rinderpest some decades ago, they are now apparently more resistant to disease. ■

INTO THE FUTURE

The future of some species of cattle may lie in their domestic versions—animals that have been bred over the centuries originally from wild stock. These animals differ from those of the wild beasts, generally being smaller, more tractable, and less afraid of their human taskmasters.

Probably the greatest success in this regard is the water buffalo. There are at least 130 million domestic water buffalo today, found across the wild species' natural range as well as Africa, Central and South America, Australia, Japan, and such islands as Mauritius and Madagascar. In many areas there are also feral herds—descendants of abandoned stock or of escapees into the wild. The domestic water buffalo is usually smaller than its wild relative and ancestor, although size varies with the location and according to whether the animals have been bred for their milk and meat or for their work potential.

PREDICTION

FOREST FEARS

The future of domesticated forms of wild cattle seems assured, as they provide a useful service in agriculture and stock farming. However, if the deforestation of Southeast Asia continues at the present rate, the truly wild forms will lose their habitats and their chances of survival will decline accordingly.

Banteng were first domesticated on the islands of Bali, Java, and Sumbawa, and later introduced to nearby islands and to northern Australia. These "Bali cattle" are smaller than the wild form and have a more variable coat color. The gaur's domesticated form is the gayal, also smaller with shorter legs and a less pronounced hump on its shoulders.

The domesticated versions of these various wild species may readily mate with one another to produce fertile young, although the wild yak take aversion to its tamer relatives; wild yak bulls have been known to attack and kill domestic yaks.

There are today some 12 million domestic yaks in existence, set against no more than a few hundred wild ones. Sturdy and surefooted, they are crucial to inhabitants of the snowy uplands of Tibet and neighboring areas. They provide meat, milk, wool, and hides, and the feces are burned for fuel. The yaks seen in zoos are often descendants of domestic stock rather than of those captured in the wild. ■

DOMESTIC CATTLE

Besides the domestic forms of wild species of cattle, there are some 800 different breeds of cattle known in the world today. Many of these, particularly those recognized as European breeds, have descended from the aurochs. The black bulls of the Iberian Peninsula and British park cattle both resemble the aurochs in appearance. Among the best known, and certainly the most revered, are the zebus, the sacred cattle of India that roam the streets unhindered. They have a characteristic hump over the shoulders and a large dewlap hanging down between the forelegs, and may be a variety of colors. Although they are not allowed to be killed in India, they have been imported to other countries, notably the United States where they have been used in the development of other breeds.

Selective breeding of cattle has been part of humankind's heritage for centuries and is likely to continue as the search for the "perfect" beast continues. In the main, domestic cattle are bred for milk or meat, with relatively few still being used around the world as work animals. As fads and requirements change—a desire in more recent times, for example, for leaner meat—so stockbreeders experiment with crossing breeds to establish new strains to suit the market. There are estimated to be more than 1.2 billion domestic cattle in the world today.

Illustration Evi Antoniou

INDEX

Published by Marshall Cavendish Corporation
99 White Plains Road
Tarrytown, New York 10591-9001

The material in this series was first published in the English language by Marshall Cavendish Limited, of 119 Wardour Street, London W1V 3TD, England.

Library of Congress Cataloging-in-Publication Data

Encyclopedia of mammals.
p. cm.
Includes index.
ISBN 0-7614-0575-5 (set) ISBN 0-7614-0578-X (v. 3)

Summary: Detailed articles cover the history, anatomy, feeding habits, social structure, reproduction, territory, and current status of ninety-five mammals around the world.
1. Mammals—Encyclopedias, Juvenile. [1. Mammals—Encyclopedias.] I. Marshall Cavendish Corporation.
QL706.2.E54 1996
599'.003—dc20

96-17736
CIP
AC

Printed in Malaysia
Bound in U.S.A.